GROUP DYNAMICS AND ORGANIZATIONAL CULTURE

Group Dynamics and Organizational Culture

Effective Work Groups and Organizations

Athena Xenikou

Assistant Professor of Psychology, Air Force Academy, Greece

Adrian Furnham

Professor of Psychology, University College London, UK

First published 2013 by
PALGRAVE MACMILLAN

Palgrave Macmillan in the UK is an imprint of Macmillan Publishers Limited,
registered in England, company number 785998, of Houndmills, Basingstoke,
Hampshire RG21 6XS.

Palgrave Macmillan in the US is a division of St Martin's Press LLC,
175 Fifth Avenue, New York, NY 10010.

Palgrave Macmillan is the global academic imprint of the above companies
and has companies and representatives throughout the world.

Palgrave® and Macmillan® are registered trademarks in the United States,
the United Kingdom, Europe and other countries.

ISBN 978–1–4039–8733–4

This book is printed on paper suitable for recycling and made from fully
managed and sustained forest sources. Logging, pulping and manufacturing
processes are expected to conform to the environmental regulations of the
country of origin.

A catalogue record for this book is available from the British Library.

A catalog record for this book is available from the Library of Congress.

10   9   8   7   6   5   4   3   2   1
22   21   20   19   18   17   16   15   14   13

Printed in China

To the memory of my father, Stamatiou Xenikou
— Athena

To the memory of my mother, Lorna Goodwin
— Adrian

Contents

Figures, Tables and Boxes

Figures

Tables

Boxes

x

Acknowledgements

We wish to thank a number of individuals and organizations whose support has enabled the production of this book. Our two institutions, the Department of Aviation Sciences, Air Force Academy, Greece, and the Department of Psychology, University College London, UK, have been supportive and encouraging working environments for each of us.

Our deepest thanks go to three anonymous readers of the book who made challenging suggestions as to how it might be improved, and to our students who heard most of the book in lectures and seminars and criticized it relentlessly. Many thanks should also go to Ursula Gavin at Palgrave Macmillan for her editorial advice and encouragement throughout the production of this book and to Kate Boothby, who copy-edited this book, for carefully reading the typescript.

Athena Xenikou and Adrian Furnham

Introduction: The Psychology of Work Groups and Organizations

1

Chapter outline

Introduction
Group dynamics
    Performance and decision-making in work groups
    Conflict and negotiation in work groups
    Work group creativity and innovation
The larger organization
    Organizational culture and leadership
    Performance and organizational culture
    Organizational change
Summary
Questions

Chapter objectives

The main objectives are to:

- define the field of the psychology of organizations;
- explore the origins and nature of group dynamics;
- introduce basic psychological processes that take place in groups, and relate them to group efficiency;
- explore understanding the larger organization using a culture perspective;
- attempt to understand leadership in organizations, organizational efficiency and change through the lens of organizational culture.

Introduction

How does working in an organization influence the thoughts, feelings and behaviour of individual employees? What work group characteristics and processes make groups more or less effective? In what ways does the larger organization 'set the stage' for work groups to operate? How does organizational culture affect work outputs and employee satisfaction and well-being?

The psychology of organizations is the study of how organizations influence the thoughts, feelings and, most importantly, behaviours of all those working within them. Also, it focuses on how individual members and small- or medium-sized groups within the organization constantly interact with organizational factors such as formal structure, organizational culture, strategy or technology and production systems to produce organizational behaviours, outputs and individual or organizational changes.

Organizations are social entities that are more or less compartmentalized or divided up by function or activity. Most comprise specific departments, divisions, sections and various work groups. Individual employees usually work as part of one or two groups in the organization, such as finance, human resources and marketing. To a large extent, employees see the organization as an extension of the groups in which they spend most of their working time. Many feel they belong to their group within the organization. Employees' perceptions of the organization they work for, in turn, influence their cognitions, emotions and observable behaviour.

Research has shown that employees tend to generalize about the image of the larger organization from attributes of their immediate supervisor and the section, division and work group to which they belong – something that is not necessarily a reasonable thing to do. It is therefore of great importance to study groups at work, their functioning and processes, as well as the interaction between group members. Psychologists have always distinguished between inter- and intra-group behaviour: that is, the behaviour between groups and the behaviour of individuals within groups, respectively.

Work groups, it is argued, increase efficiency as long as they are characterized by high-quality group processes, such as sharing a vision, participation and involvement, respect for personal identity, social support and trust among group members. For example, top management teams reach decisions of high quality when group processes are hierarchically decentralized and lateral communication is taking place.

However, it is rather naïve to suggest that efficiency depends only on group dynamics. Indeed, a number of individual and organizational factors need to fit together and constantly adapt to one another for an organization to run smoothly, to achieve high levels of performance and to offer quality of working life to its members. These include task variables, such as the abilities and skills required to perform a task, personal motivations and preferences, task complexity, autonomy and feedback on output performance. Moreover, the organizational system of rules and procedures, incentives and rewards, policies and leadership, and formal and informal prescriptions relates to all of these factors, and these combine in ways that render an organization as functional and high performing, or dysfunctional and maladaptive. There needs to be a fit between various individual, group and organizational factors that is inevitably dynamic, so that efficiency in terms of productivity, economic or other performance and employee satisfaction is achieved.

The first principal objective of this book is to examine small- and medium-sized groups and teams at work by looking at their characteristics, functioning and primarily the psychological processes that occur within them; that is, group dynamics. We shall investigate how these psychological processes directly affect the work product or outcome of the group, and how that outcome influences group dynamics.

The second main objective is to look at the larger organization in which these groups and teams operate, and reveal the values and priorities set by organizations, as well as the role of leadership in the formation, maintenance and change of these values and practices. We consider it essential to understanding group functioning and effectiveness, as well as organizational effectiveness, to have a grasp of the larger context in which groups are situated. One may take a critical stance and argue that switching between the group and organizational levels of analysis constitutes a serious conceptual problem. That is, do we best understand how organizations operate by trying to understand how work groups behave or, rather, the overall structure, processes and strategy of the organization?

However, most organizational problems do not fall neatly into the boundaries erected by our attempt to be rigid in disciplinary terms. Indeed, a plethora of organizational studies have been carried out which examine organizational behaviour by applying a multilevel analysis; that is, investigating the individual, group and organizational units of analysis simultaneously. Baron and Greenberg (1990) are among the many others who have suggested that the field of organizational behaviour seeks knowledge of all individual, group and organizational aspects of behaviour in organizational settings to enhance effectiveness and individual well-being. Of course, we need constantly to be conscious of whether the unit of analysis is the group or the larger organization since many processes significantly differ when occurring at the group or the organizational level.

Group dynamics

What motivates or enables individual employees to explore and exploit their talents when working in group settings? What are the factors that help employees working in teams to fulfil their potential, and set even more challenging goals? What are the major determinants of group efficacy? What are the main threats to continual effective group work?

Groups in organizations are sources of powerful forces that need to be managed because they can be both constructive and destructive. These powerful forces may affect individual employees, as well as the larger organization, in either positive or negative ways. Group dynamics refer to all the psychological processes that take place in groups. Kurt Lewin (1951), importing gestalt ideas to social psychology, put emphasis on describing the total situation; that is, the configuration of forces, not its isolated elements, when studying socio-psychological phenomena. Groups, therefore, are social entities that in some respects are greater than the sum of their parts. The social environment constitutes the psychological field in which various facilitating and inhibitory forces are activated, eventually determining human behaviour.

Although Lewin's ideas have been very influential in organizational psychology, the importance of group processes at work has been highlighted primarily by the human relations school of thought, which originated from the seminal Hawthorne studies. These studies were conducted for almost a decade from the beginning of the 1920s to the start of the 1930s, and they revealed that social factors at work had a more profound effect on productivity in comparison to physical conditions, such as the level of illumination or ventilation. They changed the way people thought about work. The emerged human relations approach argued that work productivity depends on the formal and informal social environment that exists at work, and the extent to which the organization is prepared to meet employees' needs for recognition, respect, acceptance and group membership. There are, however, a number of criticisms of the Hawthorne experiments; perhaps the most serious concerns the research methodology employed since there were only a few observations of some small samples of work groups. Moreover, the basic assumption of the human relations perspective about the cooperative or social nature of human beings has been fiercely challenged. Nevertheless, it is important to acknowledge that there have been few subsequent studies that have had such an influence on management thinking and work psychology (Duncan, 1978).

Since the Hawthorne studies in the 1930s, researchers have spent considerable effort in trying to understand how the psychological processes that take place in groups affect group products or outcomes, and how work outcomes influence group dynamics. Employees usually talk about 'group atmosphere' as a key factor that affects how well they work together. Team spirit and group engagement often seem to be major determinants of group work performance and team members' beliefs in their collective efficacy. At this point we should make a note that, in general, the terms 'work team' and 'work group' are used interchangeably in the relevant literature (see, e.g., Cohen & Bailey, 1997; Sundstrom, McIntyre, Halfhill, & Richards, 2000). Although an important conceptual distinction can be made – that is, teams can be defined as groups with higher levels of interdependence and integration – researchers have not paid much attention to this distinction.

To give an answer to the question 'What is a group?', one should consider four basic elements that cannot be left out. First, a group consists of at least two individuals (two is a dyad; three or more a group) who are involved in social interaction which exerts influence on each others' beliefs, attitudes and behaviours, and perceive themselves as being a group. Some theorists also add 'interdependence' as an essential element of groups but others argue that we should define them more loosely by using the terms 'social interaction' and 'influence' rather than 'interdependence' in order to incorporate all different types of groups.

For example, formal, as opposed to informal, groups are most often characterized by putting effort into achieving specific tasks and objectives, and having a stable structure, roles and hierarchy that endure over time and across situations. On the other hand, informal groups concern people who have something in common and normally function to support friendship, mutual help and understanding, and the social verification of specific values and beliefs. Formal groups often appear in the organizational chart. They have a name, and sometimes even a uniform. But most people belong to informal groups at work, spending time together in breaks or out of work. There are, for instance, interest groups whose members come together on the grounds of having mutual interests and perhaps ideologies, such as union representation or gender discrimination at work. Of course, informal groups may naturally involve into formal groups and possess all the particular characteristics attributed to the latter.

Most work groups in organizations are formally organized to accomplish various tasks and objectives that contribute to the organization's collective purpose. However, the interaction among members within work groups, as well as with members of other formal or informal groups in the organization, may be a major contributor to the quality of group outputs. Even though it is necessary for a group to contain members who have the abilities and skills to perform group tasks, group processes resulting from the interaction between individual members are also important. If group processes are dysfunctional, the benefits of putting together a group of highly competent individuals are offset.

Part I elaborates on the psychological processes taking place in groups and teams at work, as well as their outcomes. More specifically, it examines work group performance in general, as well as decision-making (Chapter 2), conflict and negotiation (Chapter 3), and group creativity and innovation (Chapter 4).

Performance and decision-making in work groups

Group performance has mainly been modelled as an input–process–output analysis, which considers performance to be a function of group 'inputs' (such as members' abilities, personal motivation and group size), contextual factors (the larger organization, task characteristics), group processes and group 'outputs' (products, decisions and services). Research has shown that group performance is enhanced through shared vision and goal interdependence because it promotes cooperation, good communication and social support. Poor integration of group member's efforts can lead to a drop in motivation and output. To deal with motivational losses in group settings, tasks have to be meaningful to and self-involving for group members, and the management of performance needs to focus on the uniqueness of skill-based individual inputs, the evaluation of individual contributions and group evaluation and collective rewards.

An important aspect of work group performance is the quality of the decisions that the group makes since groups are vital parts of the larger organization. Research on group dynamics has systematically shown that in group discussions, members tend to stick to their initial preferences regarding which group decision should be made, and by the end of a meeting they tend to feel more strongly about the rightfulness of their initial choice (group polarization). An explanation of this group phenomenon is that individual members give more weight to arguments favouring their initial position in group discussion, while neglecting the arguments against it. Some argue that the quality of decisions in real groups can be improved by making group members familiar with this type of knowledge about group dynamics, and asking them to consciously direct their attention to arguments against their initial preferences. In our experience, however, simply telling the group how individual members' initial preferences are reinforced by group discussion is usually not enough to tackle the problem. Special training and experience-based learning should be provided to employees to build competencies leading to high-quality group decision-making. Paradoxically, bad decision-making by groups also takes place when members feel strongly attracted to each other, as well as to the group as a whole (highly cohesive groups), and usually under the auspices of a charismatic and directive leader. This group phenomenon is called 'groupthink' and has been attributed primarily to exceedingly high levels of group cohesiveness.

Research on work group effectiveness has been criticized (e.g., Ilgen, 1999) on the grounds of focusing on the identification of group characteristics (e.g., group composition) and organizational context as determinants of effectiveness, while neglecting the importance of interaction processes taking place within groups. Even though the rationale of an input–process–output model is widely used to investigate work group effectiveness, the dynamic nature of the combination of input variables, which is represented in group processes, has not been adequately explored.

Conflict and negotiation in work groups

Conflict in groups at work is a process that often (but not always) exerts negative effects, interfering with communication and morale; but it also may produce positive outcomes, such as avoiding groupthink and making better group decisions. Indeed, effective conflict management can improve coordination, resulting in improved group performance. Problem solving is considered as the most effective strategy for resolving conflicts. However, research has shown that other conflict management styles, such as avoidance, can be helpful depending on the type of conflict (relationship conflict) and the time frame (short-term vs long-term orientation). Often it is organizational culture, situational factors and immediate goods that determine whether conflict or cooperation will occur.

It has been shown that a moderate level of task conflict – that is, debate and disagreement over the job or project the group has to carry out – has positive effects on group performance, such as the quality of decision-making, problem solving and task accomplishment. On the other hand, there is also substantial evidence demonstrating that *relationship conflict* – that is, clashes of personal preferences and differences in values and beliefs – is destructive to both task performance and social-emotional factors at work. An interesting point is that task conflict transforms rather easily into relationship conflict; therefore, one has to be careful not to cause relationship conflict by triggering conflict over the task.

A key point with respect to conflict is managing its inevitable occurrence – deriving the benefits of conflict while minimizing its harmful effects, but not eliminating it entirely. It is simplistic to see all conflict at work as bad, and all problems as solvable. Bargaining or negotiation is the most common approach to resolving organizational conflicts. Many factors influence the course and outcomes of bargaining, including specific tactics used by participants, their perceptions of each others' interests and priorities and their overall approach to bargaining – 'win–lose' or 'win–win'. Third-party interventions, such as mediation and arbitration, can also prove useful in resolving conflicts.

Window on the workplace

The Tavistock model of groups

The Tavistock model of groups (Bion, 1961) helps us observe, understand and intervene on group dynamics in real-life work groups operating in organizations. The basic premises of the model are:

- The group behaves as a system – an entity that is in some respects greater than its parts.
- The group should be perceived as focal and the individuals as background in order to observe group dynamics.
- The primary task of the group is survival.
- The group has a manifest overt aspect and a latent covert aspect. The former contains the tasks, goals and objectives pursued by the group. The latter comprises group members' hidden agendas; that is, unconscious desires, wishes and fantasies. The hidden agendas concentrate primarily on the role of leadership and authority in groups, the desire to fight or flee from the task, and the pairing/bonding between two group members who are expected to complete the task on behalf of the group.

The Tavistock model offers a practical guide applied by consults to analyse group behaviour in organizations. An example illustrating how this approach

(cont'd)

is utilized to understand group dynamics at work and increase awareness of group phenomena is as follows:

Applying the Tavistock model to understand group dynamics at work

The management team of a public Health Organization has decided to hire a human resource consultant to handle some problems that have emerged with the newly formed steering committee at its pediatric clinic. The steering committee has been running for a year, and consists of five members who are all doctors specialized in pediatrics holding equal hierarchical status in the clinic. The committee's task is to supervise the functioning of the clinic, work towards the expansion of the clinic's activities, diagnose potential problems and malfunctions, and take action towards their solution. One of the doctors, Nick Stevenson, is the head of the committee whose role is to coordinate group activities, while other group members do not hold any formal group responsibilities. The committee normally functions by forming project groups which work on the basis of accomplishing an agreed upon task, such as managing the website of the clinic on the internet. The five doctors have been rather well acquainted with each other even before being appointed into this committee or indeed joining the organization, since all five of them are well-known and respected doctors in their profession, who are also scientifically active doing research, attending scientific conferences and publishing their work in prestigious journals.

The problems began when Nick Stevenson and Stephanie Struck, one of the committee members, started having several arguments about relatively unimportant (and irrelevant) issues. Stephanie has become more and more aggressive towards Nick, as well as other members of the committee, with no apparent reason. For her part, Stephanie is anxious to secure her status in the group and succeed Nick when he retires in about two years. Stephanie is coming up with complaints of any sort about how the group functions and the opportunities that she has to actively participate in achieving group objectives and make a contribution to the clinic. The management team of the hospital, and the general manager in particular, is very frequently the recipient of such complaints by Stephanie, who seems to be very concerned with the political movements that, she thinks, will bring her to the top.

The hired consultant Sophie Scott is using the Tavistock group approach to observe and describe group processes occurring in groups at work, as well as provide interventions for the group to consider. Sophie has collected information on the committee group by observing several of their meetings, participating silently in some of them, conducting interviews with various informants within the hospital and checking on past meeting minutes that were made available to her. She has consulted only to the group, not to

(cont'd)

individual members, and only within prescribed time boundaries. Her task is to confront the group by drawing attention to *group behaviour* rather than individual members' characteristics, ambitions, desires or fantasies, and offer interventions for enabling more efficient group function.

Sophie has concentrated on the ways authority is vested in the group leader by other members so as to unravel the covert processes that operate in the committee. Even though Nick, as the head of the committee, has the formal responsibility to merely coordinate group activities towards the achievement of its goals, other group members expect of him to behave as an authority figure and save the group from the misbehaviour of Stephanie, which will eventually lead to a serious drop in the group's motivation to pursue its goals. The group behaves as if it is incompetent and hopes that it will be *rescued* by a leader who will instruct and direct towards task completion. The basic motivation of the group to either fight (active engagement) or flight (withdrawal, avoidance, passivity) from the task depends on the exercise of authority by the committee's head. If Nick becomes a directive and authoritative leader confronting the dysfunctional behaviour of Stephanie, group members will be alleviated from a psychological burden and the group's motivation to fight will rise. Sophie has proposed a number of intervention suggestions to group members that can be summarized as follows:

- Concentrate on your behaviour when having committee meetings rather than your intentions and beliefs. You might be surprised by how your behaviour in the group setting differs from what you expected it to be.

- Perceive the group-as-a-whole and do not focus on individual members' characteristics, and inferred values and intentions.

- Acknowledge the restricted role of the committee's head as a group coordinator rather than an authority figure.

- Work towards increasing the group's motivation to fight rather than flight from the task at hand.

- Take your share of responsibility in how the group is functioning and put effort to make it more effective.

Work group creativity and innovation

How can groups use their creative resources effectively? Innovation is a multistage process during which new and valuable ideas are generated (creativity phase) implemented (implementation phase) and usually reformulated since problems often arise when new ideas are put into practice. Groups can be an invaluable source of creativity and innovation because of the cross-fertilization of ideas and the cognitive stimulation that results from members' interaction.

Brainstorming is a group creativity-enhancing technique widely used by organizations to stimulate creative thinking among their employees. However, when organizational members brainstorm there are a number of psychological mechanisms that have been systematically shown to negatively interfere with the production of novel ideas. One such mechanism social psychologists call 'production blocking', and this refers to the negative effect that oral communication between group members has on the production of new ideas. That is, the generation of new ideas by one member may be inhibited by the demanding task of thinking of new ideas and simultaneously listening to the ideas of others. Other factors that reduce the effectiveness of brainstorming include 'evaluation apprehension' (the anxiety about being judged) and 'social loafing' (letting others in the group do the work).

To achieve creativity it is necessary that employees have expertise and a deep knowledge in a specific domain, that they exhibit divergent thinking and that they possess an appropriate combination of personality traits (specifically, curiosity and conscientiousness). The way in which jobs are designed can be a contributory factor to creative performance. Autonomy and control over the means to do the job, challenging tasks and an opportunity to verify one's personal competencies are also beneficial to creative thinking. However, for innovations to be successful it is essential that the social environment is characterized by high-quality group processes, such as a common vision, teamwork, trust, regard for personal identity and support for innovation. There is also a need to promote 'organizational climates' that make employees:

- feel safe in taking interpersonal risks and discussing problems openly;
- approach work proactively.

Apart from investigating how the effectiveness of groups at work is determined by the wider organization, this book aims to explain the effectiveness of an organization as a complex and dynamic system, which is always more than the sum of its parts.

Organizations are entities consisting of many groups, departments and sections that need to be well coordinated and integrated, as well as differentiated and pluralistic, for the whole system to run efficiently. We believe that an organizational culture approach to the study of organizations provides the opportunity to look at the organization as a social system of various conflicting values and preferences, which are characterized by a dilemmatic nature. The challenge is to develop an organization that promotes apparently conflicting values – such as autonomy and control, innovation and stability, and achievement and cooperation – to some extent by different departments, sections and informal groups in order to gain in efficiency.

Part II looks at the larger organization, in which work groups and teams are embedded, by taking an organizational culture perspective (Chapter 5). More specifically, we examine the role of leadership in shaping organizational culture (Chapter 6), the impact of culture on organizational performance (Chapter 7) and the dynamics of organizational change (Chapter 8).

The larger organization

It is possible to look at organizations from many different angles – to focus on the technology, the social system or culture, the authority and power, and the employees and their characteristics. Morgan (1986) vividly presented eight popular metaphors for the organization as follows:

1. culture: a set of basic assumptions, values, attitudes and beliefs about important aspects of organizational life;
2. machine: a machine that is designed and operated to make employees conform to its needs;
3. organism: a live and adaptive entity, like the human body;
4. brains: a rational, smart, creative and self-critical system;
5. political system: a system with a set power, authority, order and sources of social influence;
6. psychic prison: a set of fantasies and myths about its own image;
7. flux and transformation: a system that grows, develops, transforms and regenerates;
8. vehicle for domination: a system that imposes its will on its members by domination and control.

We argue that the study of organizations as dynamic cultures holding values, preferences, behavioural norms and practices regarding the way they deal with their members and with the external environment has offered a lot in aiding an understanding of the complex dynamics of organizational behaviour, including leadership, organizational performance and change.

Organizational cultures are contextual influences that operate on both individuals and groups to influence their behaviour. On the other hand, organizational members and groups may act towards maintaining or changing the essence of their organization's culture. For example, an important aspect of leadership is to work on the organizational values and practices; that is, to maintain and enhance the positive aspects of culture and to change the negative ones. Many would argue that changing culture is impossible, and that we cannot easily distinguish positive or functional aspects of a culture from negative or dysfunctional ones. However, it is worth making an attempt to examine organizational efficiency and change from an organizational culture perspective because the organizational culture concept encompasses many aspects of organizational life in a rather coherent way.

Organizational culture and leadership

Clearly, leadership influences the value system and practices of the organization, which in turn influences who is to become a leader. But how can leaders promote the adoption of their values by other organizational members? In the early history of an organization it is most often the leaders who formulate the philosophy and practices of the new organization, and select organizational members on the basis of sharing their beliefs about how the organization should operate. However, as the organization grows and usually becomes bigger and departmentalized, organizational practices get established and values are taken for granted. During this stage, organizational culture seems to be more of a cause rather than an effect of leadership.

There are a number of mechanisms that leaders have at their disposal when they try to communicate and establish their values and priorities. The allocation of rewards, status and scarce resources; reactions to critical incidents and crises; role modelling; and formal statements of philosophy are but a few of the means that leaders can utilize to promote their values and vision. These mechanisms are particularly useful when a leader faces the difficult task of changing an already well-established culture that has proved to be dysfunctional and maladaptive.

An interesting question is how an individual member can gain the power associated with the leadership role to be in a position to use the abovementioned mechanisms to change organizational culture. In general, mature organizations have cultures that are stable and therefore difficult to change. This is particularly the case when they have had a history of success over long periods of time.

However, it seems that there are cultures in mature organizations that are more receptive to organizational changes via strong, determined and visionary leadership. It is argued, for example, that organizations with supportive and adaptive cultures are conducive to transformational leadership; that is, individual leaders who show personal integrity, competence and self-confidence, articulate a persuasive vision, inspire others with their vision, behave creatively and show concern for others. Therefore, organizational members characterized by the attributes of transformational leadership might stand a better chance of becoming leaders of organizations with supportive and adaptive cultures, and of changing ineffective aspects of their organization's culture.

Performance and organizational culture

Researchers have shown considerable interest in the culture–performance link, putting forward two main questions. The first is whether organizational effectiveness is related to the strength of organizational culture, which is usually defined in terms of how widely and intensively organizational values are shared by its members. The second research question examines the content of culture in relation to its performance; that is, investigating whether there are functional and dysfunctional dimensions of organizational culture and identifying their content.

A number of studies have demonstrated that culture strength is associated with effectiveness, possibly because it leads to implicit coordination of individual employees and groups at work. However, strong cultures can possess dysfunctional elements and, therefore, culture strength needs to be examined in relation to its content in order to understand organizational effectiveness. A review of the literature identified two main dimensions of culture as predictors of effectiveness; namely, a 'humanistic orientation' and an 'achievement orientation'. The humanistic orientation involves participation in decisions, cooperation, teamwork, creativity, social support and constructive social relations at work. The achievement orientation, on the other hand, promotes values and practices such as goal setting, task organization, efficiency, organizational objectives and feedback.

The contingency approach to the culture–performance link has argued that organizational effectiveness is largely determined by the fit between the organization and its environment, and focused on a third dimension of organizational culture, namely, adaptability. This is an organization's capacity to change in response to external demands and to undertake a learning process by responding to these demands. It is possible that an organization fits its external environment but does not possess the capability of changing when its environment changes. Therefore, culture–environment fit is conducive to organizational effectiveness but the cultural trait of adaptability reflects more than a mere organization–environment fit.

Organizational change

The ability to change and adapt to new circumstances is essential to organizational success and survival, especially when the economic, technological and social conditions are rapidly transforming. The organization is a sociotechnical system that needs to be adaptable to important changes in the external environment or to challenges arising from within.

The targets of organizational change are usually the *structure, technology* and *people*. Whether or not an organization aims to change its structure, technology or people, culture and climate change are cardinal factors in the process of change. Armenakis, Harris and Mossholder (1993) have persuasively proposed that beliefs, perceptions and attitudes are critical to successful change.

It is well argued that we cannot change organizations unless we understand their organizational culture. Once organizational culture is understood, one should focus on specific behaviours rather than trying to change values and beliefs. Beliefs (attitudes and values) often follow behaviour. Moreover, changing group behaviour is more feasible than changing individual behaviour. Individual members are more willing to alter the way they do their job or behave towards their supervisor or colleagues when other members have adopted novel practices.

Changing a complex social system, such as an organization, is a difficult task. Some argue that changing an organization's culture is not feasible and that the best one can do is to be aware of the multiple ways in which behaviour is interpreted within the cultural frames of a particular organization. Resistance to change is often observed and to a large extent involves the multiple forces that exist and act within organizations. For example, organizational members in places of authority might resist change because of a desire to maintain their power, while non-management employees might feel that their jobs are at risk.

Case study

Understanding the DLM airlines' culture through the examination of a planned change

DLM is a European airline that switched from a product-and-technology to a market-and-service orientation under the leadership of a new president. Before the implementation of change, planning and sales had been based on conducting a maximum number of flights with the most modern equipment available. Pilots, technicians and disciplinarian managers were the organization's heroes. However, as organizational performance was deteriorating, the president decided that to deal with the competitive business environment the organization had to focus on its customers' needs.

Employees with face-to-face customer contact are the main recipients of customers' complaints, suggestions and desires. They were never previously asked for their opinions and were rather treated as disciplined soldiers, who had to follow rules. But the new way of conducting business recognizes that they are on the 'front line', so the organization has to support instead of order them around. They are empowered to deal with customer problems on the spot and are expected to take initiatives towards solving these problems, while checking with their superiors afterwards.

Interviews with middle managers and non-management employees were carried out three years after the turnaround. All members of staff are uniformed, disciplined, formal and punctual; they seem to enjoy working in a disciplined environment. When talking about the company's past, they do not show any signs of nostalgia. They appear to be proud of the company and at least part of their identity is derived from being a member of the organization. The president is often mentioned as a company hero, who has managed to save the corporation from a declining route. Social relations among DLM-ers outside work are strongly encouraged. Despite the high value placed on discipline, relations between colleagues tend to be positive and supportive. A colleague who confronts a crisis in their private life is supported by others and by the company. Managers at various hierarchical levels are visible and generally accessible, although more managers have trouble accepting their new role than do non-managers.

(cont'd)

New employees are introduced to the company's policies and practices via a formal introduction and training programme, which includes simulated encounters with client complaints. This also serves as a screening device to check whether the new employee has the values and skills necessary for the profession. Employees are expected, as well as encouraged, to show a problem-solving attitude towards clients. They show considerable excitement about finding original ways to solve customer complaints, in which some rules can be twisted to achieve the desired goal. Promotion is from the ranks and is on the basis of competence and collegiality.

Source: Adapted from Hofstede, Neuijen, Daval Ohayv, and Sanders (1990).

Summary

Groups are powerful forces within organizations that can promote or inhibit the achievement of organizational objectives, including economic or other indicators of performance and quality of working life. Understanding group dynamics can increase the chances of obtaining desirable consequences from group interaction. Decision-making, problem solving and innovation are but a few important processes that occur in groups and are largely determined by human psychology. Work groups encounter conflicts over tasks or personal issues, which, in turn, have a major impact on the quality of group products. If organizational members understand group dynamics in organizations, they can use groups more effectively to accomplish the goals of the organization, as well as their personal goals.

Organizations, however, are complex social (and technical) systems that need more than effective work groups to run smoothly. Improved group performance does not guarantee improved organizational performance (Guzzo & Dickson, 1996). It is vital that departments, sections and work groups are well coordinated and integrated for superior performance to be achieved.

Organizational culture – representing a system of basic beliefs, values and practices – can be fundamental in building a coordination mechanism. Cultures that promote an achievement and humanistic orientation have the potential to integrate organizations and lead to efficiency given that they simultaneously promote adaptability to environmental influences and innovation. Focusing on achievement or the human factor in organizations may seem at times conflicting and dilemmatic in nature. For example, encouraging employees to take parental leave may interfere with the effective functioning of a department. However, in the long run, efficiency is enhanced by working environments that show individualized consideration and concern for the needs of employees, and respect for personal identity, given that the importance of achievement is well embedded in organizational culture.

Questions

1. What is group dynamics and why should we be examining it? What are the key defining elements of groups?

2. How do groups reach decisions, and by what means can we improve the quality of group-decision making?

3. Can we identify psychological processes occurring in groups that (a) promote creativity and innovation and (b) ensure that conflict is beneficial to the group?

4. Does the construct of organizational culture fulfil expectations of understanding what organizations basically are?

5. Are leaders important influences on organizational cultures? Name some of the mechanisms that they have at their disposal in reinforcing or changing aspects of an organization's culture.

References

Armenakis, A. A., Harris, S. G., & Mossholder, K. W. (1993). Creating readiness for organizational change. *Human Relations*, **46**, 681–703.

Baron, R., & Greenberg, J. (1990). *Behavior in Organizations*. Boston, MA: Allyn & Bacon.

Bion, W. (1961). *Experiences in Groups*. New York: Basic Books.

Cohen, S. G., & Bailey, D. E. (1997). What makes teams work: Group effectiveness research from the shop floor to the executive suite. *Journal of Management*, **23**, 239–290.

Duncan, W. (1978). *Essentials of Management*. Hinsdale, IL: Dryden Press.

Guzzo, R. A., & Dickson, M. W. (1996). Teams in organizations: Recent research on performance and effectiveness. *Annual Review of Psychology*, **47**, 307–338.

Hofstede, G., Neuijen, B., Daval Ohayv, D., & Sanders, G. (1990). Measuring organizational cultures: A quantitative study across twenty cases. *Administrative Science Quarterly*, **35**, 286–294.

Ilgen, D. R. (1999). Teams embedded in organizations: Some implications. *American Psychologist*, **54**, 129–139.

Lewin, K. (1951). *Field Theory in Social Science*. New York: Harper & Row.

Morgan, R. (1986). *The Image of Organizations*. London: Sage.

Sundstrom, E., McIntyre, M., Halfhill, T., & Richards, H. (2000). Work groups: From the Hawthorne studies to work teams of the 1990s and beyond. *Group Dynamics: Theory, Research, and Practice*, **4**, 44–67.

Part I
Group Processes and Outcomes

Performance and Decision-Making in Work Groups

2

Chapter outline

Introduction
Definition and types of work groups
Individual versus group performance
   Social facilitation/inhibition
   Group productivity: Steiner's theory
   Social loafing and motivation gains in groups
Decision-making in groups
   Risky shift and group polarization
   Groupthink
Work group effectiveness in organizational contexts
Some practical implications for groups at work
Summary
Questions

Chapter objectives

The main objectives are to:

- understand the defining characteristics of work groups, and be able to describe various types and different functions of work groups;

Parts of this chapter appear in 'Xenikou, A., & Hantzi, A. (2004). Groups, Productivity in. In C. Spielberger (ed.), *Encyclopedia of Applied Psychology* (vol. 2, pp. 137–142). San Diego, CA: Elsevier.'

(cont'd)

- identify the conditions under which either individual or group performance produces better results, and describe the factors that explain these differences in performance;
- describe the psychological processes that take place in group decision-making;
- explain the phenomenon of 'groupthink', and identify practical ways to prevent its occurrence;
- describe theory addressing the topic of work group effectiveness, and explain how it may be applied in organizational settings to increase efficiency at work.

Introduction

The explicit and implicit structure of organizations places people in groups, something that we find natural and normally enjoy. We are social creatures: we prefer to live and work in groups. But the question for organizations is when, whether, how and why we work more efficiently and happily in groups. More specifically, we need to describe the different types of groups that organizations often utilize to do tasks like designing new products, delivering services and making strategic decisions, as well as the factors that make these groups work successfully.

The complexity and flux of the global business environment has led to a more extensive use of work groups in organizations. For example, project teams have the ability to save time by doing multiple activities simultaneously, rather than sequentially, as they bring together members of the organization with different and complementary backgrounds and expertise. Similarly, management executive teams are considered to be in a better position than individual managers to achieve the strategic objectives of the organization since they represent a greater pool of knowledge, cognitive abilities and expertise.

West (2001) suggests that the current enthusiasm of the business world for work groups and team working reflects a deeper recognition that this way of working offers the promise of greater progress than can be achieved through individual endeavour or mechanistic approaches to work. However, he also points to the fact that organizing work by using work groups has become a fad, and very often the necessary conditions for enabling groups to be efficient are neglected. Further, it seems to be much easier in collectivist rather than individualistic cultures.

Definition and types of work groups

Sundstrom, De Meuse, and Futrell (1990) define work teams as small groups of interdependent individuals who share responsibility for specific outcomes for their organizations. There are, for example, work groups which are responsible for the production of goods or the delivery of services to customers. Production groups consist of employees who collaborate on producing a final output and share responsibility for its quality. Organizations also make use of project groups whose members synchronize their efforts to carry out specialized projects and offer a variety of expert knowledge and experience to tackle organizational problems.

Work groups have various characteristics, such as size, roles, cohesiveness and norms, and are structured in different ways. There are explicit structures that describe the roles that group members occupy, their relative status and power, as well as communication channels that exist within any given group. Besides the explicit structure of the group, there are also other forces that determine power differentials and communication networks, as, for example, the time one has spent being a member of the group and sharing common beliefs or ideologies with powerful group members.

Most work groups have a formal structure, are task-orientated and have been consciously and formally organized by organizational decision-makers for a reason. Furthermore, their activities (should) contribute directly to organizational objectives and goals. There are many issues that work groups need to address over time. Groups can even change the way they do some of these things, but they have to deal with these problems in one way or another:

- *Participation.* Are members expected to actively participate in group discussions and decision-making? Do members feel that their contributions are unique and indispensable for group functioning?
- *Decision-making.* How are decisions made? Is it the leader who makes the important decisions? Does the group operate on democratic rules?
- *Conflict handling.* How are disagreements handled? Are members of higher status challenged on the validity of their arguments?
- *Communication.* Which are the formal and informal channels of communication? Are there preferred modes of communication, such as face-to-face communication?
- *Division of labour.* How are group tasks assigned to members? Is it usually the case that subgroups are formed for handling various group tasks?
- *Process monitoring.* How are task processes monitored and checked? Is feedback regularly provided?
- *Performance evaluation.* Are the criteria on which members evaluated clear? How frequently are members evaluated and by whom?
- *Goal comprehension.* Is it important that each group member understands group goals? How crucial is it that group members are motivated by and committed to these goals?
- *Social relations.* How close, friendly and causal should group interaction be? Are group members expected to become friends or is it that formal relations are encouraged within the group?

In a recent review of research on work group effectiveness, Sundstrom, McIntyre, Halfhill, and Richards (2000) identified six types of work groups distinguished mainly by the tasks the groups have to carry through:

- *Production groups* comprise front-line employees who repeatedly produce tangible output, such as automobile assembly groups and chemical processing crews.
- *Service groups* consist of employees who cooperate to conduct repeated transactions with customers, as in maintenance groups and telecommunications sales groups.
- *Management teams* usually consist of an executive or senior manager and the managers or supervisors who report directly to them and coordinate work units through policy making.
- Similar to *task forces, project groups* carry out specialized and time-limited projects and their members come from different departments, as in engineering project teams and new-product development groups.
- *Action and performing groups* usually consist of expert specialists, who carry out complementary roles in conducting complex tasks, such as rescue units, investigative units and surgery teams.
- *Advisory groups*, such as quality circles and employee involvement groups, are most of the times put together by managers to make recommendations about various problems rather than implementing them.

Sundstrom et al. suggested that possibly different factors have an effect on the performance of the six types of work groups they identified. For instance, some groups, such as project groups, need creativity and innovation to be successful at dealing with their task requirements, while other groups, such as sales groups, have to use good communication strategies to be effective with customers. However, it remains unclear which factors are important for the effectiveness of different types of work groups.

Although theory and research on group dynamics have accumulated considerable knowledge on individual versus group performance and decision-making – for instance, social facilitation/inhibition effects, social loafing, group polarization and groupthink – it is an open question as to what extent this knowledge has been utilized in most work settings in understanding work group effectiveness.

There is a plethora of studies that have attempted to study the complexity of group life in organizational settings and unravel the conditions that lead to high-performing real work groups. However, as noted by Ilgen (1999), research on work groups in organizational contexts has focused on the identification of group characteristics (e.g., group composition) and context variables (e.g., reward systems) that are related to effectiveness while neglecting the interaction processes taking place within groups, as well as their dynamic nature.

This chapter aims at integrating the models and findings of work group effectiveness literature with knowledge that social psychology has provided on the interaction processes that take place within groups. In the following two sections, the accumulated social psychological knowledge on individual versus group performance is presented, as well as the processes that occur in group decision-making. Then, we examine the available findings on work group effectiveness and combine these latter findings to group dynamics.

Individual versus group performance

Most people have at some point wondered if it is more productive to work as part of a team or alone. Are decisions made by groups better than those made by separate individuals? Is the quantity and quality of group products superior to the products generated by individuals? These are simple, but challenging, questions that social psychology has faced from its start. Researchers have worked hard for decades to answer whether group performance is superior to aggregated individual performance. Inevitably, the results are both equivocal and complex but there are clear patterns. In work settings, it is important, in terms of work design, to be in a position to know whether groups are more effective than individuals, as well as the conditions that are related to the superiority of either group or individual performance.

Social facilitation/inhibition

The most elementary issue concerning the impact of social factors on individual task performance is whether the mere presence of others influences individual performance. Social facilitation and inhibition (SFI) refer to the positive and negative effects that audiences (as well as coactors) may have on individual task performance. Think, for example, of how an open office layout influences the motivation and performance levels of individual employees. Imagine one wall of an office has brick replaced by glass so that what goes on in the office can be observed by those outside it.

Interest in how the presence of others affects individual performance dates back to 1898 when Tripplett conducted one of the first experiments in the field of social psychology. Tripplett had children spin fishing reels either alone or in coactive pairs and found that participants performed better coactively. He also timed competitive cyclists racing alone or against others. They always achieved better times when competing against talented rivals. Following Tripplett's work, many researchers replicated the finding that the mere presence of others facilitates individual performance.

However, later on others demonstrated the social inhibition of individual performance under similar conditions. In 1965 these apparently inconsistent results were explained by Robert Zajonc, who proposed that the presence of others facilitates individual performance in the case of simple tasks, whereas it impairs performance at complex tasks. Zajonc put forward a drive theory of social facilitation, suggesting that the mere presence of others increases generalized drive or physiological arousal. Arousal, in turn, leads to the generation of dominant responses – that is, responses which are well learned, habitual or innate. Simple tasks are successfully performed when dominant responses are generated, whereas complex tasks being more demanding in nature cannot be accomplished by the emission of dominant responses.

A number of other theoretical accounts of how task complexity affects individual performance at social settings have been provided. Zajonc had such a great impact that some of these theoretical accounts did not challenge the 'drive' approach of his theory and presented factors considered as determinants of drive/arousal. For example, (1) people's concern with evaluation and (2) distraction/conflict caused by attending both to the task at hand and other people were factors proposed by different theoretical approaches to account for elevated arousal at social settings. Recent theories have challenged the biologically based explanation offered by Zajonc's theory, and have focused on cognitive and attentional factors as determinants of SFI effects.

There is a strong empirical basis suggesting that task complexity is related to the manifestation of SFI effects as proposed by Zajonc. However, it has been found that physiological arousal is not necessarily increased by the presence of others irrespective of task complexity. Complex tasks do lead to an elevated drive when others are present, whereas simple tasks do not seem to provoke increased levels of physiological arousal. In sum, Zajonc's proposition that task complexity plays an important role in explaining SFI effects has been strongly supported by the findings, but the exact mechanism(s) leading to facilitation and impairment of simple and complex tasks, respectively, has not been identified. On a practical level, we can suggest that for achieving greater efficiency employees should be enabled to control their working environment by either allowing or not allowing the presence of their colleagues. Jobs most often contain both simple and demanding tasks to be performed by an individual employee and, therefore, making a choice on working in the presence or absence of others can elevate individual performance.

Group productivity: Steiner's theory

Although the literature on social facilitation suggests that under certain conditions one feature of group settings (i.e., the presence of others) enhances individual performance, most of the work on group performance argues that when people work together in groups they do not perform at the maximum level of their potential. Steiner (1972) proposed an influential analysis of group productivity, which focuses on the notion of a group's potential productivity, the maximum possible performance level that the group can achieve. Potential productivity is determined by group members' resources and task demands.

Member resources concern the capabilities, knowledge and skills of group members that can be useful at completing the task at hand. Task demands mainly refer to the criterion that is used to estimate a group's performance level. The criterion of performance at a weight-lifting construction task is the total weight lifted, whereas in the case of a brainstorming task it is the number of novel ideas generated by the group.

Steiner's model assumes that a group is not in a position to achieve its potential productivity due to process loss (faulty group process), and that a group's actual productivity is potential productivity minus losses due to faulty process. Process loss refers to coordination, as well as motivation, losses. When performing in groups it is necessary for group members to coordinate their actions to achieve the desired group goal. For example, at a rope-pulling task group members have to synchronize their actions to achieve their full potential. This need for coordination inevitably leads to loss in productivity since group members cannot often pull at exactly the same time or direction. Regarding motivation losses, individuals are considered to exert less effort when working as part of a team than when working alone.

Steiner also provided a task classification or taxonomy (see Table 2.1), which aimed at further assisting researchers in the investigation of group productivity. According to Steiner's classification, there are three task characteristics that can be used to categorize different tasks. The first task feature is whether a task can be subdivided to separate parts performed by different people. The tasks that cannot be subdivided are unitary, whereas the tasks that can be subdivided are divisible. An example of a unitary task is finding a solution to a numerical problem such

Table 2.1   Steiner's task classification

Task characteristics	Task taxonomy
Can a task be subdivided to separate parts performed by different people?	Yes→ Divisible tasks No→ Unitary tasks
Does the task performance criterion concern quantity/speed of production or a correct/optimal solution?	The performance criterion concerns Quantity/speed of production → Maximizing tasks Correct/optimal solution → Optimizing tasks
How are group members' inputs related to group product?	Members make separate contributions and the best contribution must be chosen → Disjunctive tasks Group performance is determined by the contribution of the least capable member → Conjunctive tasks The individual contributions are simply added together → Additive tasks

Source: Adapted from Steiner (1972).

as an accounting mistake. A task, on the other hand, that is certainly divisible among co-workers is assembling a car.

The second task feature used to classify tasks is the performance criterion mentioned earlier, leading to a distinction between maximizing and optimizing tasks. When a task performance criterion concerns the quantity or speed of production, the task is considered to be a maximizing task; the weight-lifting task is a good example of a maximizing task. On the other hand, optimizing tasks put a demand for a correct or optimal solution (e.g., finding an accounting error).

Third, the way that group members' inputs are related to the group product leads to four different types of tasks: disjunctive, conjunctive, additive and discretionary tasks. In a disjunctive task, members make separate contributions and the best contribution must be chosen (e.g., a reasoning problem). In conjunctive tasks, group performance is determined by the contribution of the least capable member (e.g., executing an action plan). In additive tasks, the individual contributions are simply added together (e.g., the number of products that have been sold by group members), and finally, in discretionary tasks individual inputs are combined in any way the group chooses (e.g., brainstorming outputs).

Steiner's model has been criticized on the basis that it explicitly makes the assumption that groups never reach their full potential, which is the total of all group members' maximum performance. It has been argued that groups might be in a position not only to achieve performance at the highest level of their potential but also to overperform it. The model has put emphasis on coordination and motivation losses that influence group performance, while discounting the possibility that groups may exhibit 'motivation gains'.

Social loafing and motivation gains in groups

Do people put in less effort towards accomplishing a task or reaching a goal when they work as members of a group? There is ample evidence suggesting that individuals tend to loaf when working in groups occupied with a wide variety of tasks, such as physical tasks, cognitive tasks and perceptual tasks. Maybe people in groups feel less pressure towards performing well or/and individual output is not identifiable, which, in turn, leads to lower levels of motivation. However, researchers have also identified certain conditions in which individuals overperform when working in groups, as, for example, in the case of a group member compensating for the low performance of other members to accomplish a highly valued group goal.

Social loafing

Productivity loss in group settings has been defined in terms of both coordination and motivation losses. The first experiments on group productivity were conducted during the last decades of the nineteenth century by Ringelmann (1913). In these experiments individuals were asked to pull a rope either alone or in groups of various sizes. The results showed that when individuals worked in groups, the collective output was less than the sum total of the typical individual performance measured when individuals pulled the rope alone. This finding can be explained as the result of coordination loss. However, subsequent research showed that this finding is caused by the joint effect of coordination problems and reduced effort exerted by group members.

Regarding motivation losses, there is a difference between the effort that individuals exert when working collectively and working coactively (or individually). When people work collectively their individual contributions are combined to form a group product, whereas when they work coactively their individual inputs are not combined to a single product. Individuals' tendency to produce lower effort when working collectively compared to working coactively (or individually) has been called 'social loafing' by Latané and his colleagues (1979).

Social loafing has been observed in a wide variety of tasks, including physical tasks (e.g., rope pulling, shouting, clapping), cognitive tasks (e.g., idea generation tasks), perceptual tasks (e.g., maze performance) and evaluative tasks (e.g., evaluation of editorials), suggesting that social loafing is a robust phenomenon. As a general phenomenon not restricted to physical tasks, it poses the important practical question of why and when less effort is exerted in group settings.

A number of theoretical explanations have been proposed to explain why social loafing takes place in groups. It has been suggested that social loafing occurs because:

- The pressure people feel as group members to accomplish the task at hand is less intense than the pressure one feels when working alone.
- The presence of other group members is drive reducing because others share the responsibility for carrying out the task.
- There is reduced identifiability or evaluation potential in collective action compared to individual action.
- Group members feel their contributions to the group product not to be essential but dispensable.

An interesting question is whether people are generally aware of their social loafing. Subjects' self-reports tend to fail to acknowledge the difference in their efforts between the collective and the coactive conditions or to underestimate the magnitude of the difference. Therefore, participants either do not appear to be aware that they loaf or are unwilling to report that they do loaf. It has been shown that self-reports on effort are more likely to be consistent with actual performance when people have an expectation of how well their co-workers will perform on the task. This suggests that usually social loafing reflects a nonconscious process, whereas in some cases people do make a conscious decision to reduce their collective effort. In practical terms, organizational members participating, for example, in new product teams or quality circles tend to psychologically rely rather heavily on other group members to accomplish group objectives and engage non-consciously in social loafing but there are a number of ways to deal with social loafing as shown in Box 2.1.

Box 2.1   Ways to deal with social loafing at work

- identify and evaluate individual contributions
- ensure uniqueness of individual inputs
- provide feedback on individual or group performance
- have small rather than large groups
- devise meaningful and self-involving tasks
- attempt to ensure close ties among group members

Free-rider and sucker effects

Apart from social loafing, two other effects have been reported, namely, the free-rider effect and the sucker effect (see Baron & Kerr, 2003). The free-rider effect concerns the enjoyment of the benefits resulting from the successful group performance without contributing to it. The free-rider effect might be seen as the result of a person's conscious decision to indulge in social loafing.

On the other hand, members of a group who work hard to accomplish group goals run the risk that others may free-ride on their efforts and become suckers. The expectation that others withhold efforts in performance groups can lead to the individual reducing his or her contribution to the group in order to prevent being a victim of free-riding (the sucker effect).

Social compensation

Even though research on group performance has focused on productivity loss in group settings due to reduced motivation, there are findings showing that motivation gains can also result from performing within groups (Karau & Williams, 1993). Williams and Karau (1991) demonstrated conditions under which people may actually increase their efforts when working collectively compared to when working individually (coactively). They call this effect 'social compensation'. Social compensation refers to a group member compensating for (making up for) the low performance of other members in order to accomplish the desired group goal.

One factor that might produce social compensation is the expectation that other group members are performing insufficiently. The perception of inadequate co-worker inputs may be derived from a general lack of trust in the reliability of others to perform well when their contributions are pooled with those of others, or/and direct knowledge of co-workers' insufficient efforts or inabilities. A group member may be new, tired, sick or handicapped, so others try to make up for this. The second factor that may be necessary to produce social compensation is that the group product is in some way important to the individual. If the group output is not meaningful and important to group members, then one does not expect social compensation to occur.

Social compensation is not expected to occur in all situations in which individuals believe their co-workers are contributing less than their fair share. Besides group product meaningfulness previously mentioned, other factors are important for compensation to take place. Social compensation is more likely to occur

- when the individual has to remain in the group working collectively;
- when the group size is relatively small;
- at earlier stages of the collective effort.

Finally, people may be motivated to compensate in some cases for their own prior underperformance rather than the underperformance of other group members. This could be seen as a sort of guilt reduction.

According to social compensation, when group members of unequal strength work on an important task, the most competent member will often compensate for the insufficient contribution of the other group member(s). There are, however, findings showing that under specific conditions the weaker member of the group tries hard to match the performance level of the stronger member (the Köhler effect). One necessary condition for this effect to occur is that the group product must be meaningful and important to its members. The second condition is that the discrepancy in ability between the group members must be of a moderate degree. A high discrepancy in individual performance is not expected to lead to more effort exerted by the weakest members because people believe that there is a limit to the discrepancy in ability that can be compensated through increased effort (Stroebe, Diehl, & Abakoumkin, 1996). Therefore, we can possibly apply these findings in real work settings, and design work groups on the criterion of members' ability discrepancy – moderate magnitude of discrepancy is desirable – and meaningfulness of task objectives to obtain high levels of job motivation.

The social loafing paradigm has been criticized on the basis that little effort is expended by researchers in making participants feel that they are part of a meaningful group. In the paradigm, a number of individuals combine their efforts for a group output without interacting with each other, competing with other groups or expecting any form of future interaction. Even though the findings of research on social loafing are discussed in terms of group membership, it seems that participants mainly act on the basis of their personal identity rather that a group-based sense of self. Motivation and performance losses described by research on social loafing might be the result not of faulty group processes but of individuals acting as persons rather than group members. It has been demonstrated that when social identity is made salient there are motivation gains leading to the accomplishment of the desired goal (Worchel, Rothgerber, Day, Hart, & Butemeyer, 1998).

Decision-making in groups

Since many decisions in organizations are made by groups, it is important that organizational members are familiarized with the knowledge that social psychology has accumulated on how groups reach decisions. For example, Papadakis and Barwise (2002) examined the influence of top management teams on strategic decision-making and found that both the competitive aggressiveness of the team and educational level of managers had an impact on how rational, comprehensive and decentralized the strategic decision was, alongside with other contextual factors (see Box 2.2 for some rules of group decision making). A basic question is whether groups make better decisions than individuals since groups have more resources in comparison to individuals alone. Commonsense suggests that groups make more reasonable, and therefore better, decisions than individuals but research on group decision-making has shown that groups often tend to polarize group members' initial preferences.

Box 2.2   Rules of group decision-making: Can group decisions be objectively evaluated?

A group task may be solving a problem or reaching a decision for which there exists a demonstrably correct answer (intellective tasks). For example, a group of accountants might be looking for an important accounting error that has troubled the finance department of a corporation. On the other hand, there are tasks that are purely judgemental since there is not a demonstrably correct answer or some time is needed before one is in a position to objectively evaluate whether a preferred solution is the best among a number of alternatives (judgemental tasks). That is the case of decisions usually made by an organization's board of directors concerning the strategies that will be employed to outperform competitors

Laughlin and Ellis (1986) demonstrated that in the case that the group is facing an intellective task with obvious demonstrable correct answer, group decision-making is predicted by the 'truth-wins' rule. That is, if there is a group member who knows the correct answer the group will collectively agree on it given that the solver has the motivation to share his knowledge and the other group members have the ability and motivation to recognize a correct solution. Moreover, if the correct answer to an intellective task is not so obviously demonstrable, then the 'truth-supported wins' rule predicts group decision-making. Since the correct solution is not that easily shown, the mutual support between two correct group members increases their ability to demonstrate that their solution is correct.

Finally, for judgemental tasks, since there is no objective basis for assessment, the principle that predicts group decision-making is 'majority rules'. As the demonstrability of whether a group response is correct is low, the number of group members favouring a solution is important for that solution to be adopted by the group.

Risky shift and group polarization

Stoner (1961) utilized a set of 12 life-situation problems, which were originally developed to examine individual risk-taking, to test the hypothesis that groups are more cautious than individuals. An example of a life-situation problem used in Stoner's experiment is the following: An electrical engineer is faced with an opportunity of joining a new company with an uncertain future which, if it is successful, could offer greater chance for advancement than his present, more secure, position offers. Participants were asked to give advice to the actors in various life situations on the preferred course of action in private, and then to reach unanimous decisions in six-member groups. The results showed that group decisions were more risky than the mean of the individual group members' prior decisions. The finding that group discussion leads group members to prefer more risky decisions than they had advocated as individuals was termed the 'risky-shift phenomenon'.

However, later research demonstrated that group discussion might sometimes also lead to more cautious decisions in comparison to the mean of individual members' initial positions. Stoner (1968) talked about 'risky' and 'cautious' shifts in group decisions, reflecting on the finding that group discussion may result in either more risky or more cautious shifts depending on whether widely shared values favour a risky or a conservative decision. The term 'group polarization' has been introduced to capture the phenomenon that group discussion tends to produce more extreme decisions compared to the mean of group members' initial preferences, in the direction favoured by the mean (Moscovici & Zavalloni, 1969). For instance, if a top management team has to make a decision on pursuing a risky business opportunity the decision that will eventually be reached by the group will be more extreme than the average of top managers' opinions, and in the direction already favoured by the group.

There are three main theoretical approaches that explain why group polarization takes place. First, in accordance with persuasive arguments theory (Burnstein & Vinocur, 1977), people hold a number of supportive arguments in favour of their position which they express publicly in group discussion. During this process group members probably hear new arguments favouring their initial position and consequently group opinion polarizes. A second perspective focuses on the mechanisms of social comparison (Festinger, 1954) and proposes that group members tend to compare their own opinions to the opinions of other group members. As individual members realize that others in the group hold the same opinions, they tend to become more extreme to gain greater social approval and avoid disapproval (Sanders & Baron, 1977). Third, self-categorization theory (Turner, Hogg, Oakes, Reicher, & Wetherell, 1987) suggests that group discussion leads to the formulation of a group norm that distinguishes the group as a unit from other groups. In order to achieve a clear differentiation between our group and other groups, the final decision reached by the group may become extreme.

Research on group polarization has not concluded on which theoretical explanation is more adequate, or whether a combination of all is necessary, to understand this group phenomenon. Certainly, some strong new ideas and theories are needed to fully understand the mechanisms behind group decision-making. However, the suggestions offered by each theory can be taken seriously into account to promote the quality of decisions in real work groups. For example, it can be made explicit to group members that because people tend to give more weight to arguments favouring their initial position in group discussion, they need to consciously redirect their attention to arguments against it. However, as already mentioned, simply informing people of how their opinions become polarized when participating in group discussions is not enough to deal with this bias. Training and more experience-based learning seem to be necessary to avoid the pitfalls of group decision-making.

Groupthink

Another important line of research on group decision-making has suggested that highly cohesive groups, in which members are attractive to each other or have a strong desire to continue being part of the group, under specific conditions make bad-quality, or even disastrous, decisions. This phenomenon is called 'groupthink' by Janis (1982) and refers to the deterioration of mental efficiency, reality testing and moral judgement that results from group pressures.

Janis developed the concept of groupthink by qualitatively analysing historical materials of political and military decision-making. An example of a historical case that Janis included in his analysis is the Bay of Pigs invasion that was decided by the American President J. F. Kennedy and his group of advisers. In the Bay of Pigs invasion a rather small group of Cuban exiles were sent to invade this Cuban coast but in a short while were all killed or captured resulting in the mission being a total failure. Another frequently cited example of groupthink is the dramatic explosion of the space shuttle Challenger, which has been described as a sequence of bad decisions made by groups of people working for NASA (Esser, 1998).

Which are the conditions that cause groupthink to emerge in group decision-making? Groupthink is likely to occur when cohesive groups of individuals having directive rather than participative leadership work under pressure to reach a decision, while being isolated from other sources of information, such as experts, and following limited search and appraisal procedures. As a result the group has an illusion of unanimity and invulnerability (i.e., they all agree and are right), puts pressure on dissenters to conform to the 'group's position' (i.e., put down those with different views) and stereotypes out-groups such as market competitors. Janis suggests that under these circumstances defective decision-making processes take place leading to ill-made decisions. Among these defective decision-making processes are selective bias in examining information, incomplete survey of objectives and alternatives, failure to elaborate on risks of preferred solutions and failure to reassess initially rejected solutions.

Groups of individuals sharing similar backgrounds and opinions such as employees with similar professional qualifications, irrespective of the individual members' abilities, are quite vulnerable to groupthink. In order to prevent groupthink from taking place a number of things can (and should) be done:

- It is important that leaders and other powerful group members do not express their preferences until other members have the chance to put forward their thoughts so that pressure to conform to the dominant position is weakened.

- Leaders should also explicitly encourage group members to share any reservations they might have about a preferred course of action and to express openly and frequently their ideas concerning possible alternatives.

- Experts can be invited to give new information on various topics on which the group has to decide.

- The group can be divided in two subgroups so that different perspectives may emerge on dealing with the issue at hand.

- A devil's advocate may be appointed whose duty is to look for possible drawbacks in the preferred solution and the risks that this solution entails.

Of course, groupthink has been extensively criticized and other constructs, besides cohesiveness, have been suggested as explanations for the bad decision-making in groups, such as collective efficacy (Whyte, 1998). However, although the model is based on relatively weak empirical data – primarily the examination of case studies – it is a compelling, coherent and probably oversimplistic perspective of real-world groups and organizations (Paulus, 1998).

Work group effectiveness in organizational contexts

An issue that has strongly been put forward is whether findings regarding group processes and outcomes from laboratory experiments can be readily and easily generalized to real groups and teams operating in organizational settings. Being specific, it is advocated that even though organizational features external to the team can be important determinants of work group effectiveness, they are rarely examined in laboratory settings (Cohen & Bailey, 1997; Sundstrom et al., 1990). Therefore, field research on real groups operating in organizational contexts proliferated, and different types of work groups in various industry sectors were examined to find the elements that are associated with group effectiveness.

A considerable number of models of work group effectiveness were presented during the 1980s and the 1990s (Campion, Medsker, & Higgs, 1993; Campion, Papper, & Medsker, 1996; Cohen & Bailey, 1997; Gladstein, 1984; Hackman, 1987). Most of the models were built on an input–process–output analysis that is the dominant theoretical perspective on group performance. The input–process–output models suggest that input and process variables have an impact on outcomes such as group performance. Specifically, input refers to the attributes of the individual members of the group such as cognitive ability, skills, expertise, experience and personality; process concerns the social interaction of group members and how their individual characteristics are combined to produce a number of group outcomes; and finally, output refers to the various group products such as decisions, services and suggestions that the group generates to respond to task and, in general, organizational demands.

An input–process–output model of work group effectiveness has been suggested by Campion and his colleagues (Campion et al., 1993, 1996) that intended to integrate and extend a number of earlier models, as well as the findings of various studies on work group effectiveness. They proposed and tested a conceptual framework consisting of the following clusters/themes of work team characteristics related to group effectiveness:

- *Job design characteristics* concern self-management of work groups and members participation in decision-making, as well as characteristics related to the nature of the task at hand, namely task variety, significance and identity.
- *Interdependence* is the degree to which

  (a) group members have to cooperate to accomplish the work (task interdependence),
  (b) individual members' goals are linked to the groups' goals (goal interdependence),
  (c) feedback is provided and rewards are distributed on the basis of individual or collective performance (interdependent feedback/rewards).

- *Composition* captures membership heterogeneity in terms of abilities and experiences, flexibility in terms of members' ability to perform each other's jobs and relative size of the group.
- *Organizational context* refers to organizational resources, such as training and managerial support, and communication and cooperation between groups within the organization.

In accordance with an input–process–output perspective, the four themes above are the inputs to the group, while a fifth element called 'process' describes how those things that go in the group, the inputs, interact to produce the group outputs. 'Process' includes various characteristics, such as the confidence with which a group approaches its tasks (potency), social support, workload sharing and good communication/cooperation within the group (see Figure 2.1).

Campion and his colleagues tested the assumptions of their model using samples of work groups primarily from the financial services sector. They examined the relationship between work team characteristics proposed in their model and a number of team effectiveness criteria including productivity, employee satisfaction and management ratings. The findings showed that all team characteristics were related to some criterion of effectiveness, and that process and job design themes were more predictive in comparison to the other work group characteristics.

On the other hand, Cohen and Bailey (1997) presented a heuristic model of group effectiveness that moves away from the input–process–output approach by

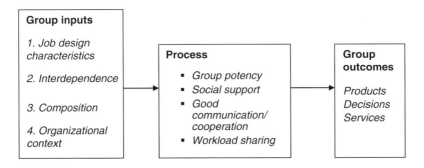

Figure 2.1   Campion and colleagues' model of work group effectiveness (adapted from Campion et al., 1993, 1996)

depicting group design factors as having a direct and an indirect impact on outcomes via group processes and psychosocial traits. The model refers to a number of variables including environmental factors (e.g., turbulence, industry characteristics), task design and group composition (e.g., group autonomy, group size) and organizational context (e.g., rewards, supervision), which directly and indirectly influence effectiveness. The indirect effect of these factors on effectiveness is mediated by group processes such as conflict (see Chapter 3) and internal and external communication, and group psychosocial traits, namely norms and shared mental models. It is also suggested that group processes can become embedded in 'psychosocial traits' such as group norms and beliefs. These are in effect aspects of organizational culture, which we will talk about later. Finally, effectiveness outcomes can reciprocally influence group processes, psychosocial traits, and even design factors. For example, the composition of top management teams is likely to change when the organization is performing badly (see Figure 2.2).

Both models of work group effectiveness proposed by Campion and his colleagues and Cohen and Bailey can be criticized on the grounds that they conceive group processes much more as another stable group characteristic rather than a dynamic psychological phenomenon. Group processes concern how individual members' perceptions, beliefs and behaviours are influenced and changed when group members interact and communicate with each other rather than the socio-psychological traits of groups partially emerging from group interaction and social influence, such as group potency or sharing workload. Socio-psychological traits of groups, such as group values of social support, are expected to have an impact on how supportive group members are to each other, but need to be clearly differentiated on a conceptual basis from group processes to help us understand group dynamics. Group polarization in decision-making and motivational losses or gains in group settings are clearly group processes describing how groups function, while social support or participation in decision-making may be processes occurring in groups but also can be attributes of groups or organizations to the extent that they are values promoted

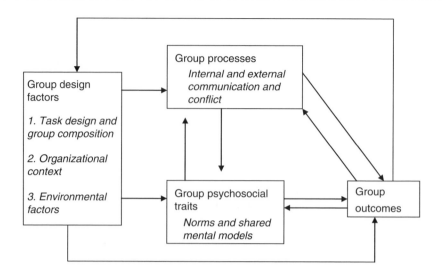

Figure 2.2   Cohen and Bailey's model of work group effectiveness (adapted from Cohen and Bailey, 1997)

by these social units. This conceptual distinction between group attributes and processes is indeed very useful towards the direction of integrating the knowledge of social psychology on group dynamics with the findings on work group effectiveness.

Let us now consider in more detail research on work group effectiveness, and then integrate it with the literature on group processes to gain a better understanding of group performance. As far as group work design characteristics are concerned, Janz, Colquitt, and Noe (1997) found that group autonomy and interdependence, which are the most widely used team design characteristics, reduced the positive effects associated with each other. For teams placed in highly interdependent circumstances, there was no relationship between autonomy and team job motivation, whether that autonomy related to discretion over goals, budgets, training needs and/or product development. However, it is worth noting that autonomy for people, that is decision-making over staffing, was positively related to job motivation regardless of interdependence levels. Similarly, Wageman (1995) investigated the relationship between task interdependence and group effectiveness in groups of service technicians. The findings showed that highly interdependent groups performed well in the case of collective rewards, whereas members of independent groups demonstrated high performance when rewards were distributed on an individual basis (see also 'Constructive controversy' in Chapter 3).

In terms of group composition, research has examined the effect of individual members' cognitive abilities, experiences, background and personality traits, as well as group size, on work group performance. Group members' individual cognitive ability and the personality trait of conscientiousness were related to higher group effectiveness (Barrick, Stewart, Neubert, & Mount, 1998; Neuman & Wright, 1999). As far as ability is concerned, Tziner and Eden (1985) showed that uniformly high-ability military crews surpassed performance effectiveness anticipated on the basis of members' ability, whereas uniformly low-ability crews fell far short of expectations based on individual ability. They concluded that teaming high-ability members not only ensures superior performance in each position but also enhances the accomplishment of group performance more than expected. Also, research on group size has advocated for using the smallest possible number of people who can do the task (Hackman, 1987) because group performance seems to decline as a result of adding members to the group beyond the ones needed for accomplishing the task at hand.

Among the most studied predictors of group performance has been cohesiveness – that is, 'the resultant forces which are acting on members to stay in a group' (Festinger, 1950). In a meta-analytic study of the relation between group cohesiveness and performance, Mullen and Copper (1994) found that the cohesiveness–performance effect was significant, but of small magnitude, and that the effect was stronger in real and small groups. Besides group cohesiveness researchers have extensively studied whether members' shared beliefs regarding group collective ability (collective potency or efficacy) and team psychological safety influence group effectiveness. Perceptions of group collective ability have been found to be positively related to group productivity, employee satisfaction and managerial judgements of effectiveness (Campion et al., 1993; Hyatt & Ruddy, 1997). Moreover, team psychological safety, defined as a shared belief that the team will not embarrass, reject or punish someone for speaking up, has been shown to be associated with learning behaviour, which in turn is related to higher team performance (Edmondson, 1999).

The impact of group activities and strategies directed towards other groups within the organization, such as top management and other functional or divisional groups, on team effectiveness has been highlighted by Ancona and Caldwell (1992). They argued that the frequency of communication with outsiders is not the only factor that influences team performance but it is the content and purpose of communication that matters. By studying new-product teams in high-technology organizations they showed that a 'comprehensive' strategy of external communication is related to better performing teams over the long run. The comprehensive strategy focuses on external interaction both to persuade powerful others in the organization that the team's work is important and to coordinate, negotiate and obtain feedback from outside groups on task accomplishment. In other words, a group may engage in activities that enhance group competence to powerful others and try to control images of itself, while at the same time look for information sharing and feedback on task through lateral communication.

Finally, in line with the proposition that work groups can best be understood in relation to external surroundings, Sundstrom and his colleagues (1990) have suggested that organizational culture is probably an important contextual feature that has an impact on group effectiveness. For instance, organizational cultures that encourage innovation or reflect shared expectations of success may especially foster group performance. Xenikou and Simosi (2006) found that a cultural achievement orientation mediated the relationship between transformational leadership and business unit performance. In other words, organizational culture was the mechanism through which leadership behaviour had a positive impact on group effectiveness.

The findings on work group effectiveness show that the perceived nature of group task, participation in decision-making, cooperation within the group and beliefs in group collective competence are factors associated with high group performance. Similarly, the literature on group motivation gains proposes that complex and self-involving tasks performed by groups that are psychologically meaningful to their individual members are conditions leading to group effectiveness.

Therefore, a central theme that might emerge out of these research findings is that groups outperform individuals when the task at hand is stimulating, as well as complex, and at the same time group members value the fact that they are part of a given group. Perceptions of collective group competence are directly related to the value a member places on group membership because individual members can enhance their self-esteem by belonging to a successful group. In practical terms, groups are expected to be better performers than individuals when the group task at hand is self-involving and the group is of great importance to its members.

Some practical implications for groups at work

Despite the fact that most research on group performance has emphasized the inefficiency of groups compared to individuals, groups feature in most essential aspects of everyday life. Their central role in real-world contexts might have to do with the fact that many tasks cannot be accomplished by individuals working alone. If one considers how many people with different skills are involved in making a car or building a house, then it becomes clear that getting rid of groups cannot (ever) be a practical solution to increase performance.

Regarding groups at work, how can we use the accumulated knowledge on group performance to understand how groups function and to propose ways on a practical level for groups to become more effective?

In organizational settings, brainstorming groups, for example, are extensively used to stimulate employees to think creatively. In brainstorming groups, members are asked to generate as many ideas as possible, not to criticize others' ideas and to build on ideas presented by other group members. Research by Diehl and Stroebe (1987) has showed that brainstorming groups produce half the ideas produced by the same number of individuals who brainstorm alone (nominal groups). This productivity loss in brainstorming groups has been discussed as a coordination and motivation loss resulting from mutual production blocking, evaluation apprehension and social loafing. Mutual production blocking arises from the constraint that only one group member can talk at a time in a brainstorming group. Individuals are also concerned about potential evaluation by other group members and therefore may limit the number and type of ideas that they share in the group. Finally, group members may have low motivation because of social loafing or free-riding.

Although there is ample evidence showing brainstorming groups to be less effective than nominal groups, organizations of all kinds make wide use of brainstorming groups. A reason that might explain organizational members' confidence in brainstorming groups is that members of such groups are more satisfied with their performance in comparison to individuals who brainstorm alone. This discrepancy between satisfaction and productivity can be accounted for by the greater ease of idea generation in brainstorming groups compared to nominal groups. Since brainstorming is widely used at work, some advice needs to be given on the conditions that make brainstorming groups more effective:

- Firstly, the size of the group should be kept as small as possible, not exceeding four members.
- Secondly, because time pressure negatively affects the productivity of brainstorming groups, groups should decide when it is the best time to stop.
- Finally, it is advisable that group members be heterogeneous in their knowledge about the brainstorming topic so that members can have a stimulating impact on each other (see also Chapter 4).

Moreover, our knowledge on group productivity can be applied to training at work in order to improve organizational effectiveness. There are interventions designed to increase productivity through learning which were found to have strong positive effects, such as group training programmes. It has been suggested that in group training programmes learning is associated with a transactive memory system – knowledge shared by group members on who is good at what. When members of a work group are trained together, they develop complementary specializations that enable the group to share knowledge and skills. In this way, the group as a whole makes use of social compensation – that is, individual members compensate for each other's inadequacy. However, a practical problem related to group training at work involves the disruption that employee turnover has on the smooth operation of the work group.

The business world has acknowledged the importance of one's ability to work within groups as a key factor to success. In this sense, groups are seen as capable of accomplishing more than the sum of their individual parts. However, the bulk of research on group performance suggests that, more often than not, groups are not as efficient as they could potentially be.

Summary

It is a well-known fact that the use of work groups is extensive in organizations. Groups at work might have quite different goals to accomplish, therefore various types of work groups do exist, such as production groups, brainstorming groups and service groups. Since groups are widely used by organizations the knowledge on how groups work, as well as the conditions that are related to superior group performance, is of great value to management.

In general, the findings have shown that groups are more effective than separate individuals because groups learn faster, produce a greater quantity and quality of work, and make fewer errors. However, groups rarely accomplish their full potential since their performance is not as high as the sum-total of the maximum individual performance of each group member. It has been suggested that coordination losses and motivation losses are responsible for groups performing less efficiently than expected. Therefore, groups have to work on how to coordinate and motivate their members to achieve high levels of effectiveness. Groups do lead to motivation and productivity gains when tasks are self-involving and the group is important to its members.

Most significant decisions in organizations are usually made by groups, such as management executive teams or boards of directors. Consequently, it is beneficial to an organization if its members are conscious of the psychological processes that affect group decision-making. Social psychologists have shown that group discussion tends to polarize the initial preferences of group members. In other words, people tend to hold more extreme opinions following group discussion and in the same direction as their initial preferences. Moreover, groups and especially their leaders should be paying attention to the negative effects that group cohesion may have on the quality of decision-making. When the group leader is directive and group members are very likeable to each other, there is a high probability that the group will ignore valuable information and make bad decisions.

How can we make work groups more effective? The conditions under which the group becomes psychologically important to its members are key factors to work group effectiveness. Groups are important to their members if individual goals are linked in some way to group goals, members have to cooperate to accomplish group goals and rewards are provided on the basis of collective performance. When group members believe in their collective efficacy to achieve group goals, they tend to identify with the group because, by doing so, they expect to accomplish the desired goals and at the same time they feel more valuable as persons (enhancement of self-esteem). Of course, perceptions of collective efficacy are to a great extent determined by past group successes, which are largely the result of individual members' cognitive abilities, discrepancies in members' abilities (social compensation) and personality traits.

Questions

1. Describe various types of work groups. With reference to an organization you know well, give examples of various work groups.
2. Which are the conditions related to the superiority of either individual or group performance at work?

3. Does the mere presence of other people (either as an audience or coactors) enhance individual performance? Discuss how these findings relate to the case of teleworking.

4. What is social loafing and why does it take place? In your opinion, is social loafing a serious threat to work group performance? Explain your answer.

5. How can social loafing be reduced or overcome in work settings?

6. How does individual decision-making differ from group decision-making?

7. Which work group characteristics and processes seem to matter most in achieving high performance?

Window on the workplace

Strategic decision-making by top management teams

Tim Lane is the CEO and one of the five owners of a medium-sized corporation operating in the petroleum industry. His father was running the company for nearly 20 years until he became ill and retired. Since then Tim has managed the corporation with the aid of a top executive team consisting of a finance, sales and personnel director. The four men get along very well on a professional as well as personal level, and they have harmoniously worked together for nearly five years accomplishing most of the objectives set by the corporation's business plan.

Even though the petroleum industry sector is a stable rather than dynamic business environment, the international economic recession has put a lot of pressure on the company to adopt new business revenues. For the corporation to survive through the difficult economic conditions, Tim believes that they have to adopt a more aggressive strategy towards their competitors, and thoroughly explore the opportunities of collaborating with companies in the greater region of the Balkans on an import–export basis. He has recently made some business contacts with petroleum corporations operating in Albania and Turkey.

But, because of the economic recession, the importance of accurately judging how serious, trustworthy, and financially robust is a potential collaborator has become even greater than before. Should the company proceed with entering international partnerships on an import–export basis, and if so, what financial guarantees should be asked for?

(a) Analyse the parameters of the situation and,

(b) Describe how the CEO and the top management team can work towards reaching a high-quality decision.

References

Ancona, D. G., & Caldwell, D. F. (1992). Bridging the boundary: External activity and performance in organizational teams. *Administrative Science Quarterly*, **37**, 634–665.

Baron, R. S., & Kerr, N. L. (2003). *Group Process, Group Decision, Group Action*. Buckingham: Open University Press.

Barrick, M. R., Stewart, G. L., Neubert, M. J., & Mount, M. K. (1998). Relating member ability and personality to work-team processes and team effectiveness. *Journal of Applied Psychology*, **83**, 377–391.

Burnstein, E., & Vinocur, A. (1977). Persuasive argumentation and social comparison as determinants of attitude polarization. *Journal of Experimental Social Psychology*, **13**, 315–332.

Campion, M. A., Medsker, G. J., & Higgs, A. C. (1993). Relations between work group characteristics and effectiveness: Implications for designing effective work groups. *Personnel Psychology*, **46**, 823–850.

Campion, M. A., Papper, E. M., Medsker, G. J. (1996). Relations between work team characteristics and effectiveness: a replication and extension. *Personnel Psychology*, **49**, 429–452.

Cohen, S. G., & Bailey, D. E. (1997). What makes teams work: Group effectiveness research from the shop floor to the executive suite. *Journal of Management*, **23**, 239–290.

Diehl, M., & Stroebe, W. (1987). Productivity loss in brainstorming groups: Toward the solution of a riddle. *Journal of Personality and Social Psychology*, **53**, 497–509.

Edmondson, A. (1999). Psychological safety and learning behavior in work teams. *Administrative Science Quarterly*, **44**, 350–383.

Esser, J. K. (1998). Alive and well after 25 years: A review of groupthink research. *Organizational Behavior and Human Decision Processes*, **73**, 116–141.

Festinger, L. (1950). Informal social communication. *Psychological Review*, **57**, 271–282.

Festinger, L. (1954). A theory of social comparison processes. *Human Relations*, **7**, 117–140.

Gladstein, D. L. (1984). Groups in context: A model of task group effectiveness. *Administrative Science Quarterly*, **29**, 499–517.

Hackman, J. R. (1987). The design of work teams. In J. W. Lorsch (ed.), *Handbook of Organizational Behavior* (pp. 315–342). Englewood Cliffs, NJ: Prentice-Hall.

Hyatt, D. E., & Ruddy, T. M. (1997). An examination of the relationship between work group characteristics and performance: Once more into the breech. *Personnel Psychology*, **50**, 553–585.

Ilgen, D. R. (1999). Teams embedded in organizations: Some implications. *American Psychologist*, **54**, 129–139.

Janis, I. L. (1982). *Groupthink* (2nd edition). Boston: Houghton Mifflin.

Janz, B. D., Colquitt, J. A., & Noe, R. A. (1997). Knowledge worker team effectiveness: The role of autonomy, interdependence, team development, and contextual support variables. *Personnel Psychology*, **50**, 877–904.

Karau, S. J., & Williams, K. D. (1993). Social loafing: A meta-analytic review and theoretical integration. *Journal of Personality and Social Psychology*, **65**, 681–706.

Latané, B., Williams, K., & Harkins, S. (1979). Many hands make light work: The causes and consequences of social loafing. *Journal of Personality and Social Psychology*, **37**, 822–832.

Laughlin, P. R., & Ellis, A. L. (1986). Demonstrability and social combination processes on mathematical intellective tasks. *Journal of Experimental Social Psychology*, **22**, 177–189.

Moscovici, S., & Zavalloni, M. (1969). The group as a polarizer of attitudes. *Journal of Personality and Social Psychology*, **12**, 125–135.

Mullen, B., & Copper, C. (1994). The relation between group cohesiveness and performance: An integration. *Psychological Bulletin*, **115**, 210–227.

Neuman, G. A., & Wright, J. (1999). Team effectiveness: Beyond skills and cognitive ability. *Journal of Applied Psychology*, **84**, 376–389.

Papadakis, V. M., & Barwise, P. (2002). How much do CEOs and top managers matter in strategic decision-making? *British Journal of Management*, **13**, 83–95.

Paulus, P. B. (1998). Developing consensus about groupthink after all these years. *Organizational Behavior and Human Decision Processes*, **73**, 362–374.

Ringelmann, M. (1913). Recherches sur les moteurs animes: Travail de l'homme (Research on animate sources of power: The work of man). *Annales de l' Institut National Agronomique*, **XII**, 1–40.

Sanders, G. S., & Baron, R. S. (1977). Is social comparison relevant for producing choice shifts? *Journal of Experimental Social Psychology*, **13**, 303–314.

Steiner, I. D. (1972). *Group Process and Productivity*. New York: Academic Press.

Stoner, J. A. F. (1961). *A comparison of individual and group decisions involving risk*. Unpublished Master's thesis, Massachusetts Institute of Technology, School of Industrial Management.

Stoner, J. A. F. (1968). Risky and cautious shifts in group decisions: The influence of widely held values. *Journal of Experimental Social Psychology*, **4**, 442–459.

Stroebe, W., Diehl, M., & Abakoumkin, G. (1996). Social compensation and the Köhler effect: Toward a theoretical explanation of motivation gains in group productivity. In E. Witte, & J. H. Davis (eds.), *Understanding Group Behaviour: Small Group Processes and Interpersonal Relations* (pp. 37–65). Mahwah, NJ: Lawrence Erlbaum Associates.

Sundstrom, E., De Meuse, K. P., & Futrell, D. (1990). Work teams: Applications and effectiveness. *American Psychologist*, **45**, 120–133.

Sundstrom, E., McIntyre, M., Halfhill, T., & Richards, H. (2000). Work groups: From the Hawthorne studies to work teams of the 1990s and beyond. *Group Dynamics: Theory, Research, and Practice*, **4**, 44–67.

Tripplett, N. (1898). The dynamogenetic factors in pacemaking and competition. *American Journal of Psychology*, **9**, 507–533.

Turner, J. C., Hogg, M. A., Oakes, P. J., Reicher, S. D., & Wetherell, M. S. (1987). *Rediscovering the Social Group: A Self-Categorization Theory*. Oxford, England: Blackwell.

Tziner, A., & Eden, D. (1985). Effects of crew composition on crew performance: Does the whole equal the sum of its parts? *Journal of Applied Psychology*, **70**, 85–93.

Wageman, R. (1995). Interdependence and group effectiveness. *Administrative Science Quarterly*, **40**, 145–180.

West, M. A. (2001). The human team: Basic motivations and innovations. In N. Anderson, D. S. Ones, H. Sinangil, & C. Viswesvaran (eds.), *Handbook of Industrial, Work, and Organizational Psychology* (pp. 270–288). London: Sage.

Whyte, G. (1998). Recasting Janis's groupthink model: The lead role of collective efficacy in decision fiascoes. *Organizational Behavior and Human Decision Processes*, **73**, 185–209.

Williams, K. D., & Karau, S. J. (1991). Social loafing and social compensation: The effects of expectations of co-worker performance. *Journal of Personality and Social Psychology*, **61**, 570–581.

Worchel, S., Rothgerber, H., Day, E. A., Hart, D., & Butemeyer, J. (1998). Social identity and individual productivity within groups. *British Journal of Social Psychology*, **37**, 389–413.

Xenikou, A., & Simosi, M. (2006). Organizational culture and transformational leadership as predictors of business unit performance. *Journal of Managerial Psychology*, **21**, 566–579.

Zajonc, R. B. (1965). Social facilitation. *Science*, **149**, 269–274.

Conflict and Negotiation in Groups at Work

3

Chapter objectives

The main objectives are to:

- analyse the conflict process by referring to its basis elements, that is perceptions/cognitions, emotions and responses;

- distinguish between task and relationship conflict, and describe the dimensions on which conflict can be assessed;

- understand the factors, as well as mechanisms, which lead to positive or negative effects of conflict;

- appreciate the significance of the cooperative and competitive elements comprising most conflict situations;

- identify and assess styles of conflict management;

(cont'd)

- describe types of third-party intervention;
- explore and understand cognitive biases interfering with negotiations.

Introduction

In large as well as small organizations, conflict between organizational members is usually frequent and certainly inevitable at some time or another. Managers have reported that they spend about 20 per cent of their time dealing with some form of interpersonal conflict (Baron, 1989). It is important that managers realize that conflict can be an enemy but also an ally in their efforts to have their organization work efficiently. It can be both a constructive and a destructive force. Indeed some managers deliberately engineer conflict to bring about change. The management of conflict in organizations between individual employees, groups of employees or organizational departments can potentially contribute to an organization's ability to deliver goods and services to clients. Employees throughout the organization need, however, to collaborate and manage conflict if they are to provide high-quality services. In Chapter 2 we elaborated on group performance and put emphasis on the quality of the interactive processes that occur between members of work groups. The main concern is that putting together a group of competent people does not guarantee that a high-quality group output is produced. These highly competent people need to be well coordinated and keep their motivation high to deliver good decisions, products or services. One important aspect of group interaction is conflict and how it is handled within work groups. Dealing with conflict constructively contributes to the coordination necessary to achieve organizational objectives.

Individuals and groups in dispute frequently use negotiation to resolve their conflict. In negotiation, disputants hold different initial beliefs and preferences, which are considered as an obstacle to each other's attempts to gain or retain a desired state, and interact in order to settle their differences (Thompson, 1990). It is important that parties in conflict realize that various components of a settlement may be valued differently by each party and mutually beneficial trade-offs can be the outcome of a negotiation. A necessary condition for the occurrence of trade-offs is that the two parties interact and communicate with each other in an open and constructive way. The communication between the conflicting parties helps an understanding of each other's perspective, finding some common ground, creating a shared understanding of the situation and detecting differences in the value placed on various negotiation outcomes. However, communication should be considered as a means to achieve settlement and mutual satisfaction, which is a necessary rather than a sufficient factor. Communication seems to produce a number of positive negotiation outcomes because it can potentially be a factor promoting trust and positive feelings between the disputants. On the other hand, the interaction and communication of the conflicting parties may also lead to the escalation of a destructive conflict when trust is not a product of the social interaction.

The conflict process

Traditionally, conflict has been assumed to be inevitably destructive: a win–lose dual. Conflict is something that causes pain and reduces cooperation and friendship. As people with opposing interests compete against each other, both sides can be seriously damaged in one way or another. The destructive consequences of conflict are thought to be especially pervasive in the case that conflicting parties belong to the same group, since cooperation and coordination of group members are essential prerequisites for group success. However, Deutsch (1973) argued against viewing conflict situations as necessarily reflecting opposing interests, suggesting that in every conflict there are both competitive and cooperative elements. Deutsch has defined conflict as 'incompatible activities, where one person's actions interfere, obstruct, or in some way make the behaviour of another less effective'. Thus, conflict is not the opposite of cooperation and there is cooperative potential inherent in almost every conflict.

It is interesting, however, to notice that the negotiation literature has shown that people in conflict usually assume their interests are strictly opposed to those of the other party, even when the two parties have compatible interests (Thompson & Hrebec, 1996). Imagine, for example, how an employee might be competitive towards other people in their department when working in work groups, because of assuming that they are as much motivated as he/she is to get promoted. However, this is not necessarily an accurate description of other people's motives since individuals differ significantly in the priorities they set in their lives. It seems, therefore, that people have a tendency to disregard the cooperative potential inherent in conflict, which might be responsible for the fact that using conflict positively in organizations has proven difficult.

Conflict is a process that usually begins when one party perceives that another party has negatively affected, or is about to negatively affect, something that they care about, leading to various thoughts, emotions and possible responses to the conflict situation (Thomas, 1992). De Dreu et al. (1999) define conflict as the tension an individual or group experiences because of perceived differences with another individual or group; conflict issues produce feelings such as pride, resentment, anger and fear, as well as cognitions that relate to the other side in the conflict and involve stereotypes. Moreover, Rahim (2001) suggests that conflict is inevitably an interactive process manifested in incompatibility, disagreement or dissonance within or between social entities.

Consider a hypothetical scenario of an emerging conflict between two directors of a large financial organization to illustrate the theoretical points made above (see also Box 3.1):

> In a large financial organization the personnel department has received numerous requests from branch managers asking for the immediate recruitment of a substantial

number of personal financial advisors (PFAs). The job of a PFA is to inform customers about the various financial products that the organization offers to its customers and to give advice on which products seem to be more suitable to each individual client. Branch managers have reported to the personnel department that customers have to wait for an average of 30 min to be served by a PFA at the bank branches.

It has been a month now since the board of directors decided that the selection tools for the recruitment of the PFAs had to be improved. The research and development (R&D) manager argued that PFA performance evaluation during the last eight years showed that the way PFAs are selected should change. The selection tools that are used currently do not seem to pick the best people for the job, as the overall PFA performance is average. More importantly, the best PFAs working for the bank at the moment do not hold high scores on the selection tools. On these grounds all the directors agreed that the R&D people should work on a new battery of selection tools for PFA selection.

However, the launching of a new marketing campaign by the bank has attracted new customers visiting the bank's branches, which has caused further delays in service. As the marketing campaign is particularly successful the problem is not expected to be a temporary one sorting out itself in a few weeks.

The personnel manager decided to go to the R&D manager's office to gather information about the time schedule of the project and to make sure that his colleague knew about the pressure put on the branches because of PFA shortage. During the one hour that the meeting lasted the R&D manager said that they needed another two months to finish the project, but under the circumstances he was going to put a lot of pressure on his people to have the selection tools ready within a month. The personnel manager argued back that the branches could not possibly wait for another month as customers were making complaints on a daily basis for delays in service. Both men felt particularly frustrated by the situation, and there was a lot of tension while they continued trying to find some way to resolve the issue.

The personnel manager believed that he was unreasonably obstructed by the R&D people to go ahead with the recruitment of new PFAs, who were so badly needed by the bank branches. He thought that the people at the R&D unit were more like researchers than business people, and they weren't willing to understand that for a corporation to be successful the realities of the business world were more important over some academic rigour. On the other hand, the R&D director believed that personnel people were bureaucrats primarily interested in carrying through the procedure and completing the task at hand rather than making sure that what they did was effective and functional.

The meeting between the two directors ended without finding a common ground on how the problem could be handled, and the two men agreed on taking the issue to the board of directors to resolve it.

The scenario presented above shows the possible incompatible activities of the R&D and personnel people. The conflicting elements of the situation are apparent, whereas the directors do not seem to have found the cooperative

Box 3.1   Conflict scenario between sales and production managers of a manufacturing firm

The sales department has promised a major customer an early delivery date on a given item. When informed of this during a meeting, the production supervisor feels frustrated because that delivery date would throw off his whole production schedule. He has carefully planned his schedule to maximize the productive capacity of his resources. Therefore, since the production manager believes that covering the sales department's promise is incompatible with the efficiency of his own department he tries to make the sales manager change the promised delivery date. Annoyed at this response, and disturbed by the idea of disappointing the customer, the sales manager resists this influence attempt and tries to convince the production manager to meet the delivery date. The discussion of this issue took an hour of the meeting during which both parties become more hostile and argumentative. By the end they did not reach any decision.

Negotiations between the department heads are largely taking place during biweekly meetings chaired by the vice-president of operations. This procedure shapes the behaviour of both parties as complaints accumulate until meeting time. Social pressures from other department heads help to keep the competition from escalating uncontrollably, but the prevailing organizational norms do not encourage problem solving. The production manager tends to be somewhat more competitive than the sales manager. This difference is partly due to the production manager's personality: he is an older up-from-the-ranks manager who fought his way out of poverty. Both managers are greatly encouraged by their departmental colleagues to behave competitively, and the members of the two departments have come to view the other department as an enemy. Underlying many of the issues that arise between the two department heads is some very real conflict of interest resulting from tight performance measures and tightening organizational resources. Both parties have high stakes in these issues, since their departmental performance evaluations depend heavily on production cost efficiency (for production) and meeting delivery dates (for sales).

The conflict between the sales and production managers has consumed an hour of the meeting, preventing the department heads from addressing a number of important agenda items. As the production and the sales manager could not come to an agreement, it appears that the sales department will be unable to keep its promise to one of the organization's important customers. Moreover, relations between the two department heads have become even more antagonistic, and the sales manager seems to be even more frustrated and disenchanted with how the organization operates.

The vice-president of the operations, the immediate supervisor of the two managers, is chairing the meeting in question. The vice-president suppresses the conflict for the remainder of the meeting to move on to other topics. He schedules a meeting with both department heads for later in the day, when

---

Box 3.1   (cont'd)

he attempts to help the two clear the air and reach an agreement that will be acceptable to both departments and will not alienate the customer in question.

The vice-president mandates regular meetings between the sales and production departments, requiring the sales and production managers, along with their immediate subordinates, to meet jointly at a fixed time each week to discuss the scheduling of major upcoming orders. He also calls in a staff specialist to re-examine the performance evaluation systems for the two department heads.

(1) Analyse the conflict situation with reference to:

   (a) conflicting parties' perceptions/cognitions, emotions and behaviour,

   (b) styles of conflict management,

   (c) organizational norms and

   (d) vice-president interventions.

(2) Identify the conflicting elements of the situation and the potential cooperative elements.

Source: Adapted from Thomas (1992).

---

elements that can potentially lead to conflict resolution. The personnel manager focuses on the recruitment of new personnel to staff the bank branches, while the R&D director believes that the organization's priority should be to develop a valid instrument to select the best people for the job. There is also tension, feelings of frustration and lack of trust, and the two parties seem to experience a state of dissonance. Finally, it is interesting to notice the role that stereotypical beliefs play in the evolution of conflict as the parties in dispute believe that the image of 'researcher' or 'bureaucrat' can explain a lot in the behaviour of their opponents.

The interaction of the disputing parties is not usually limited to one conflict episode. According to Thomas (1992), a conflict episode begins with the party's awareness of the conflict. This awareness may be triggered by a threat to the party's self-interest but may also involve a variety of other types of concerns (such as differences in values or judgement). Awareness leads to various thoughts and emotions of the party regarding the conflict situation and possible responses to it. The thoughts and emotions result in the formulation of intentions with respect to coping with the conflict, which are then enacted in the form of observable behaviour. The other party then reacts to this behaviour, initiating a more or less prolonged interaction with the other. During the course of this interaction, the party's thoughts and emotions may change, altering intentions and behaviour accordingly. When the interaction on a given issue stops, some set of outcomes has occurred. The outcomes of a given episode set the stage for subsequent episodes on the same issue.

As sequences of conflict behaviour unfold it is important to examine whether people have a tendency to reciprocate each other or to react in a complementary fashion. Weingart, Thompson, Bazerman, and Carroll (1990) found that negotiators mostly engage in reciprocation irrespective of their opponent's behaviour. However, De Dreu et al. (1999) argue that in many disputes conflicting parties may be tempted to take advantage of each other's cooperative behaviour and to respond with dominating behaviour. They also suggest that parties in dispute may suspect ulterior motives behind each other's yielding or problem-solving behaviour and attempt to defend themselves with dominating responses. De Dreu et al. conclude that there is a general tendency in conflict behaviour to reciprocate, but with constructive behaviour sometimes being 'undermatched'. In explaining the circle of action and reaction of conflicting parties, De Reuver (2006) suggested that the concept of 'power' could play an important role. In fact De Reuver found that line managers reacted in a complementary fashion to their superiors by avoiding confrontations with dominant superiors, while they dominated more with submissive subordinates than with dominant subordinates.

Conflict most often occurs in 'mixed-motive' situations where persons have both competitive (win–lose) and cooperative (win–win) interests; the competitive elements produce the conflict (eye-for-an-eye), whereas the cooperative elements create the incentives to negotiate for an agreement (Tjosvold, 1998). The disputing parties tend to behave in a reciprocal way irrespective of the distributive or integrative behaviour of the other party. There is also, however, a tendency to take advantage of others by acting in a competitive way when they behave cooperatively.

Conflict and work group effectiveness

According to a traditional viewpoint, as already mentioned, conflict is something destructive (even irrational) that needs to be avoided if groups and individuals are to perform effectively. The traditional perspective suggests that conflict interferes with information processing capacity and impedes task performance, while at the same time conflict leads group members to dislike each other, feel rather dissatisfied and intent to leave the group. Later on the human relations school argued that conflict is inevitable and that under specific circumstances it can prove to be beneficial to team performance. Finally, the interactionist view considers conflict as potentially desirable so that groups can accomplish higher levels of performance, and it proposes that conflict should be encouraged since building a superficial consensus leads to poor results.

Most research on organizational conflict during the last 20 years has attempted to identify the situations in which conflict is mostly beneficial and those in which conflict is destructive to organizational functioning. Conflict may, for example, enhance understanding of decisions, improve decision quality

(Amason, 1996) and stimulate group innovation (De Dreu & West, 2001; Lovelace, Shapiro, & Weingart, 2001), while, on the other hand, it can damage quality of working life by causing organizational stress and feelings of burnout (De Dreu, Van Dierendonck, & De Best-Waldhober, 2002; Dijkstra, Van Dierendonck, & Evers, 2005). There has been a lot of effort put on the investigation of the specific and interacting factors that lead to the positive or negative effects of conflict on groups.

Task conflict, relationship conflict and group performance

In some of the earlier and most important work on groups Bales (1950) argued that social interaction taking place in small groups could be broadly categorized into two types: socio-emotional and task-oriented. In other words, group members contribute to group functioning through social and task inputs. On the same line of thinking, it has been suggested that there are two basic types of conflict in work teams, that is task conflict and relationship conflict. It is quite possible that the former leads to the latter. Task conflicts pertain to controversy over the job the group focuses on, whereas relationship conflicts are based on animosity surrounding interpersonal relationships among co-workers (Jehn, 1995). Task conflict involves disagreements among group members about the content of their decisions and includes differences in viewpoints, ideas and opinions. Relationship conflict entails problems members have with others' personalities, dispositions and value priorities. Besides task and relationship conflict some other types of conflict have been suggested, such as conflict over resources and process conflict over the means to accomplish tasks; however, most research on the association between types of conflict and performance deals with these forms of conflict as parts of task conflict.

There is empirical evidence showing that task conflict can, under certain conditions, be beneficial to group performance (Amason, 1996; De Dreu et al., 1999; Jehn, 1995, 1997; Jehn & Mannix, 2001), whereas relationship conflict is systematically related to low levels of group effectiveness (De Dreu & Van Vianen, 2001; Jehn, 1997; Rau, 2005). Task conflict, a realistic questioning of members' opinions and ideas, seems often to be beneficial to group performance by increasing the cognitive understanding of group tasks, the careful evaluation of alternatives as well as constructive criticism of processes. When group members engage in task conflict the information processing capacity of the group is reinforced, leading to a high quality of decision-making and task accomplishment. On the other hand, the main reason why relationship conflict negatively influences team performance is because it results in less helping behaviour: sharing of information, resources and so on. In other words, relationship conflict tends to undermine performance because it hinders prosocial behaviour, including helping (De Dreu & Van Vianen, 2001).

It is important, however, to note that the link between task conflict and group performance is far from clear (De Dreu & Weingart, 2003). Research suggests that task conflict has a positive effect on group performance given that:

- team members believe that their goals are cooperative rather than competitive (Alper, Tjosvold, & Law, 2000);
- intensity of conflict is moderate (Jehn & Mannix, 2001);
- team members trust each other and feel psychologically safe in their team (Edmondson, 1999);
- there are norms promoting openness and tolerance of diverse viewpoints (Jehn, 1997; see Box 3.2);
- emotionality – that is, the amount of negative affect exhibited and felt during the conflict – is kept low (Jehn, 1997; see Box 3.2);
- the conflict issue is important (Jehn, 1997; see Box 3.2);
- resolution potential of the conflict is high (Jehn, 1997; see Box 3.2).

Box 3.2   Episodes of conflict types and dimensions based on interview data

Conflict types

Task conflict: 'We usually fight about work things – interpreting our reports, disagreeing about government regulations.'

'We constantly fight about accounts and which numbers to use and how to interpret them. We really only fight about this work stuff.'

Relationship conflict: 'Like any situation, there are some of us that don't get along, and so we don't talk at all.'

'Her attitude just stinks. It's a personality conflict in the first place. I'd rather be working for anyone else but her. I just can't stand her attitude and her voice. We just clash.'

Process conflict: 'I don't think we have a lot of interpersonal problems, but we do have disagreements, like right now on this reorganization about how some of these teams are set up. There's some conflict on the composite of the team and who should do what.'

Conflict Dimensions

Acceptability: 'Any kind of negative attitude is frowned upon and that means bringing up problems and fighting all the time. Bad attitude, uncooperative, general bad attitude is very bad, difficult and is discouraged. Otherwise people would be fighting like cats and dogs.'

Emotionality: 'We've gone at it a couple of times over things. There is a lot of yelling and frustration. Emotions run high; people don't use their heads.'

Box 3.2   (cont'd)

Importance: 'and I think it is going to have severe consequences so I'll voice my opinion. It's a very big disagreement and the conflict is a very important one.'

   Resolution potential: 'But they don't manage each other well, they don't want to attack a problem so it never goes away. When they should speak up to resolve this, they don't. They don't want to be bothered with it.'

Source: Interview data adapted from Jehn (1997).

Task complexity has also been suggested as an important variable that determines whether task conflict is beneficial to group life. Jehn (1995) originally found that in groups performing routine tasks, disagreements about the task were detrimental to group functioning, while in groups performing nonroutine tasks, task conflicts were in some cases beneficial. However, De Dreu and Weingart (2003), in a meta-analysis of studies that examine the relationship between task conflict, relationship conflict and team performance, found that both task and relationship conflicts were negatively related to team performance, and that task conflict interfered less with the execution of simple, well-learned tasks than with more complex, nonroutine tasks. Therefore, there are inconsistent results in the literature concerning the moderating role of task complexity in the relationship between task conflict and team performance. These inconsistent results can possibly be explained by investigating the relation between task conflict and group performance under various levels of task complexity, as well as goal interdependence, psychological safety and within-team trust, emotionality, conflict acceptability and conflict issue importance. Conflict is a complex, multi-determined problem. Many factors determine when, why and how it occurs or is solved.

   The conflict literature distinguishes between task and relationship conflict partly on the ground that the two types of conflict were demonstrated to have different performance consequences. However, the empirical data show that the two types of conflict are often positively correlated (Amason, 1996; Janssen et al., 1999; Jehn, Northcraft, & Neale, 1999; Pelled, Eisenhardt, & Xin, 1999). Since moderate task conflict is beneficial to group performance while relationship conflict is detrimental, one has to be careful not to trigger relationship conflict by increasing task conflict (Gebert et al., 2006).

   Simons and Peterson (2000) studied the transformation of one type of conflict into another by interviewing top management groups in the hotel and motel industry. They found that task conflict is misattributed as being personal in nature or motive and thus leads to relationship conflict if there are low levels of intragroup trust. They identified intragroup trust as the psychological mechanism that links task and relationship conflicts. On a practical level, managers and group leaders can prevent task disagreements from being misinterpreted as personal attacks by enhancing trust between group members and creating a climate of psychological safety. When group members trust each other and feel safe in their group, task conflict does not escalate into relationship conflict and the group performs effectively.

Thus, task conflict has been shown to have positive effects on group effectiveness given that certain factors are seriously taken into account, whereas relationship conflict has consistently generated a negative effect on group performance. However, one has to be careful when offering practical advice to managers because a strategy of stimulating task conflict may backfire by transforming disagreements over tasks to personal attacks. Consequently, groups should be encouraged to focus on confronting problems rather than avoiding or smoothing over the issues so that they can benefit from the diverse ideas of group members. But, for example, expressing different viewpoints and various alternatives may have a negative impact on group effectiveness if group members do not feel respected and psychologically safe in their work group.

Constructive controversy

In search of the conditions that enable conflict to have a positive effect on group performance Tjosvold and his colleagues (Tjosvold, 1990, 1997, 1998; Tjosvold, Dann, & Wong, 1992; Tjosvold, Morishima, & Belsheim, 1999) have argued that conflict is beneficial to group functioning when group members believe that their ultimate, salient work goals are cooperative. Departing from Deutsch's (1973) theory of cooperation and competition Tjosvold proposed that conflict can have positive effects on organizational functioning when organizational members deal with their disputes by engaging in 'constructive controversy'. Constructive controversy is stimulated when group members in dispute believe that their goals are ultimately cooperative so that the attainment of a goal by one member facilitates other members to achieve their own goals, that is, win–win. Despite the fact that group members disagree, they perceive their objectives to be common, discuss their opposing views openly, try to cope with their incompatible activities and resolve their conflicts constructively. Opposing positions do hinder, temporarily, the group from making a decision, but constructive controversy helps people combine their ideas to resolve conflicts in a positive way (for a review, see Tjosvold, 1997).

Constructive controversy is conceptually based on Deutsch's theory of cooperation and competition. The theory argues that how people interact depends on their beliefs about how the attainment of desired goals is related to other people achieving their own goals (goal interdependence). When people cooperate they perceive their goals to be positively linked, so that as one person moves towards goal attainment the other person is also getting closer to achieving a desired goal. On the other hand, when people compete with each other, they believe their goals are negatively related, so that one's successful goal attainment makes others less likely to reach a desired goal. Finally, independence occurs when people believe that their goals are not related either in a positive or negative way. In cooperation, group members are open to influence, they mutually support each other and group performance is high. On the other hand, in competition, people are often closed-minded because they aim to outperform each other, and groups are ineffective. Independence reflects indifference to the actions of others and group performance is the product of individual work rather than the combination of group members' inputs.

Considerable evidence points to the positive effect of constructive controversy on group functioning. For example, Tjosvold et al. (1992) found that employees in different departments of a large telecommunications company discussed their differences openly and used their conflicts to serve customers when they believed that their business goals were cooperative. More specifically, organizational members who developed cooperative goals while still in dispute were able to interact open-mindedly and effectively, make progress on their task, work efficiently and serve customers. They also strengthened their work relationship as they felt confident they could collaborate in the future. In contrast, competitive and independent conflicts were characterized by closed-minded interaction, little task progress, inefficiency and reduced confidence in future conflict management. Various specific conditions lead to the perception of goals as cooperative, competitive and independent. Common tasks and compatible objectives, shared vision and aspirations, tasks requiring coordination and teamwork, feelings of understanding and complementary roles are reasons for cooperative goals. Incompatible objectives and insisting on doing it one's own way are antecedents for competitive and independent goals. Individual tasks and objectives also lead to independent goals (see Box 3.3).

Box 3.3   Conditions leading to the perception of goals as cooperative, competitive and independent (Tjosvold et al., 1992)

Cooperative goals

- Shared vision and aspirations
- Common tasks and compatible objectives
- Tasks requiring coordination and teamwork
- Complementary roles
- Feelings of understanding

Competitive goals

- Incompatible objectives
- Insisting on doing it one's own way

Independent goals

- Individual tasks and objectives
- Incompatible objectives
- Insisting on doing it one's own way

Cooperative goal interdependence has been shown to facilitate the adoption of new technological innovations, as well as the effective handling of informal grievances. When new technological innovations are implemented employees often confront considerable problems and need to discuss solutions with each other to make the technology work. For example, in a study of how new technology is implemented, employees of a retail chain in cooperative interdependence were able to use new scanning technology efficiently because they exchanged information and hammered out ideas about how to solve the many problems the technology created (Tjosvold, 1990). Regarding the handling of grievances, Tjosvold et al. (1999) studied how supervisors and employees in a large forest products company dealt with complaints. The findings showed that employees and supervisors who emphasized their cooperative interdependence were able to negotiate open-mindedly to develop integrated solutions and successfully handled their informal grievances. On a practical level, supervisors who are trained to demonstrate clearly to employees that they have common objectives and want to discuss issues for mutual benefit are apt to develop cooperative goals with employees.

The construct of 'conflict efficacy' has been suggested to be the psychological mechanism that mediates the impact of a cooperative/competitive approach to conflict on team performance (Alper et al., 2000). In a study of self-managing teams in the production department of an electronic manufacturer, Alper et al. found that when team members manage their conflicts in a cooperative way they feel confident in dealing with conflicts in the future, which leads to long-term effective group performance. Therefore, groups that rely on cooperative approaches to conflict management develop efficacy that they can deal with their conflicts; this efficacy in turn results in effective team performance.

A cooperative approach to conflict management might be an essential aspect of an organizational culture that promotes cooperation rather than competition among organizational members. Since an organizational culture of cooperation is associated with effective organizational functioning (Cooke & Rousseau, 1988; Petty, Beadles, Lowery, Chapman, & Connell, 1995; Smart & John, 1996), future research can possibly examine whether:

- a cooperative approach to conflict management characterizes an organizational culture of cooperation and
- such an organizational culture is related to organizational performance via the mechanism of conflict efficacy.

In an attempt to combine the two separately developed research literatures of task/relationship conflict and constructive controversy, Janssen et al. (1999) examined how task and relationship conflict shape the role of positive interdependence in management teams. The findings showed that cooperative interdependence fosters effective group decision-making only if relationship conflict interferes with task conflict, but not in the case of one-sided task conflict, one-sided relationship conflict or no conflict at all. In other words, whether or not group members believe that their goals are positively interdependent has an impact on group performance given that task conflict escalates into relationship conflict or relationship conflict is reflected in task conflict. In positive interdependence because team members move towards their goals as a consequence of actions of others, they develop positive attitudes towards each other and become receptive to information, suggestions and ideas provided by other persons.

When task conflict and relationship conflict coexist, which has been shown empirically to be the rule rather than the exception, positive interdependence facilitates the resolution of conflict by the development of positive attitudes among group members and the cognitive receptivity to other members' suggestions. For example, think of a project group commissioned to design the spring collection of a corporation in the fashion industry having a dispute over the quality of the textiles to be used. If group members believe that the success of the collection depends on the input of every member of the group, then interaction among members is intense and individuals are receptive to others' suggestions.

Constructive controversy is, therefore, based on the perception of a positive interdependence among team members. This cooperative approach to conflict management involves open discussion, understanding others, integrating views and reaching agreements. Research has shown that customer service, handling of employee grievances, new technology adoption and production of goods are effectively carried out when organizational members believe that they share common objectives. A cooperative approach to conflict seems to be especially conducive to effective group performance in the case that task and relationship conflict are simultaneously unfolding their dynamics within a team.

Conflict management and negotiation in the workplace

Conflict management is the behaviour primarily oriented towards the reduction and resolution of conflict. The literature on conflict management and negotiation has suggested that there are a number of distinct strategies or styles that characterize the behaviour of disputing parties. For example, when core departments in organizations such as marketing and production pursue different goals, they can choose either to collaborate by finding some common ground and integrating their different perspectives or to dominate by enforcing one's position. Negotiation is often the process through which organizational departments and individual employees try to settle their differences and, eventually, coordinate their efforts.

Conflict management strategies

Conflict is a process, as already noted, that begins when a party becomes aware that another party has negatively affected something that the party cares about. A family of theories called dual concern models (Pruitt, 1983) have argued against the idea that cooperation and competition are the only conflict management strategies, as suggested by Deutsch's theory (1973). These models propose that when two parties are in a dispute one party's intentions to satisfy (a) its own concerns and (b) the other party's concerns affect the conflict management strategies that the party chooses to adopt.

Blake and Mouton (1964) were among the first to suggest that when managers deal with conflict they adopt five different styles of conflict management: forcing, confronting, withdrawing, smoothing over and compromising. These five styles of conflict management reflect the dimensions of concern for people and concern for production. For example, a finance manager may choose to settle his or her differences with the personnel manager on the necessity of hiring new employees by using a strategy of compromise or even avoidance. Pruitt (1983) proposed that when two parties are in a negotiation the strategic choice of each party is determined by each party's 'concerns about its own outcomes as well as about the other's outcomes'. Parties in negotiation can adopt one (or more) of the following four strategic choices: contending, yielding, problem solving and inaction.

Thomas (1992) presenting a classification of the conflict management strategies that can be adopted by a party in an organizational conflict situation focused on two orthogonal dimensions of intent: cooperativeness and assertiveness. Cooperativeness is the extent to which the party attempts to satisfy the other party's concerns, whereas assertiveness is the extent to which a party attempts to satisfy its own concerns. Various combinations of assertiveness and cooperativeness produce five strategic intentions, which are as follows: competing, accommodating, compromising, collaborating and avoiding (Thomas, 1976; see Box 3.4).

Box 3.4   Various conflict management strategies/styles as presented in the relevant literature

Blake &   Smoothing over
Mouton
(1964)   Compromising

                            Confronting

                                    Forcing

                                            Withdrawing

Deutch   Cooperation
(1973)
                    Competition

Pruitt   Problem Solving
(1983)
                Yielding

                        Contending

                                Inaction

Thomas   Collaborating
(1992)
                Compromising

                        Accommodating

                                Competing

                                        Avoiding

A 'competing' intention (uncooperative, assertive) is an attempt to win one's position. In goal conflicts the intention is to achieve one's goal at the sacrifice of the other's goal, while in judgement conflicts one tries to convince the other that one's conclusion is correct. The opposite of competing is an 'accommodating' intention (cooperative, unassertive), which is an attempt to satisfy the other's concern at the expense of one's own. This intent may represent an attempt to help the other attain their goals at the expense of one's own or to support the other's opinion despite any reservations. A 'compromising' intention (intermediate in both cooperativeness and assertiveness) is considered by Thomas (1992) to be midway between competing and accommodating. Compromising aims at achieving moderate but incomplete satisfaction of both parties' concerns, in other words giving up something but also holding out for something. In contrast, 'collaborating' represents an attempt to fully satisfy the concerns of the two parties to achieve an integrative solution. In goal conflicts, parties try to find a win–win solution that allows both parties to achieve their goals, and in judgement conflicts the aim is to generate a new idea that incorporates the valid insights of both parties. The final intention, 'avoiding' (uncooperative, unassertive), reflects a desire to neglect the concerns of both parties in the conflict situation. This strategic intention reflects a party's desire to avoid any involvement and to allow events to take their own course.

Thomas (1992) suggested that collaboration produces more effective conflict outcomes for the organization in the long term since it enhances a sense of justice, decision quality and satisfaction of parties involved in a dispute. However, in the short term the choice of strategic intentions needs to be based on various situational conditions such as the importance of the conflict issue, power dynamics or facing an emergency. Each of the strategic intentions is likely to be appropriate in some circumstances. For example, collaboration may not be feasible when there is insufficient time, the conflict issue does not allow integrative solutions and the parties do not trust each other. It is actually a useful managerial skill to know which strategic intention to implement under different circumstances. Thomas (1977) presented a list of situations in which to adopt the five strategic intentions as reported by a group of chief executive officers (see Table 3.1). For example, competing is considered as appropriate to adopt when quick, decisive action is vital (i.e., emergencies) or on issues vital to company welfare when you know you are right. On the other hand, accommodating is more appropriate when issues are more important to others than yourself or harmony and stability are especially important.

Even though most conflict management strategies can be constructive depending on the importance of the relationship, the complexity of the issue and time pressure, the literature on the effectiveness of conflict management suggests that collaboration or problem solving is a key to effective organizations (Alper et al., 2000; Nauta & Sanders, 2000; Rubin, Pruitt, & Kim, 1994; Tjosvold, 1997; Thomas, 1992). More recently, the effectiveness of conflict management strategies has been examined in relation to the type of conflict that occurs. In a meta-analysis of the association between relationship conflict and team performance De Dreu and Van Vianen (2001) found that collaborating

Table 3.1   Situations in which to adopt the five strategic intentions, as reported by 28 chief executives

Competing
>   When quick, decisive action is vital (i.e., emergencies)
>   On issues vital to company welfare when you know you're right
>   Against people who take advantage of noncompetitive behaviour

Collaborating
>   To find an integrative solution when both sets of concerns are too important to be compromised
>   To merge insights from people with different perspectives
>   To work through feelings that have interfered with a relationship

Compromising
>   When opponents with equal power are committed to mutually exclusive goals
>   To achieve temporary settlements to complex issues
>   As a backup when collaboration or competition is unsuccessful

Avoiding
>   When potential disruption outweighs the benefits of resolution
>   To let people cool down and regain perspective
>   When others can resolve the conflict more effectively

Accommodating
>   When issues are more important to others than yourself – to satisfy others and maintain cooperation
>   When harmony and stability are especially important
>   To allow subordinates to develop by learning from mistakes

Source: Adapted from Thomas (1977).

and contending (competing) responses to relationship conflict were negatively related to team functioning and effectiveness, while avoiding responses to relationship conflict were positively related to team functioning and performance. They, however, agree with Thomas (1977) that the time frame of the conflict can be an important factor in our attempt to examine conflict management effectiveness. They postulate that avoiding responses to relationship conflict fosters team effectiveness in the next couple of months (in the short term), but leads to intensely escalated relationship conflicts several months later.

Theories on conflict management strategies have been criticized on the ground that they deal with conflict taking primarily a cognitive perspective, while neglecting the central role of affective (emotional) reactions to conflict episodes. The intensity and type of emotions aroused in the sequence of events that unfold during conflict episodes are expected to be important factors in the process of managing conflict effectively.

In sum, apart from cooperation and competition there are a number of other conflict management strategies that one can adopt when in a conflict situation. Disputing parties may choose to avoid dealing with the conflict issue and postpone taking any action towards the resolution of conflict or accommodate to the desires of the other party while neglecting their own interests. In general, problem solving (collaborating/integrating) has been shown to be the most effective strategy for confronting conflicts that arise within organizational settings. However, one should keep in mind that other conflict management strategies may prove to be beneficial depending on the importance of the relation, the conflict type and the dynamics of conflict in terms of time frame. For example, avoidance can be an effective strategy when dealing with a relationship conflict in the short term to allow the disputing parties to cool down and gain a different perspective on the issues at hand.

Third-party intervention

A rather common way to manage conflict within organizations is to make use of third-party intervention, which can indeed prove useful in resolving organizational conflicts. Giebels and Janssen (2005) argue that third-party help can be regarded as another conflict management style since conflicting employees can take the initiative to ask a third party to help them derive structure and meaning in the conflict situation. When people are engaged in a conflict they need to derive meaning in a complex, ambiguous and stressful situation, and therefore discussions with third parties is an important dynamic in the conflict management process (Volkema, Farquhar, & Bergmann, 1996). Imagine, for example, a situation where two employees taking part in a project group are involved in a task dispute that transforms into a relationship conflict primarily because they are both very suitable candidates for filling up a highly prestigious supervisor position, which has recently become available. Seeking third-party intervention, such as the mediation of a conflict resolution expert, may help both parties re-evaluate the situation and allow them to cooperate to accomplish the group's objectives.

There are various roles that third parties can adopt when intervening in conflict between organizational parties, and a distinction is made between third parties with process control (i.e., mediator) and decision control (i.e., arbiter). In mediation the third party controls the interaction between the disputing parties, as well as the negotiation process, but allows them to make their own decisions. Although mediators often make their recommendations for resolving the conflict, they typically lack the authority to impose a settlement on the disputants. On the other hand, an arbiter acts more autocratically by making and enforcing a decision for settling the dispute between the conflicting parties.

Managers as well as consultants usually play the role of third parties in a conflict between organizational members or departments. Even though managers have the power to play the role of the third party in organizational conflicts, they do not necessarily have the specialized skills to deal with conflicts effectively. For this reason, many organizations employ specially trained consultants to act as mediators in organizational conflicts. These mediators are often known as 'ombudspersons' and their objective is to help the disputants, either individuals or groups, to settle their differences by themselves. Ombudspersons are usually experts in conflict resolution who also offer assistance to managers in their efforts to deal with work-related conflicts. The role of ombudspersons can be especially effective in mediating organizational conflicts as findings show that experts acting as third parties in a conflict resolution intervention were more influential than colleagues of the disputing parties (Arnold & O'Conor, 1999).

Window on the workplace

The ACAS Arbitration Scheme

Advisory, Conciliation, and Arbitration Service (ACAS) is a body largely funded by the British Department for Business, Enterprise, and Regulation Reform (BERR) and governed by an independent council appointed by the Secretary of the State for BERR. ACAS was given powers to draw up the ACAS Arbitration Scheme, which has been approved by the British Parliament, in the Employment Rights (Dispute Resolution) Act 1998. The ACAS Arbitration Scheme can be used as an alternative to going to an Employment Tribunal hearing to resolve disputes about alleged unfair dismissal or requests to work flexibly.

The scheme was introduced because it was felt that there was a need for a speedy, informal, private, and generally less legalistic alternative to an Employment Tribunal hearing. The scheme is also designed to provide a final outcome to cases more quickly as there are very few grounds for challenging the arbitrator's decision and appeals can only be made in limited circumstances.

In ACAS arbitration the arguments put by both parties are heard by an arbitrator who, by using their knowledge, skills, and experience, will come to a decision on the case. The arbitrator's decision is issued in the form of an award and is a binding judgement of the parties' dispute. As arbitration is a method for deciding between two conflicting claims in which the arbitrator's decision is binding upon the parties, there has to be agreement by both parties that they wish the complaint to be heard by an arbitrator.

Negotiation behaviour and cognitive biases

For all parties involved in conflict management, either disputing or third parties, it is particularly useful to know the way people usually think when they act as negotiators. When organizational members, either as individuals or groups, deal with conflict situations they normally engage in a negotiation or bargaining process to resolve the conflict. All conflict management strategies involve interaction and communication between the parties in dispute, aiming at dealing with the parties' differences in one way or another. Even in the case of avoidance, the communication breakdown that occurs is usually a temporal withdrawal from the conflict issue.

In order to be able to understand the negotiation process and help the parties work together effectively one has to take into account the structure of the bargaining situation. The degree of conflict between parties' interests determines the structure of the bargaining situation (Thompson, 1990). If parties' interests are mutually exclusive the negotiation is called fixed-sum or purely distributive. In fixed-sum or purely distributive negotiations parties' goals, values, preferences or priorities are incompatible, and therefore it is very much unlikely that both parties can be satisfied with the negotiation outcome. In contrast, when parties' interests are perfectly compatible the situation is a pure negotiation. Pure negotiation offers ample opportunities for mutually beneficial trade-offs and possibly enables negotiators to grow a larger pie. Most of the times parties' interests are neither completely opposed nor purely compatible, in which case the situation is an integrative or variable-sum negotiation.

Although conflict normally occurs in mixed-motive situations and negotiators often have very different priorities and valuation of resources, research in negotiation has shown that negotiators tend to assume that the other party places the same importance on the negotiation issues as they do. This tendency has been termed the 'fixed-pie error' (Bazerman & Neale, 1983; Thompson & Hastie, 1990). In a review paper on negotiation Bazerman, Curhan, Moore, and Valley (2000) summarize research on the systematic ways in which negotiators as decision-makers deviate from rationality and suggest that negotiators tend to:

- falsely assume that the negotiation 'pie' is fixed and miss opportunities for mutually beneficial trade-offs between the parties;
- falsely assume that their preferences on issues are incompatible with those of their opponent;
- be more concessionary to a positively framed specification of the negotiation than to a negatively framed specification;
- be inappropriately affected by anchors in negotiation;
- be inappropriately affected by readily available information;
- be overconfident and overly optimistic about the likelihood of attaining outcomes that favour themselves;
- escalate conflict even when a rational analysis would dictate change in strategy;
- ignore the perspective of other parties;
- reactively devalue any concession made by the opponent.

Bazerman and his colleagues (Bazerman et al., 2000) have outlined a psychological understanding of negotiation designed to prescribe strategies that can help the negotiators carry out integrative trade-offs and grow a larger pie to be divided by the parties in dispute. If negotiators are aware of the systematic ways that individuals as decision-makers tend to deviate from rationality when in a negotiation, and especially if they are trained to deal with these biases, then conflicts can be rather positively settled to everyone's interest. Moreover, Bazerman proposes that it is important to study how players define and create the negotiation game to help them negotiate constructively. More specifically, one needs to examine negotiator relationships, attributions about the other, knowledge of the bargaining structure and understanding of the self, as well as the personality, intelligence and biography of all parties involved. For example, as already mentioned, the negotiators' perception of whether the structure of the situation allows for integrative trade-offs can have a significant effect on the way they behave in the negotiation.

From a practical standpoint, managers and their subordinates can attend training programmes in negotiation and conflict resolution in order to manage conflicts at work more effectively. As negotiators or third parties in organizational negotiations they can learn how to:

- expand the pie by introducing new issues or by splitting existing issues into smaller ones;
- give in on less important issues and remain firm on the more valuable ones;
- create a positive relationship with the other party to get their way on the key issue;
- minimize the risks and costs associated with concessions demanded from the other side;
- invent a solution that meets both sides' relative priorities and interests (Rubin et al., 1994).

Summary

Organizational conflicts are often assumed by managers to have negative effects on the functioning of work groups, organizational departments as well as the whole organization. However, conflict can be an ally as well as an enemy in managers' efforts to run an effective organization. Disagreements among group members about the content of their decisions, debates over the job or project the group has to carry out, differences in perspectives, ideas and opinions, that is task conflicts, do have a positive effect on group performance, such as decision-making and innovation (see Chapter 4) under certain circumstances. Relationship conflicts, on the other hand, reflecting problems members have with others' personalities and value priorities, are destructive to group problem solving and task accomplishment. As task and relationship conflicts are closely related, one type of conflict can be transformed into another type. Therefore, one has to be careful not to trigger relationship conflict by stimulating task conflict. Group performance is also enhanced when organizational members have a cooperative approach to conflict and therefore engage in constructive controversy. Constructive controversy seems to have an especially positive impact on group performance when task and relationship conflict are simultaneously taking place within a group.

The literature on conflict management and negotiation suggests that there are various strategies or styles that characterize the behaviour of conflicting parties.

In general, problem solving or collaboration has emerged as the most effective strategy for handling organizational conflicts. Other conflict management strategies may also be effective depending on the importance of the relationship, type of conflict as well as time frame. For example, avoidance is a useful way to deal with relationship conflicts in the short term so that conflicting parties can cool down and gain some perspective on the issues at hand. Organizations quite often use third-party intervention to manage conflicts, which is actually regarded by some researchers as another conflict management style. If negotiators and third parties have a sound knowledge of the systematic ways in which negotiators, as decision-makers, deviate from rationality, they can be in a better position to achieve mutually beneficial settlements. Training programmes on the psychology of negotiating can help organizational members limit the negative effects of such systematic biases on resolving conflicts at work.

Questions

1. Under which conditions and via which mechanisms does conflict have a positive effect on organizational functioning? Describe situations where it would be to the advantage of a manager to stimulate conflict.
2. Which factors lead to the negative effects of conflict? In practical terms, describe steps that an organization can take to manage conflict effectively.
3. Does the type of task the group performs affect whether task conflict is beneficial? Use knowledge presented in Chapter 2 on types of group task to explain your answer.
4. Is there a possibility that task conflict changes into relationship conflict and vice versa?
5. Which are the conflict management strategies or styles proposed by dual concern models? Critically evaluate the dual concern models to conflict resolution.
6. What is the role of ombudspersons in organizational conflicts?
7. In which ways can we use the knowledge of how people think as negotiators to improve resolving conflicts at work?

References

Alper, S., Tjosvold, D., & Law, K. S. (2000). Conflict management, efficacy, and performance in organizational teams. *Personnel Psychology*, **53**, 625–642.

Amason, A. C. (1996). Distinguishing the effects of functional and dysfunctional conflict on strategic decision making: Resolving a paradox for top management teams. *Academy of Management Journal*, **39**, 123–148.

Arnold, J. A., & O'Conor, K. M. (1999). Ombudspersons or peers? The effect of third-party expertise and recommendations on negotiation. *Journal of Applied Psychology*, **84**, 776–785.

Bales, R. (1950). *Interaction Process Analysis: A Method for the Study of Small Groups*. Reading, MA: Addison-Wesley.

Baron, R. A. (1989). Personality and organizational conflict: Type A behavior pattern and self-monitoring. *Organizational Behavior and Human Decision Processes*, **44**, 281–297.

Bazerman, M. H., Curhan, J. R., Moore, D. A., & Valley, K. L. (2000). Negotiation. *Annual Review of Psychology*, **51**, 279–314.

Bazerman, M. H., & Neale, M. A. (1983). Heuristics in negotiation: Limitations to effective dispute resolution. In M. H. Bazerman & R. J. Lewicki (eds.), *Negotiating in Organizations* (pp. 51–67). Beverly Hills, CA: Sage.

Blake, R. R., & Mouton, J. S. (1964). *The Managerial Grid*. Houston, TX: Gulf.

Cooke, R. A., & Rousseau, D. M. (1988). Behavioral norms and expectations: A quantitative approach to the assessment of organizational culture. *Group and Organization Studies*, **13**, 245–273.

De Dreu, C. K. W., Harinck, F., & Van Vianen, A. E. M. (1999). Conflict and performance in groups and organizations. In C. L. Cooper & I. T. Robertson (eds.), *International Review of Industrial and Organizational Psychology* (Vol. 14, pp. 69–414). Chichester, UK: John Wiley.

De Dreu, C. K. W., & Van Vianen, A. E. M. (2001). Managing relationship conflict and the effectiveness of organizational teams. *Journal of Organizational Behavior*, **22**, 309–328.

De Dreu, C. K. W., Weingart, L. R. (2003). Task versus relationship conflict, team performance, and team member satisfaction: A meta-analysis. *Journal of Applied Psychology*, **88**, 741–749.

De Dreu, C. K. W., & West, M. A. (2001). Minority dissent and team innovation: The importance of participation in decision making. *Journal of Applied Psychology*, **86**, 1191–1201.

De Dreu, C. K. W., Van Dierendonck, D., & De Best-Waldhober, M. (2002). Conflict at work and individual well-being. In M. Schabracq, J. A. M. Winnubst, & C. L. Cooper (eds.), *International Handbook of Work and Health Psychology* (pp. 495–515). Chichester, UK: Wiley.

De Reuver, R. (2006). The influence of organizational power on conflict dynamics. *Personnel Review*, **35**, 589–603.

Deutsch, M. (1973). *The Resolution of Conflict*. New Haven, CT: Yale University Press.

Dijkstra, M. T. M., Van Dierendonck, D., & Evers, A. (2005). Responding to conflict at work and individual well-being: The mediating role of flight behaviour and feelings of helplessness. *European Journal of Work and Organizational Psychology*, **14**, 119–135.

Edmondson, A. (1999). Psychological safety and learning behavior in work teams. *Administrative Science Quarterly*, **44**, 350–383.

Gebert, D., Boerner, S., & Kearney, E. (2006). Cross-functionality and innovation in new product development teams: A dilemmatic structure and its consequences for the management of diversity. *European Journal of Work and Organizational Psychology*, **15**, 431–458.

Giebels, E., & Janssen, O. (2005). Conflict stress and reduced well-being at work: The buffering effect of third-party help. *European Journal of Work and Organizational Psychology*, **14**, 137–155.

Janssen, O., Van de Vliert, E., & Veenstra, C. (1999). How task and person conflict shape the role of positive interdependence in management teams. *Journal of Management*, **25**, 117–142.

Jehn, K. A. (1995). A multimethod examination of the benefits and detriments of intragroup conflict. *Administrative Science Quarterly*, **40**, 256–282.

Jehn, K. A. (1997). A qualitative analysis of conflict types and dimensions in organizational groups. *Administrative Science Quarterly*, **42**, 530–557.

Jehn, K. A., & Mannix, E. A. (2001). The dynamic nature of conflict: A longitudinal study of intragroup conflict and group performance. *Academy of Management Journal*, **44**, 238–251.

Jehn, K. A., Northcraft, G. B., & Neale, M. A. (1999). Why differences make a difference: A field study of diversity, conflict, and performance in workgroups. *Administrative Science Quarterly*, **44**, 741–763.

Lovelace, K., Shapiro, D. L., & Weingart, L. R. (2001). Maximizing cross-functional new product teams' innovativeness and constraint adherence: A conflict communications perspective. *Academy of Management Journal*, **44**, 779–793.

Nauta, A., & Sanders, K. (2000). Interdepartmental negotiation behaviour in manufacturing organizations. *The International Journal of Conflict Management*, **11**, 135–161.

Pelled, L. H., Eisenhardt, K. M., & Xin, K. R. (1999). Exploring the black box: An analysis of work group diversity, conflict, and performance. *Administrative Science Quarterly*, **44**, 1–28.

Petty, M. M., Beadles, N. A., II, Lowery, C. M., Chapman, D. F., & Connell, D. W. (1995). Relationships between organizational culture and organizational performance. *Psychological Reports*, **76**, 483–492.

Pruitt, D. G. (1983). Strategic choice in negotiation. *American Behavioral Scientist*, **27**, 167–194.

Rahim, M. A. (2001). *Managing Conflict in Organizations*. Westport, CT: Quorum Books.

Rau, D. (2005). The influence of relationship conflict and trust on the transactive memory: Performance relation in top management teams. *Small Group Research*, **36**, 746–771.

Rubin, J. Z., Pruitt, D. G., & Kim, S. H. (1994). *Social Conflict: Escalation, Stalemate, and Settlement*. New York: McGraw-Hill.

Simons, T. L., & Peterson, R. S. (2000). Task conflict and relationship conflict in top management teams: The pivotal role of intragroup trust. *Journal of Applied Psychology*, **85**, 102–111.

Smart, J. C., & St. John, E. P. (1996). Organizational culture and effectiveness in higher education: A test of the 'culture type' and 'strong culture' hypotheses. *Educational Evaluation and Policy Analysis*, **18**, 219–241.

Thomas, K. (1976). Conflict and conflict management. In M. D. Dunnette (ed.), *Handbook of Industrial and Organizational Psychology* (pp. 889–935). Chichester, UK: Wiley.

Thomas, K. W. (1977). Toward multi-dimensional values in teaching: The example of conflict behaviours. *Academy of Management Review*, **2**, 484–490.

Thomas, K. W. (1992). Conflict and negotiation processes in organizations. In M. D. Dunnette and L. M. Hough (eds.), *Handbook of Industrial and Organizational Psychology* (pp. 651–717). Palo Alto, CA: Consulting Psychologists Press.

Thompson, L. (1990). Negotiation behavior and outcomes: Empirical evidence and theoretical issues. *Psychological Bulletin*, **108**, 515–532.

Thompson, L., & Hastie, R. (1990). Social perception in negotiation. *Organizational Behavior and Human Decision Processes*, **47**, 98–123.

Thompson, L., & Hrebec, D. (1996). Lose–lose agreements in interdependent decision making. *Psychological Bulletin*, **120**, 396–409.

Tjosvold, D. (1990). Making a technological innovation work: Collaboration to solve problems. *Human Relations*, **43**, 1117–1131.

Tjosvold, D. (1997). Conflict within interdependence: Its value for productivity and individuality. In C. De Dreu & E. Van de Vliert (eds.), *Using Conflict in Organizations* (pp. 23–37). London: Sage.

Tjosvold, D. (1998). Cooperative and competitive goal approach to conflict: Accomplishments and challenges. *Applied Psychology: An International Review*, **47**, 285–342.

Tjosvold, D., Dann, V., & Wong, C. (1992). Managing conflict between departments to serve customers. *Human Relations*, **45**, 1035–1054.

Tjosvold, D., Morishima, M., & Belsheim, J. A. (1999). Complaint handling on the shop floor: Cooperative relationships and open-minded strategies. *The International Journal of Conflict Management*, **10**, 45–68.

Weingart, L., Thompson, L., Bazerman, M., and Carroll, J. (1990). Tactical behavior and negotiation outcomes. *International Journal of Conflict Management*, **1**, 7–31.

Volkema, R. J., Farquhar, K., & Bergmann, T. J. (1996). Third-party sensemaking in interpersonal conflicts at work: A theoretical framework. *Human Relations*, **49**, 1437–1454.

Group Creativity and Innovation

4

Chapter outline

Introduction
The concepts of innovation and creativity
Factors affecting organizational creativity and innovation
    Cognitive abilities and personality factors
    Task characteristics
    Intrinsic motivation
    Group composition and processes
    Organizational level factors
Creativity-enhancement techniques
    Brainstorming
    Other creativity-enhancement techniques
Summary
Questions

Chapter objectives

The main objectives are to:

- describe innovation as a cyclical process and the role that creativity plays in it;

- identify the factors that influence creativity at work and innovation by referring to the individual, group and organizational level of analysis;

- explain how group processes enable or inhibit individual employees from using their creative potential to address issues at work;

(cont'd)

- examine the different techniques available to stimulate creativity in the workplace;
- critically evaluate the contribution of brainstorming to organizational creativity.

Introduction

Many observers have noted how quickly the world of work is changing. This has, and will, continued to occur for various reasons, including economic, technological, legal and social change. To survive, organizations have to change and adapt to new circumstances. To thrive, they have to be the tireless adaptors and innovators on new products, processes and approaches. Thus, we have examples from 'low-cost cultures' where innovations on the part of a few people have fundamentally changed the whole industry. Innovations constantly ask why things are done in a particular way and whether they may be done differently – faster, cheaper and more simply.

All innovations, such as new programmes, products or services, begin with creative ideas produced by a person or a group of people and then are successfully implemented with the aid of wide resources within organizations (Amabile, Conti, Coon, Lazenby, & Herron, 1996).

Organizational creativity and innovation have become critical means of competitive advantage in various industrial sectors since they allow organizations to adapt and develop in a rapidly evolving environment. The innovations may be in terms of products as well as organizational processes. A number of well-known management innovations exist, such as Total Quality Management (TQM) and team-based work, which are frequently adopted and further developed by organizations to promote efficiency. Innovations seem to change managerial cognitions on what actions are possible and beneficial, and thus allow organizational change to occur (Greve & Taylor, 2000). However, one should note that although innovation is a precursor for organizational change, organizational change is a broader construct since much of it is not innovation. For example, mergers are often related to major changes in organizational functioning but innovation is not a necessary element of these changes.

It has been suggested that there are cultural, ethnic and gender differences in creativity which are attributable in part to social forces and processes (Kaufman, 2009). The question remains as to how, when, where and why these processes operate. This chapter examines innovation and creativity in the workplace by focusing on the interaction between employees working in group settings (see Box 4.1). Employees' individual characteristics, task properties, group sociopsychological traits and the context of the larger organization are regarded as basic elements of this interaction reflected in group processes. The dynamics of coordination and motivational considerations in group performance, group decision-making, and conflict and negation raised in previous chapters provide a foundation for issues analysed in this chapter.

Box 4.1   Creativity and innovation at work

Brilliant ideas are clearly not enough in the business world. They need to be translated into practical actions, processes or products. Most people think of business creativity as new product development, but equally important is process innovation and structural change. It may be equally important to innovate one's relationships with clients, suppliers and so on, or how the organization goes about strategic planning. Sherwood (2001) has identified 12 points worth considering (or debating against) on creativity and innovation:

- Creativity is about bright ideas; innovation is about the wisdom in identifying the commercially viable ones and bringing them to fruition.
- Innovation applies to all aspects of business activity, including how one manages.
- Everybody, irrespective of their level of creativity, can contribute to the business of innovation.
- People can learn the tools and techniques that enhance the process of creativity and innovation.
- People innovate better in groups. Innovation requires the coordination of many organizational resources.
- Some organizational cultures are better suited to innovation than others, being better at the deployment of teams and the promotional process.
- The heart of business creativity is searching for new patterns in existing patterns and components.
- Innovation never (or very rarely) starts from a Greenfield/blank-sheet start.
- Paradoxically, the core of much innovation is not learning new habits but rather unlearning familiar habits.
- The innovative, unlearning organization adopts a slow, deliberate process involving a great deal of time, energy, leadership and effort.
- Innovation organizations make time for, and work at, innovative processes.
- Innovative, unlearning organizations really do have unassailable, ultimate, competitive advantages.

Many of these points may be disputed. What is beyond dispute, however, is that all organizations have to adapt and innovate and that being the first with a really good idea offers considerable benefits.

The concepts of innovation and creativity

The competitive economic environment forces organizations to show interest in the generation and application of new products and practices so that they survive and prosper. The introduction of new and improved ways of doing things at work is called innovation (West, 2002). It involves the creation, as well as the implementation, of useful new ideas, products, material artefacts, services or procedures. Ideas for reorganizing, improving communication or assembling products in teams are seen as examples of innovation (Kanter, 1983). Researchers have proposed that there are distinct types of innovation, such as technological versus administrative innovations (Damanpour, 1991) or evolutionary versus revolutionary innovations (Zaltman, Duncan, & Holbek, 1973).

Basadur (2005) believes that creativity in the workplace involves three related processes: problem finding, then problem solving, then solution implementation. This is much more than simply generating ideas but involves few processes: anticipating problems, sensing and seeking better solutions; problem definition with fledgling solution ideas; systematic analysis and evaluation of the ideas generated; followed by the efficient and effective implementation of these ideas. Especially important is the management and maintenance of the process after the change has been implemented. Thus, 'applied creativity' is seen as a never-ending circular activity of generating creative options to new problems, conceptualizing the best solutions, optimizing the best ideas and practice and then implementing these to create successful change. It may well be, as Basadur believes, that different groups at different levels may be better suited to these different functions. Thus very senior people may be a lot better at conceptualizing while supervisors or technical specialists may be better implementers.

An often-cited definition of innovation is 'the intentional introduction and application within a role, group or organisation of ideas, products or procedures, new to the relevant unit of adoption, designed to significantly benefit the individual, the group, organisation or wider society' (p. 9; West & Farr, 1990). There are three characteristics of innovation that appear in the above definition. The first attribute of innovation is 'novelty', which can be either absolute (something totally new) or relative (something new to a specific unit of adoption, but already well-known and implemented). The second attribute is an 'application component', which refers to innovation not only as the generation of ideas but also as their implementation. The third aspect of innovation is 'intentionality of benefit', which distinguishes innovation from serendipitous change. It is planned and purposeful.

West and Farr (1990) developed a four-factor theory to describe and explain the process of innovation in organizations. These factors are:

1. Vision: A higher-order goal, which acts as a motivating force. It helps establish goals that are clear, valued, attainable and shared, as well as difficult to achieve.

2. Participant safety: The fact that the environment is interpersonally non-threatening because people can influence decisions and fully share information.

3. Task orientation: An emphasis on accountability, evaluating and modifying performance, feedback, cooperation, monitoring, improving.

4. Support for innovation: Support is both articulated and enacted in terms of time, money and assistance.

If these four factors are in place, it means the group is likely to seek for, accept and implement innovative ideas and practices.

Similarly, organizational creativity has been defined as the creation of a valuable, useful new product, service, idea, procedure or process by individuals working together in a complex social system (Woodman, Sawyer, & Griffin, 1993). Organizational creativity is, therefore, a subset of the broader domain of innovation since innovation may involve creativity as the ideation component of the innovative process. Moreover, even in the case of applying well-known and widely implemented innovations, creativity might be a necessary factor for these innovations to be adapted to a specific organizational context. For instance, setting up quality circles in an organization for the first time is an innovation since it is a new practice to the unit of adoption. It certainly does not involve the generation of a new idea, as quality circles are already widespread, but creativity might be called for when putting this innovation into practice. Indeed, idea implementation may call for as much creativity as initial idea generation (Mumford, Scott, Gaddis, & Stange, 2002).

Amabile (1988, 1996) argues that individual and small-group creativity is the most crucial element in the process of organizational innovation because the ideation component of organizational innovation depends on the generation of new ideas by individuals or small groups.

One important issue concerns whether determinants of, and the process involved in, creativity are different in different areas like arts, business, commerce or science. Second, is the question whether creativity as an ability or trait or process is normally distributed in the population as a whole, or highly skewed such that only a very few are highly creative.

Yet, creativity remains problematic; mainly because of how to decide whether a person, invention, work of art or science *is truly* creative. The question is: who makes the judgement and to what extent do they have to agree before one can say 'it' is a real manifestation of creativity? Criteria could be based on patent awards, judgements made by professionals, social recognition or even sales. Different groups have different criteria and different levels of reliability. For the scientist the whole enterprise hardly gets off the starting blocks. If one cannot adequately, robustly and reliably describe the criteria or label the product, it remains particularly difficult to understand the process.

Essentially, it seems that researchers have adopted one of four approaches to the problem:

1. *The creative person*: differential psychologists have attempted to delineate the particular and peculiar set of abilities, motives and traits that together describe the creative individual.

2. *The creative process*: this is an attempt to understand the thought (cognitive) processes that go on in the process of creativity. It is not so much an attempt at the 'who', but the 'how' question.

3. *The creative situation*: social and work psychologists are particularly interested in cultural, environmental and organizational factors that inhibit or facilitate creativity. The idea is that one can therefore construct situations that induce creativity even in the not particularly creative.

4. *The creative product*: this approach attempts to study all aspects of creativity by looking at those products that are clearly defined as creative.

This chapter will elaborate on these approaches to creative activity and particularly focus on how it may in practical terms be possible to enhance creativity in groups at work.

Innovation is often considered to be a cyclical process that involves two stages: creativity or idea generation and innovation implementation (West, 2002; see Figure 4.1). Creativity is the generation and development of new and useful ideas, whereas implementation is putting these ideas into practice. For instance, a group of engineers employed by a chemical company may make a discovery over a new material that allows electricity to run faster. This scientific discovery can be implemented in manufacturing a number of new appliances and eventually reach the market for consumer consumption.

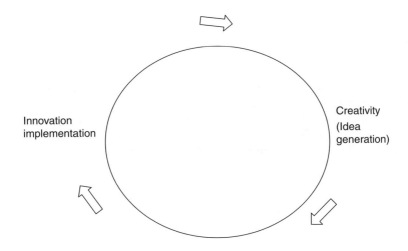

Figure 4.1   Innovation represented as a cyclical process (after West, 2002)

Researchers exploring innovation have recognized that idea generation is one stage of a multistage process on which many social factors have an effect (Scott & Bruce, 1994). Creativity takes place at the early stages of the innovation cycle when a new product, process or idea is formulated but it may also be necessary when new or adopted ideas are put into practice. Creative ideas need to be adapted, introduced and stabilized in an organizational setting for the innovation cycle to run smoothly. Therefore, acceptance of new ideas, as well as their application and implementation, is central to the definition of innovation. Innovation has a clear, social and applied component since it impacts directly or indirectly others affected by the role, or others in the work group and the organization, as, for example, in the case of administrative innovations. This necessary applied social component perhaps most sharply distinguishes it from creativity (West & Farr, 1990).

It is important to note that the stages of creativity and innovation implementation are reciprocally interdependent (West, 2002). On one hand, innovation implementation is dependent upon the quality of the creative ideas initially developed and, on the other, the application of innovations may create a need for more creative ideas to deal with unanticipated problems that arise during bringing the initial idea into use. For example, a new-product team may decide to test the quality of the new product they designed by establishing direct relationships with customers. The feedback received from their customer base, in turn, calls for more creative ideas to address the needs of customers.

In sum, innovation is a multistage process of developing and applying new and useful ways to do things at work. Creativity plays a central role in the innovative process, especially when innovation is characterized as an absolute rather than relative novelty. However, creativity may also be necessary in the case of applying well-known innovations to a new unit of adoption since putting relatively tested ideas into practice can be very challenging.

Factors affecting organizational creativity and innovation

As already noted, there are a number of factors that have been identified in the relevant literature as predictors of creative thinking and innovative behaviour. Different perspectives on whether one should put emphasis on the process of creating a novelty or on the creative product itself have provided various predictors of creativity. The process versus product criterion issue concerns thinking about creativity either as a cognitive ability of the general population or as an exceptional real-life creative achievement. Within the creativity as a process perspective the study of creativity has predominantly focused on the personality traits that influence creative behaviour, the knowledge and the mental processes on which creative thinking is based as well as the role of intrinsic motivation – viewing task engagement as interesting and involving – in facilitating creative performance.

Woodman et al. (1993) have argued that although one should advocate moving well beyond a focus solely on individual factors, theorists must nevertheless retain an appreciation for the creative person as a partial explanation for creativity in complex organizational settings. They have put forward a widely cited interactionist model of organizational creativity, in terms of which cognitive and personality characteristics of the individual interact with important social-contextual variables in formulating creative and innovative behaviour at work. In other words, antecedent conditions influence the cognitive and personality traits of individuals, and to some extent they probably determine the current situation in which the person finds himself or herself. That is, creative people choose to work in particular organizations and with particular groups. Nevertheless, social pressures towards conformity may reduce allowable variation in idea generation when organizational members try to find solutions to problems they face at work.

Finally, one should note that even though research on the factors that affect organizational creativity and innovation is ample, there is a gap in the literature as to whether there are differential predictors of certain creativity and innovation phases (Rank, Pace, & Frese, 2004). Future research needs to pay attention to this issue, as well as to whether different creativity-enhancement techniques are more beneficial for the creativity and innovation implementation phases.

Cognitive abilities and personality factors

A fundamental question in creativity research has been whether creativity is related to intellectual ability. Accumulated research has shown that moderate rather than high levels of IQ are necessary for creative accomplishment. Moreover, it has been demonstrated that the intellectual ability of providing several responses to a specific prompt, that is divergent thinking (DT), is associated with creative thinking rather than the cognitive ability to perform well in ability tests requiring one correct answer, which is convergent thinking. In an early study Wallace (1961) showed that saleswomen exhibiting high customer service obtained significantly higher mean scores on DT tests in comparison to saleswomen with low customer service. However, critics of the DT tests as predictors of creativity have argued that DT skills cannot differentiate between moderately and highly creative individuals and, therefore, can be considered only as a very partial explanation of creative behaviour.

Within the cognitive approach to creativity researchers have also studied the knowledge and the mental processes on which creative thinking is based (Mednick, 1962; Ward, Finke, & Smith, 1995). Domain-specific knowledge and expertise are a precursor of creative achievement. In fact, as knowledge combination is inherently difficult, creative people usually spend many years studying a specific domain to be able to combine knowledge in a creative manner. Deep understanding of knowledge, rather than information scanning or exposure, has been shown to increase performance in innovative teams (Taylor & Greve, 2006). Various cognitive styles, such as the ability to suspend judgement, using widely inclusive categories and breaking out of perceptual or cognitive frames, seem also to facilitate the generation of creative ideas and accomplishment.

Besides the effect of cognitive abilities and styles on creative performance, researchers have also explored the personality traits that characterize creative people. Some of the traits frequently held to be related to creative achievement are a tendency to be independent, high tolerance of ambiguity and complexity, and propensity for risk-taking (Child, 1973; MacKinnon, 1965). In the personality domain, there is a growing consensus that personality is comprised of the Big Five factors, namely, openness to experience, conscientiousness, extraversion, neuroticism and agreeableness. Research on the relationship of the five factors of personality with creative performance has shown that neuroticism is a creativity predictor in artistic populations (Feist, 1998) but successful, and possibly creative, managers and leaders are emotionally stable (Barrick & Mount, 1991; Salgado, 1998). Openness to experience seems to enhance creative behaviour in particular when it is combined with positive feedback and unclear means in doing one's job; moreover, high conscientiousness may inhibit creative behaviour when the situation encourages the conformist and controlled tendencies of employees who are high on conscientiousness (George & Zhou, 2001).

Based on research findings to date one can draw the recommended profile for a creative employee as follows: moderate to high IQ, high scores on DT tests and the ideal combination of personality traits (Batey & Furnham, 2006). However, one should keep in mind that intellectual abilities and personality factors interact with other important variables, such as task characteristics, intrinsic motivation, group composition and processes, and contextual influences stemming from the larger organization to produce creative accomplishments and innovation.

Furnham (2008) concluded:

> It seems, therefore, that there is no doubt that certain personality traits are important for explaining and predicting certain types of creativity. This may account for as much as one quarter to one third of the variance in explaining the causes of creative work. However, most personality studies have assumed that underlying personality traits are domain general. This approach has resulted in mixed evidence concerning which personality traits are important in what circumstances. As suggested, possessing certain traits, such as openness to experience or tough-mindedness (psychoticism), is probably necessarily but not sufficient for creativity as achievement. To ensure that a person fulfils his or her potential, other requisite cognitive and situational variables will need to be present.
>
> (p. 204)

Task characteristics

Task characteristics that enhance employee creativity include having a sense of autonomy or control over doing the job and viewing the work as challenging and significant (see also Chapter 2 on the effectiveness of work groups). Specifically, complex and challenging jobs characterized by high levels of autonomy, skill variety, identity, significance and feedback are expected to support and encourage higher levels of motivation and creativity than are relatively simple, routine jobs

(Hackman & Oldham, 1980). For example, Oldham and Cummings (1996) investigated creativity among 171 employees from two manufacturing facilities where creativity was assessed by patent disclosures written, contributions to an organization suggestion programme and supervisory ratings of creativity. The findings showed that complex and challenging jobs were related to these indices of creativity, as well as supervisory support for new ideas, particularly for those employees who had a personality disposition towards creativity. Ideally people prefer jobs with high autonomy and control but with few demands. These are usually the best for encouraging creativity and innovation, though relatively few in number.

On a practical level, the design of jobs may contribute to employees' intrinsic motivation and creative performance at work (Amabile, 1988; Hackman & Oldham, 1980; Oldham & Cummings, 1996) by making the numerous tasks performed within a certain organizational role as challenging as possible. However, various jobs have different creativity requirements and managers should – if they can – design and monitor work environments to ensure that the creativity levels required by a job matches the structure of the existing work environment (Shalley, Gilson, & Blum, 2000).

Similarly, work groups are more likely to develop ideas, and implement new and improved products, services and procedures, when they are autonomous – that is, they are relatively independent work units that have control over task performance (West, 2002). The tasks performed by autonomous groups are characterized by (1) completeness, which enables group members to identify with their own products, and (2) interdependence, as the various tasks performed by group members are expected to be related in content. Therefore, West proposes that the extent of group autonomy and the task requirements of completeness, varied demands, opportunities for social interaction and opportunities for learning and development will predict group creativity and innovation implementation.

Task complexity and autonomy or having control over doing one's job are characteristics of an organizational setting that promotes intrinsic motivation and creative performance. Managers and organizational consultants should design jobs in such a way that employees have control over the means and ends in carrying out their jobs, and feel excitement and intrinsic interest in performing their duties. This is of course not always possible. Jobs differ in regard to the extent that they demand the use of a variety of skills and their significance or completeness; however, even for simple and routine jobs managers can ensure that the various tasks performed within a role differ in terms of complexity.

Intrinsic motivation

Creative performance is influenced by the levels of intrinsic motivation people exhibit towards doing their job. Intrinsic motivation is motivation to perform a task for the pure love and joy in the activity. On the other hand, extrinsic motivation is doing a job for a specific reward such as money. Amabile and her colleagues (Amabile, 1996; Amabile & Gitomer, 1984; Amabile, Goldfarb, & Brackfield, 1990; Hennessey & Amabile, 1988) have actually articulated the intrinsic motivation principle of creativity which suggests that an intrinsically motivated state is conducive to creativity, whereas an extrinsically motivated state is detrimental. People are considered to be intrinsically motivated to engage in a particular task when they view their task engagement as interesting and involving. On the other hand, people are said to be extrinsically motivated to engage in a task if they perceive their task engagement as directed primarily to external goals, such as evaluation and rewards (see Box 4.2).

Box 4.2   The creativity maze

To understand the differences between intrinsic and extrinsic motivation, imagine a work problem as a maze.

One person is motivated to make it through the maze as quickly and safely as possible to get a tangible reward, as, for example, money. This person looks for the simplest, most straightforward path and then takes it. If she is in a real rush to get that reward, she might just get the most well-known path and solve the problem exactly as it has been solved before. She follows the path that others have found to lead to the exit.

That approach, based on extrinsic motivation, will indeed get her out of the maze. But the solution that arises from the process is unlikely to be creative or imaginative. It won't provide new insights about the nature of the problem or reveal new ways of looking at it.

Another person actually finds wandering around the different paths to be fun and intriguing. No doubt, this journey will take longer and include mistakes because any maze has many more dead ends than exits.

But when the intrinsically motivated person finally does find a way out of the maze – a solution – it is very likely that it will be more interesting than the rote algorithm. It will be more creative and original.

Source: Adapted from Amabile (1998).

Research has demonstrated the detrimental effect of a number of social constraints, such as competition, reward, surveillance, evaluation and restricted choice in task engagement, on the levels of creativity through the mechanism of intrinsic motivation (Amabile, 1996; Amabile, & Gitomer, 1984; Amabile, Goldfarb & Brackfield et al., 1990; Amabile, Hennessey, & Grossman et al., 1986; Hennessey & Amabile, 1988). However, there are empirical studies showing that competition does not always have a negative effect on creative performance depending on individual differences in achievement motivation (Epstein & Harackiewicz, 1992) awareness of conflict in experts (James, Chen, & Goldberg, 1992) and perceptions of masculinity (Conti, Collins, &

Picariello, 2001). Moreover, Eisenberger and Armeli (1997) have persuasively argued that reward can be conducive to creative performance when there is an explicit requirement for novel performance, or an established positive relationship between creativity and reward. It seems that extrinsic motivators can have a positive effect on intrinsic creative interest and performance when they lead individuals to view activities as more challenging and provide competence valuation (Amabile, 1996; Csikszentmihalyi, 1990; Harackiewicz & Sansone, 1991; Sansone & Harackiewicz, 1996).

Creativity is promoted when individuals perceive tasks as interesting and stimulating, which, in turn, is determined by task complexity, reward, competition, surveillance and/or restricted choice. The design of work environments advances creative behaviour when individual employees think of their jobs as something that is challenging and can potentially verify their competence in dealing with their external environments.

Group composition and processes

There is widespread belief among practitioners that organizations can promote innovation successfully by bringing together organizational members with different professional backgrounds to work in a team. For example, people from engineering-manufacturing, marketing and finance may be chosen to formulate a new-product development team. The idea is to get people out of their disciplinary-specific silos into mixed, matrix management groups. Functional diversity entails differences concerning knowledge, skills and abilities, as well as values, beliefs and attitudes. West (2002) points out that the challenge is to create sufficient diversity within the team without threatening their shared view of the task and their ability to communicate and work effectively together. He proposed that innovation is promoted by requisite knowledge diversity – that is, the amount of knowledge diversity necessary for task performance and to create variety in, and flexibility of, cognitive responses. However, when diversity begins to threaten the group's safety and integration, innovation will suffer.

Gebert, Boerner, and Kearney (2006) have noted that functional diversity management poses a dilemma. On the one hand, cross-functionality is needed for innovations; on the other hand, it may obstruct cooperation and communication within the team, which, in turn, impairs innovation. They have argued that without taking contextual conditions into account, one should not expect a positive association, but rather a nonsignificant association between cross-functionality and team innovations.

Besides functional diversity, ethnic, cultural and gender differences in organizations are thought to help employees cultivate new ideas by drawing on a larger pool of information and valuable experiences. A diverse force of skilled employees are equipped with the necessary competences and life experiences to generate and implement original and useful ideas, and, by doing so, to promote creativity and innovation. Take, for example, a group of product designers who work on finding solutions to improve a wide range of consumer products, such as computers, children's toys or kitchen appliances. A diversified and skilled staff can more adequately address the needs of a diverse customer base to which this wide range of products are marketed.

In practice, there are corporations that have diversity departments that operate on the basis of fostering diversity in the organization. These departments aim at enhancing organizational performance via understanding and valuing differences among groups of employees in the organization, which are actually thought to reflect the cultural, ethnic and gender differences of the society. However, even though it's a widespread belief – some call it a human resource fad – that organizational diversity enhances innovation, the psychological mechanisms that enable demographic, as well as functional, diversity to be beneficial to innovation are not well investigated and understood. This type of knowledge can help us address the important question, set at the beginning of this chapter, as to how, when, where and why this diversity facilitates innovation.

What we are in a position to suggest is that the quality of processes taking place in groups is an important moderator of the relation between diversity and innovation. For groups to have the ability to utilize individual creative resources effectively, as in the case of managing functional diversity, it is important that they exhibit high-quality group processes. High-quality team processes are characterized by:

- *Shared vision* (Fay, Borill, Amir, Haward, & West, 2006; Pearce & Ensley, 2004): The pursuit of goals and objectives that are appealing and felt to be worth pursuing by the team.
- *Teamwork behaviour* (Pearce & Ensley, 2004; Taggar, 2002): The ability of team members to organize and coordinate themselves together to accomplish tasks.
- *Intra-group psychological safety* (Baer & Frese, 2003; Edmondson, 1999; Fay et al., 2006; West, 2002): A personally nonthreatening work environment in which group members trust each other's intentions.
- *Regard for personal identity* (Gebert et al., 2006; Taggar, 2002): The appreciation of different ideas, viewpoints and needs, as well as the belief that expressing individuality is a positive thing.
- *Support for innovation* (Scott & Bruce, 1994; West, 1990): A psychological climate of support for innovation embracing flexibility, encouragement and tolerance of change.

Therefore, group processes seem to moderate the relationship between placing creative people in a group and the creative output produced by it. In particular, high-quality processes are the conditions that enable creative people to flourish within a team. For example, Taggar (2002) showed that when group members were inspired to elevate their goals, contributions were coordinated and there was individualized consideration for each member of the team, response novelty was high. Similarly, Fay et al. (2006) found that multidisciplinary teams in the health-care sector produced higher-quality innovations when members had a strong vision, worked closely together and there was a safe team climate. Moreover, De Dreu and West (2001) showed that minority dissent was associated with team innovation under high levels of participation in decision-making.

In conclusion, even though it is necessary for innovation that groups contain members who are creative, it is also important that teams operate under the conditions that enable the creative people to use their talents. Indeed, without the right sort of social context the benefits of putting together a group of highly creative individuals can be neutralized.

Organizational level factors

At the organizational level of analysis research investigates the effects of the larger organization on creativity and innovation. The importance of organizational structure has been emphasized (Nystrom, 1979) and the structural properties of functional differentiation, specialization and internal and external communication were shown to be positively related to innovations, while centralization was negatively correlated with innovative behaviour (Damanpour, 1991). The notion of the 'innovation dilemma' suggests that the structural variables of formalization, centralization and complexity possibly have a detrimental effect on innovation at the early stages of the process (e.g., idea generation), but promote innovation at the implementation stage (Zaltman et al., 1973). Moreover, regarding the association between innovation and organizational size, the existence of a significant positive correlation was confirmed in the case of service teams (Camisón-Zornoza, Lapiedra-Alcamí, Segarra-Ciprés, & Boronat-Navarro, 2004).

Besides structure, there are aspects of organizational climate or culture that have been shown to promote or inhibit innovation/creativity. Psychological climate perceptions of support for innovation were positively related to innovative behaviour (Scott & Bruce, 1994) and the climate dimensions of achievement motivation and risk-taking were also found to be positively related to creativity and change (Nystrom, 1990). The relation between process innovation and organizational performance was shown to be moderated by organizational climates for initiative and psychological safety; that is, only companies with a high degree of process innovativeness and high levels of climates for initiative and psychological safety did better than those companies that did not innovate (Baer & Frese, 2003).

A supportive culture that values individual creativity and achievement has been identified by a number of sources to be a facilitator of innovative behaviour (Amabile, 1988; Amabile et al., 2010; Cooke & Rousseau, 1988; West & Anderson, 1992; Xenikou & Simosi, 2006). Organizations that encourage their members to take risks, not to be afraid of failure and to set their own goals are characterized as highly innovative environments. Moreover, innovation is promoted within a cooperative social environment in which team work flourishes and open communication is perceived as a necessary factor for individual and organizational growth. Competition *can* be a conducive factor to innovation, mainly when it is manifested at an inter-organizational level (between companies), while internal competition can lead to an uncontrollable conflict within the organization hindering members perception of the organization as an entity with certain common goals.

Sherwood (2001) believed that business innovation is all about corporate culture. Some organizations welcome innovation: they have the time, money and will to do it. They know they need to revisit all sorts of issues on a regular basis: rewards and recognition, performance management, funding and budgeting arrangements. They understand about managing innovation products and embedding the process. They certainly know about the crucial role of senior management and how to reward innovation. However, most organizations are the opposite. Their problem is not so much the introduction of new ideas as the unlearning of old ones. They are reactive not proactive, full of hubris rather than humility, risk and failure averse, against things new, quick to judge and punish innovations.

In sum, attributes of the larger organization can be crucial determinants of individual and group creativity at any point in time. Centralization of power (the concentration of decision-making authority) has been shown to inhibit innovation as it decreases organizational members' awareness, commitment and involvement, whereas functional differentiation, specialization, and internal and external communication promote innovative behaviours. Organizational culture and climate have been introduced as important intervening factors affecting the outcome of innovation strategies; climate and culture dimensions of initiative, psychological safety, achievement and risk taking, cooperation and open communication were shown to be related to innovations.

Creativity-enhancement techniques

Groups are extensively tasked by particular organizations to stimulate creative thinking among their employees. There are various creativity-enhancement techniques that groups in organizational settings can apply to stimulate the generation of novel ideas. Some creativity-enhancement techniques encourage group members to view the problem from a different angle by breaking cognitive mindsets, whereas others do not necessarily provoke a radical shift in perception (McFadzean, 2001). For example, techniques that use stimuli unrelated to the task at hand are more likely to produce novel ideas than techniques that use related stimuli.

Brainstorming

In brainstorming organizational members are asked to generate new ideas in groups of a rather limited number of people. Group members are encouraged to provide as many ideas as possible without concern for quality. They are also instructed to avoid criticizing or evaluating ideas as they are presented, namely the no-criticism rule, and to build on the ideas generated by others in the group (see window on the workplace).

Hicks (1991, p. 50) has described a number of ground rules for encouraging creativity in groups. These are as follows:

- Welcome every idea no matter how wild it is – it has some merit. If nothing else, it will fire our imagination or someone else's imagination.

- Hold back on criticizing an idea – remember that it is difficult enough to get an idea past our self-censor, so don't be too quick to criticize somebody else's idea. And make sure you understand another person's idea before you evaluate it.

- Remember that we always have some knowledge or experiences that can help us solve a given problem.

- Don't be afraid to indulge in some childlike behaviour – as in wishing, imagining, mental playfulness and so on.

- Never forget that other people perceive problem situations in ways different from you – treat this as an advantage, a way of helping you establish the most appropriate one to work with.

- Always think of a mistake or failure as an opportunity to learn, not as a thing we did wrong. If we just forget about it we could do it again!

Even though brainstorming is a very popular technique among managers and business consultants for stimulating creativity in groups at work, the research literature has shown that group interaction seems to inhibit the sharing of novel ideas (Diehl & Stroebe, 1987). Groups using the brainstorming rules generate substantially fewer ideas than the same number of individuals producing new ideas in isolation. Researchers have suggested that this productivity loss might be attributable to (1) the fear that group members experience of their ideas being negatively evaluated by their peers (i.e., evaluation apprehension), (2) the difficulty of simultaneously listening to the ideas of others and thinking of one's own ideas (i.e., production blocking) and (3) the tendency of people to put less effort in carrying out a task when they work in group settings (i.e., social loafing). On these grounds it has been argued that idea generation may be best left to individuals, whereas the selection and implementation of high-quality ideas may be a task better performed in groups (Nijstad & De Dreu, 2002).

However, individuals brainstorming in groups often report that they have lots of fun trying to find new ways to improve their jobs. Moreover, Paulus and his colleagues (Paulus, Larey, & Dzindolet, 2000; Paulus & Yang, 2000) have recently argued that people generating ideas in group settings seem to experience a condition of cognitive stimulation, which actually facilitates the generation of a higher quantity and quality of novel ideas. For this cognitive stimulation to take place it is important that group members are given the opportunity to generate additional ideas on their own afterwards, in a subsequent session, following the group brainstorming session.

Other procedural techniques that have been developed to overcome the limitations of group brainstorming have focused on exchanging ideas by writing instead of talking. These techniques are usually referred to as 'brainwriting' and aim at limiting the production blocking that occurs in brainstorming groups. Writing instead of speaking facilitates the generation of novel ideas because group members have the opportunity to choose when to attend to the ideas of others. Therefore, group members are not required to perform the rather demanding task of attending to the ideas of others, building on these ideas and simultaneously generating their own ideas. Finally, brainstorming is also performed in 'electronic brainstorming groups' in which case the interaction among group members is taking place through computers, eliminating any oral communication among the interacting parties. All the procedural techniques presented above also deal to some extent with the problem of evaluation apprehension people most likely experience in brainstorming groups since ideas generated by group members are kept anonymous.

Other creativity-enhancement techniques

Brainstorming and brainwriting use free association by encouraging team members to build on and further develop the ideas that other participants present to the group. Therefore, the stimulation of ideas tends to rely on the group members' past experiences or the immediate environment. There is another creativity-enhancement technique called forced association that requires group members to coerce two or more elements together. These elements may or may not be related to one another or to the problem. McFadzean (1998) describes a forced association technique named 'object stimulation':

- The problem statement is developed and written down.
- The group members are asked to develop a list of objects that are completely unrelated to the problem.
- Each individual then selects one object and describes it in detail. The group uses each description as a stimulus to generate new ideas.
- The facilitator writes each idea down.
- This process continues until each group member has described an object or until each object has been described.
- The ideas are then related back to the problem and developed further.

For example, McFadzean describes the use of object stimulation when the group has formulated the problem statement as follows. How can we attract more customers to our car dealership? After the problem statement is developed, an object is chosen that is completely unrelated to the problem. In this case, the board game Monopoly is chosen. The object is described by group members and these descriptions are used as stimuli to generate novel and valuable ideas on how to attract more customers.

Another method to stimulate creativity described by McFadzean (1998) is called 'rich pictures' and uses a form of expression other than just verbal or written language:

- Group members are asked to write a brief statement of the problem.
- The facilitator then asks each individual to draw two pictures. The pictures may be a metaphor of the situation (e.g., a vehicle or an animal). The first drawing would be a picture of how each participant would like to see the situation in the future. The second picture would be a drawing of how the participants see the present situation.
- Each participant is asked to describe the picture of the present first. Not only should he or she describe the picture but a description should also be given of the properties of the objects drawn and why they have been drawn that way. Next, a description of the picture of the future should be given. Again, the properties and the relationships of the objects should be described.
- From the descriptions given by the participants new ideas can then be generated.

The generation of novel and useful ideas in groups can offer great satisfaction and enjoyment to individual employees. However, it is important that group leaders or facilitators make the necessary amendments so that the quantity and quality of ideas produced in organizational groups are as high as possible. Various creativity-enhancement techniques deal with the production loss observed in brainstorming groups by creating the conditions which act as stimulators for creative thinking. It should be noted that the essence of a good idea is that it is both new and useful. Some creative techniques seem to throw up interesting but essentially impractical ideas.

Summary

Creativity has been described as the foundation of innovation and a key to organizational effectiveness. Innovation is considered to be a cyclical process encompassing the search for new ideas, products, practices and processes (creativity), as well as their implementation. Indeed the implementation of creativity products may call for as much creativity as their initial generation.

The creative employee, characterized by expertise, knowledge, divergent thinking and a unique combination of personality traits, is a partial explanation for creativity in work groups and complex organizational settings. The challenge is to provide a work environment that enables employees to flourish and realize their creativity potential in full capacity (see Box 4.3). The design of jobs supports creative thinking and behaviour when employees are given autonomy and

---

Box 4.3   Tactics of leaders to promote a culture of innovation

While there is reason to suspect that leaders shape climate and culture, less research is available examining how leaders should behave to ensure a culture and climate likely to support innovation.

The following tactics can be used by leaders to encourage innovation via culture perceptions:

- Exhibiting involvement, intellectual stimulation and idea support.
- Seeking to recognize and reward people who have exhibited both creative output and the pattern of interactions known to promote creativity (e.g., risk taking, collaboration, challenging others' ideas)
- Telling stories about past accomplishments involving creativity and innovation
- Approaching crisis as an intellectual challenge by accepting risks and seeking for creative solutions
- Framing mundane decisions in terms of the impact of these decisions on openness, trust and challenge

Source: Adapted from Mumford et al. (2002).

---

control over the means to do their work, tasks are being perceived as a challenge and team members have the opportunity to verify their personal competencies. The management of cultural and functional diversity entails high-quality group processes – such as a common vision, organizing and coordinating team work, trust, regard for personal identity and support for innovation. Moreover, the size and structure of the organization has an impact on organizational creativity and innovation – that is, larger decentralized organizations with functional differentiation and specialization are more innovative. Finally, Baer and Frese (2003) point out that for innovations to be successful there is a need to develop organizational climates in which people participating in the changing process feel safe in taking interpersonal risks, are encouraged to propose new ideas, openly discuss problems and proactively approach work. In Part II of this book, we will further examine the interplay between organizational culture, as well as climate – reflected in value priorities, behavioural norms and expectations – and innovative behaviour.

On a practical level, there are various creativity-enhancement techniques that managers and business consults may use to facilitate creativity among organizational members. Brainstorming is a well-known and widely implemented technique encouraging the free flow of new ideas and cooperation between team members on generating solutions to problems in a noncritical environment. Other creativity-enhancement techniques, such as object stimulation and rich pictures, try to fire the imagination by using unrelated stimuli or drawing pictures.

Questions

1. What is the relationship between innovation and creativity? In your experience, is the originality of new ideas closely associated with their successful implementation?
2. Is creativity necessary for innovation to take place?
3. Innovation is considered to be a multistage process. Which are the main stages of the innovation process and how do they feed each other?
4. What factors influence the extent to which groups generate and implement ideas for novel and useful products, services and practices at work?
5. Should groups be used in the creativity phase of innovation? Describe some techniques that can facilitate idea generation in group settings.
6. Under which conditions do demographic diversity and cross-functionality have primarily positive effects on team innovations?
7. How can managers stimulate and encourage creativity among their subordinates?

Window on the workplace

Innovation in a product development firm

IDEO is a product design consulting firm specializing in mechanical engineering and industrial design. Clients typically hire IDEO to design part or all of a product that they would like to manufacture and sell but lack the expertise of staff levels to design.

Engineers at IDEO use brainstorming sessions to address product design problems that they face. Sessions usually last between 45 minutes and 2 hours. Typically, project engineers introduce the project and describe a design problem that troubles them. Then the other engineers offer possible solutions, often in the form of solutions they have seen in other settings. Solutions are sometimes found in similar products that are brought to brainstorms (e.g., a designer suggested adapting a design solution for a new skin stapler that was already used in a competitor's product) or in products that were brought in from different industries (e.g., a designer showed how a gas engine from a model airplane could be used to power a skin stapler). The topics of the brainstorming sessions range widely concerning video cameras, furniture, personal appliances, surgical skin staplers, blood analysers, laptop computers, remote controls, vacuum cleaners, and portable traffic control systems. Five brainstorming rules are displayed in large letters in several locations in each room: (1) defer judgment;

(cont'd)

(2) build on the ideas of others; (3) one conversation at the time; (4) stay focused on the topic; and (5) encourage wild ideas. Engineers often describe and sketch solutions on paper or on whiteboards in the room.

Designers at IDEO make connections between existing solutions and new problems over time and across people. There are routines that designers and teams use to create new products by teaming of possible solutions, remembering them, and retrieving them in new forms that fit in new combinations.

Source: Adapted from Hargadon and Sutton (1997).

References

Amabile, T. M. (1988). A model of creativity and innovation in organizations. In D. G. Gardner and L. L. Cummings (eds.), *Research in Organizational Behavior*, 10 (pp. 123–167). Greenwich, CT: JAI Press.

Amabile, T. M. (1996). *Creativity in Context: Update to the Social Psychology of Creativity*. Boulder, CO: Westview Press.

Amabile, T. M. (1998). How to kill creativity. *Harvard Business Review*, 76, 76–87.

Amabile, T. M., & Gitomer, J. (1984). Children's artistic creativity: Effects of choice in task materials. *Personality and Social Psychology Bulletin*, 10, 209–215.

Amabile, T. M., Conti, R., Coon, H., Lazenby, J., & Herron, M. (1996). Assessing the work environment for creativity. *Academy of Management Journal*, 39, 1154–1184.

Amabile, T. M., Goldfarb, P., & Brackfield, S. C. (1990). Social influences on creativity: Evaluation, coaction, and surveillance. *Creativity Research Journal*, 3, 6–21.

Amabile, T. M., Hennessey, B. M., & Grossman, B. S. (1986). Social influences on creativity: The effects of contracted-for reward. *Journal of Personality and Social Psychology*, 50, 14–23.

Amabile, T. M., & associates (2010). Breakthrough ideas for 2010. *Harvard Business Review*, 88, 41–57.

Baer, M., & Frese, M. (2003). Innovation is not enough: Climates for initiative and psychological safety, process innovations, and firm performance. *Journal of Organizational Behavior*, 24, 45–68.

Barrick, M. R., & Mount, M. K. (1991). The Big Five personality dimensions and job performance: A meta-analysis. *Personnel Psychology*, 44, 1–26.

Basadur, M. (2005). Management: Synchronizing different kinds of creativity. In J. Kaufman and J. Baer (eds.), *Creativity Across Domains* (pp. 261–279). Mahwah, NJ: LEA.

Batey, M., & Furnham, A. (2006). Creativity, intelligence, and personality: A critical review of the scattered literature. *Genetic, Social, and General Psychology Monographs*, 132, 355–429.

Camisón-Zornoza, C., Lapiedra-Alcamí, R., Segarra-Ciprés, M., & Boronat-Navarro, M. (2004). A meta-analysis of innovation and organizational size. *Organization Studies*, 25, 331–361.

Child, D. (1973). *Psychology and the Teacher*. New York: Holt-Rinehart.

Conti, R., Collins, M. A., & Picariello, M. L. (2001). The impact of competition on intrinsic motivation and creativity: Considering gender, gender segregation, and gender role orientation. *Personality and Individual Differences*, 31, 1273–1289.

Cooke, R. A., & Rousseau, D. M. (1988). Behavioral norms and expectations: A quantitative approach to the assessment of organizational culture. *Group and Organization Studies*, 13, 245–273.

Csikszentmihalyi, M. (1990). *Flow: The Psychology of Optimal Experience*. New York: Harper Perennial.

Damanpour, F. (1991). Organizational innovation: A meta-analysis of effects of determinants and moderators. *Academy of Management Journal*, **34**, 555–590.

De Dreu, C. K. W., & West, M. A. (2001). Minority dissent and team innovation: The importance of participation in decision making. *Journal of Applied Psychology*, **86**, 1191–1201.

Diehl, M., & Stroebe, W. (1987). Productivity loss in brainstorming groups: Toward the solution of a riddle. *Journal of Personality and Social Psychology*, **53**, 497–509.

Edmondson, A. (1999). Psychological safety and learning behavior in work teams. *Administrative Science Quarterly*, **44**, 350–383.

Eisenberger, R., & Armeli, S. (1997). Can salient reward increase creative performance without reducing intrinsic creative interest? *Journal of Personality and Social Psychology*, **72**, 652–663.

Epstein, J. A., & Harackiewicz, J. M. (1992). Winning is not enough: The effects of competition and achievement orientation on intrinsic interest. *Personality and Social Psychology Bulletin*, **18**, 128–139.

Fay, D., Borill, C., Amir, Z., Haward, R., & West, M. A. (2006). Getting the most out of multidisciplinary teams: A multi-sample study of team innovation in health care. *Journal of Occupational and Organizational Psychology*, **79**, 553–567.

Feist, G. J. (1998). A meta-analysis of the impact of personality on scientific and artistic creativity. *Personality and Social Psychological Review*, **2**, 290–309.

Furnham, A. (2008). *Personality and Intelligence at Work*. London: Routledge.

Gebert, D., Boerner, S., & Kearney, E. (2006). Cross-functionality and innovation in new product development teams: A dilemmatic structure and its consequences for the management of diversity. *European Journal of Work and Organizational Psychology*, **15**, 431–458.

George, J. M., & Zhou, J. (2001). When openness to experience and conscientiousness are related to creative behavior: An international approach. *Journal of Applied Psychology*, **86**, 513–524.

Greve, H. R., & Taylor, A. (2000). Innovations as catalysts for organizational change: Shifts in organizational cognition and search. *Administrative Science Quarterly*, **45**, 54–80.

Hackman, J. R., & Oldham, G. R. (1980). *Work Redesign*. Reading, MA: Addison-Wesley.

Harackiewicz, J. M., & Sansone, C. (1991). Goals and intrinsic motivation: You can get there from here. In M. L. Maehr & P. R. Pintrich (eds.), *Advances in Motivation and Achievement* (pp. 21–49). Greenwich, CT: JAI Press.

Hargadon, A., & Sutton, R. I. (1997). Technology brokering and innovation in a product development firm. *Administrative Science Quarterly*, **42**, 716–749.

Hennessey, B. A., & Amabile, T. M. (1988). The conditions of creativity. In R. J. Sternberg (ed.), *The Nature of Creativity* (pp. 11–38). New York: Cambridge University Press.

Hicks, M. J. (1991). *Problem Solving in Business and Management: Hard, Soft, and Creative Approaches*. London: Chapman & Hall.

James, K., Chen, J., & Goldberg, C. (1992). Organizational conflict and individual creativity. *Journal of Applied Social Psychology*, **22**, 545–566.

Kanter, R. M. (1983). *The Change Masters*. London: George Allen and Unwin.

Kaufman, J. (2009) *Creativity 101*. New York: Springer.

MacKinnon, D. (1965). Personality and the realization of creative potential. *American Psychologist*, **20**, 273–281.

McFadzean, E. (1998). *The Creativity Tool Box: A Practical Guide for Facilitating Creative Problem Solving Sessions*. Milton Keynes, UK: TeamTalk Consulting Ltd.

McFadzean, E. (2001). Critical factors for enhancing creativity. *Strategic Change*, **10**, 267–283.

Mednick, S. (1962). The associative basis of the creative process. *Psychological Review*, **69**, 220–232.

Mumford, M. D., Scott, G. M., Gaddis, B., & Stange, J. M. (2002). Leading creative people: Orchestrating expertise and relationships. *The Leadership Quarterly*, **13**, 705–750.

Nijstad, B. A., & De Dreu, C. K. W. (2002). Creativity and group innovation. *Applied Psychology: An International Review*, **51**, 400–406.

Nystrom, H. (1979). *Creativity and Innovation*. New York: John Wiley.

Nystrom, H. (1990). Organizational innovation. In M. A. West & J. L. Farr (eds.), *Innovation and Creativity at Work: Psychological and Organizational Strategies* (pp. 143–161). New York: John Wiley.

Oldham, G. R., & Cummings, A. (1996). Employee creativity: Personal and contextual factors at work. *Academy of Management Journal*, **39**, 607–634.

Paulus, P. B., Larey, T. S., & Dzindolet, M. T. (2000). Creativity in groups and teams. In M. Turner (ed.), *Groups at Work: Advances in Theory and Research* (pp. 319–338). Hillsdale, NJ: Hampton.

Paulus, P. B., & Yang, H. C. (2000). Idea generation in groups: A basis for creativity in organizations. *Organizational Behavior and Human Decision Processes*, **82**, 76–87.

Pearce, C. L., & Ensley, M. D. (2004). A reciprocal and longitudinal investigation of the innovation process: The central role of shared vision in product and process innovation teams (PPITs). *Journal of Organizational Behavior*, **25**, 259–278.

Rank, J., Pace, V. L., & Frese, M. (2004). Three avenues for future research on creativity, innovation, and initiative. *Applied Psychology: An International Review*, **53**, 518–528.

Salgado, J. F. (1998). Big five personality dimensions and job performance in army and civil occupations: A European perspective. *Human Performance*, **11**, 271–288.

Sansone, C., & Harackiewicz, J. M. (1996). 'I don't feel like it': The function of interest in self-regulation. In M. M. Martin & A. Tesser (eds.), *Striving and Feeling: Interactions among Goals, Affect, and Self-Regulation* (pp. 203–228). Mahwah, NJ: Erlbaum.

Scott, S. G., & Bruce, R. A. (1994). Determinants of innovative behaviour: A path model of individual innovation in the workplace. *Academy of Management Journal*, **3**, 580–607.

Shalley, C. E., Gilson, L. L., & Blum, T. C. (2000). Matching creativity requirements and the work environment: Effects on satisfaction and intentions to leave. *Academy of Management Journal*, **43**, 215–223.

Sherwood, D. (2001). *Smart Things to Know about Innovation and Creativity*. Oxford: Capstone.

Taggar, S. (2002). Individual creativity and group ability to utilize individual creative resources: A multilevel model. *Academy of Management Journal*, **45**, 315–330.

Taylor, A., & Greve, H. R. (2006). Superman or the fantastic four? Knowledge combination, and experience in innovative teams. *Academy of Management Journal*, **49**, 723–740.

Wallace, H. R. (1961). Creative thinking: A factor in sales productivity. *Vocational Guidance Quarterly*, **9**, 223–226.

Ward, T. B., Finke, R. A., & Smith, S. M. (1995). *Creativity and the Mind: Discovering the Genius Within*. New York: Plenum Press.

West, M. A. (1990). The social psychology of innovation in groups. In M. A. West & J. L. Farr (eds.), *Innovation and Creativity at Work: Psychological and Organizational Strategies* (pp. 309–333). New York: John Wiley.

West, M. A. (2002). Sparkling fountains or stagnant ponds: An integrative model of creativity and innovation implementation in work groups. *Applied Psychology: An International Review*, **51**, 355–387.

West, M. A., & Anderson, N. (1992). Innovation, cultural values, and the management of change in British hospitals. *Work and Stress*, **6**, 293–310.

West, M. A., & Farr, J. L. (1990). *Innovation and Creativity at Work: Psychological and Organizational Strategies.* New York: Wiley.

Woodman, R. W., Sawyer, J. E., & Griffin, R. W. (1993). Toward a theory of organizational creativity. *Academy of Management Review*, **18**, 293–321.

Xenikou, A., & Simosi, M. (2006). Organizational culture and transformational leadership as predictors of business unit performance. *Journal of Managerial Psychology*, **21**, 566–579.

Zaltman, G., Duncan, R., & Holbek, J. (1973). *Innovations and Organizations.* London: Wiley.

Part II
The Larger Organization

The Concept of Organizational Culture

5

Chapter objectives

The main objectives are to:

- explore the various origins of the concept of organizational culture and examine how the study of organizational culture has been influenced by them;

- define what organizational culture is and get familiar with various theoretical approaches to the concept;

- investigate the nature and meaning of the elements and dimensions of organizational culture;

- understand the usage of quantitative and qualitative methodologies, and their theoretical assumptions in the study of organizational culture;

- delve into the relationship of organizational climate with organizational culture and critically evaluate their similarities and differences.

Introduction

For three decades the concept of organizational culture has been explored, discussed and debated by researchers in different academic disciplines, business consultants as well as among line, middle and top managers. Organizational culture became popular in the early 1980s in an attempt to understand the superior performance of Japanese corporations as compared to their American and European counterparts in terms of productivity, innovation and quality. It was persuasively argued that Japanese management and workers shared a set of important values that promoted commitment to quality, problem solving and cooperative effort, which, in turn, led to high levels of performance.

Several early influential books written for managers used the idea of organizational culture during that period. Peters and Waterman's (1982) best-selling popular business book titled *In Search for Excellence* advocated that the basic philosophy of an organization has far more to do with its achievements than do technological or economic resources, organizational structure, innovation and timing. They proposed that excellent companies are characterized by clearly defined shared value systems. Apart from clarity on values excellent companies show the right sorts of values. The dominant beliefs of excellent companies include just a few basic values, namely a belief in being the best, attention to detail, the importance of people as individuals, superior quality and service, innovation, informality, the importance of economic growth and profits, and hands-on management. However, even though the book was a great success, later on these 'brilliant' companies failed to perform well. This was a blow for the theory.

Another best-selling popular business book written by Deal and Kennedy was published in the year 1982; it proposed that culture has a major effect on the success of organizations. After examining various corporations and their business environments they suggested that many companies fall into four general types of culture. These categories are determined mainly by two factors in the external environment: the degree of risk associated with the company's activities and the speed at which organizations get feedback on whether their strategies are successful. These are presented in Box 5.1. They also suggested that a strong culture is considered to be the driving force behind continuing success in business. Companies with strong cultures have rich and complex, as well as clear and explicit, value systems that are shared by their employees. However, Deal and Kennedy (1982) acknowledged that a strong culture can possibly have a negative impact on performance when the company's value system is not adapting to changing environmental (marketplace) conditions and leads to resistance to necessary changes.

Box 5.1 Deal and Kennedy's (1982) four types of organizational culture

1. *The tough-guy, macho culture.* This type of corporate is characterized by a world of individualists who regularly take high risks and get quick feedback

---

Box 5.1   (cont'd)

on whether their actions were right or wrong. The marketplace provides a variety of organizations that fall in this category: cosmetics, television, movies, advertising and management consultancy.

2. *The work hard/play hard culture.* The employees take few risks, all with quick feedback; fun and action are the rule here. The primary values of this culture focus on customers and their needs as, for example, in the world of sales organizations.

3. *The bet-your-company culture.* In this culture years pass before employees know whether decisions paid off. The business environment is characterized by high risk and slow feedback as, for example, in the case of the oil industry and aircraft constructors.

4. *The process culture.* This type of culture is a world of little or no feedback and low risk where employees find it hard to measure what they do; instead they concentrate on how it is done. Insurance companies and governmental agencies are good examples of process culture organizations.

The work of both Peters and Waterman (1982) and Deal and Kennedy (1982) was severely criticized primarily for lacking academic rigour in their study of organizational life. The empirical basis of their propositions was merely a series of vivid and capturing anecdotes involving top management of the corporations under study. A second methodological pitfall was that only successful companies were included, and there were no comparisons made between excellent and less well-performing companies (Carroll, 1983). Moreover, corporate excellence was described as the outcome of managerial effectiveness while environmental and marketplace factors, such as competitors, advances in technology, government policy and regulation, were ignored (Carroll, 1983; Hitt & Ireland, 1987; Reynolds, 1986).

Similarly, Harrison (1972) and Handy (1986) advocated that organizations are characterized by their own philosophies of management and organizational cultures, and presented four different types of organization ideologies or, in other words, cultures. The 'power culture' is highly centralized and depends on a central power source that exerts immense influence on organizational members. Within the organization those who are powerful strive to maintain absolute control over subordinates. The 'role culture' is often stereotyped as bureaucracy and identified by a strong preference for rules and procedures as the major method of influence. The 'task culture' values expertise rather than seniority or position power, and focuses on problem solving, efficiency and creativity. Finally, the 'person culture' assumes that the organization exists primarily to serve the needs of its members and organizational objectives are not considered to be more important than the personal goals of individual employees. Both Harrison (1972) and Handy (1986) argued that these types of culture are seldom found in organizations as pure types, but most organizations tend to focus on one or another of them, such as a dominant culture type emerges for each organization.

However, subsequent research has shown that there is little empirical basis to support the idea that the early proposed types of culture exist mainly because this theoretical approach puts a lot of restrictions on the combination of organizational attributes that coexist to formulate a culture type, such as a value placed concurrently on power, competition and flexibility (power culture).

Although there were methodological problems with the research of Peters and Waterman (1982), Deal and Kennedy (1982) and Handy (1986), we have to note that the basic questions addressed by following academic research were raised in connection to these authors' theoretical propositions and the discussion of the methodological problems related to their research. In particular, the relation of culture type and strength with organizational performance, the identification of the thematic dimensions of culture associated with fluctuations in organizational performance and, finally, the contingency approach to the culture–performance link are topics that have emerged, at least partially, due to the discussion of these authors' work.

What is organizational culture?

The concept of organizational culture as has been developed in organization science was primarily derived from the discipline of anthropology. Within anthropology the concept of culture has received an extensive analytical treatment, which is reflected in the fact that Kroeber and Kluckholm (1952) reviewed 164 distinct usages of the term. As far as the field of organizational behaviour is concerned, culture in organizations is defined as the way people think and act as members of a given organization, conceptualizing culture in terms of both cognition and behaviour (see Box 5.2). Schwartz and Davis (1981) suggest that culture is a pattern of beliefs and expectations shared by organizational members that create norms which powerfully shape the behaviour of individuals and groups in the organization.

Similarly, Williams, Dodson, and Walters (1989) define culture as the 'commonly held and relatively stable beliefs, attitudes and values that exist within an organization and underlie much of human activity in it'.

Smircich (1983) argues that culture is the set of meanings which is shared by group members and gives the group its own distinctive character, expressed in patterns of belief, activity, language and other symbolic forms. According to Trice and Beyer (1993), people in organizations develop cultures as they interact and share ways of managing uncertainties. Trice and Beyer conceptualize culture as (1) substance, which consists of shared systems of beliefs, values and norms; and (2) forms, which are observable ways that organizational members express cultural ideas. Moreover, Deal and Kennedy (1982) have defined culture as 'the way we do things around here', emphasizing the behavioural element in their definition of organizational culture.

Box 5.2   Definitions of the organizational culture concept

Corporate culture is a pattern of beliefs and expectations shared by organizational members that create norms which powerfully shape the behaviour of individuals and groups in the organization (Schwartz & Davis, 1981).

Culture is the commonly shared beliefs, values and characteristic patterns of behaviour that exist within an organization (Margulies & Raia, 1978).

Culture is defined as the commonly held and relatively stable beliefs, attitudes and values that exist within an organization and underlie much of human activity in it (Williams et al., 1989).

Organizational cultures consist of shared systems of beliefs, values and norms which are manifested through various cultural forms (Trice & Beyer, 1993).

Culture is a pattern of information and can greatly facilitate the exchange of understanding. Culture's main function is to try to mediate dilemmas (Hampden-Turner, 1990).

Corporate culture is 'the way we do things around here' (Deal & Kennedy, 1982).

Culture is the shared beliefs of a company's top managers about how they should manage themselves and other employees (Lorsch, 1985).

Organizational culture is a pattern of shared basic assumptions that the group learned as it solved its problems of external adaptation and internal integration that has worked well enough to be considered valid and, therefore, to be taught to new members as the correct way to perceive, think and feel in relation to those problems (Schein, 1992).

Organizational culture is the set of meanings that give a group its own ethos, or distinctive character, which is expressed in patterns of belief, activity, language and other symbolic forms through which organization members both create and sustain their view of the world and image of themselves in the world (Smircich, 1983).

Organizational culture is the patterns of meanings that link various aspects of organizational life, such as stories organizational members tell, offices layout, organization's official policies, reporting relationships, sometimes in harmony, sometimes in bitter conflict between groups, and sometimes in webs of ambiguity, paradox and contradiction (Martin, 2002).

In an attempt to formulate a definition of organizational culture Hampden-Turner (1990) examines the functions of culture. Culture is assumed to come from within people and is put together by them to reward the capacities they have in common. It gives continuity and identity to the group and at the same time balances contrasting contributions. Furthermore, culture operates as a self-steering system that learns from feedback. It works as a pattern of information and can greatly facilitate the exchange of understanding. The main function of culture is to try to mediate everyday organizational and personal dilemmas. The various issues arising within an organization take the form of dilemmas: should new products be developed more quickly to beat competitors on time; or more slowly to win on quality? The larger strategic issues have the same characteristics; the organization needs to preserve its key continuities, but it also needs periodic change. The whole area of organizational culture is constructed entirely of such dilemmas.

A definition of organizational culture that highlights some of its key functions is provided by Schein (1992) in his book *Organizational Culture and Leadership*. Organizational culture is:

> a pattern of shared basic assumptions that the group learned as it solved its problems of external adaptation and internal integration, that has worked well enough to be considered valid and, therefore, to be taught to new members as the correct way to perceive, think and feel in relation to those problems.
>
> (p. 12)

Culture is primarily considered to be what is passed on to new generations of group members. An organization's deeper assumptions that are commonly held by its members constitute the core element of the socialization process. A teaching and learning process is always going on, even though it may be quite implicit and unsystematic. These basic assumptions are utilized by the group in order to deal with the imperatives of adaptation to its external environment, as well as coordination and integration of its various units. A group's basic assumptions become a defining property of the group which permits the group to differentiate itself from other groups, and therefore value is attached to such assumptions.

There are a number of organizational theorists who believe that organizational culture is essentially the values of top management. Lorsch (1985) takes culture to mean the shared implicit and explicit beliefs of an organization's top managers about how they should manage themselves and other employees. Gordon (1985) chooses to study culture by using a managerial group because he believes that corporate values held by management are reflected in behaviour throughout the organization. Finally, Martin (1985) acknowledges that in many organizations organizational cultures are developed from the philosophies of top management and maintained through the acceptance of these philosophies by organizational members. Although we can criticize the conceptualization of organizational culture as solely the value priorities and philosophies of top management on the grounds of a stakeholder perspective emphasizing the role of management as well as employees in organizational life, it needs to be noticed that power differentials do have a strong impact on the formulation, maintenance and change of culture. For example, the values of founders are important factors shaping the cultures of organizations at the first stages of an organization's life, but once established culture becomes a frame through which leadership behaviour is reinforced. Power to influence shared meanings and activity patterns in organizations does rest in the formal structures as well as the informal social relations and networks, which are essential parts of any social group.

Another important issue regarding the definition of organizational culture is whether different groups in the organization develop their own particular cultures. As already mentioned, organizational assumptions, values, beliefs and behavioural norms are thought to be part of an organization's culture given that they are commonly shared by organizational members. However, organizations are often formulated by various subgroups such as departments, divisions, work and occupational groups. Researchers have argued that organizational cultures are treated as far too homogeneous and that different groups in organizations develop various subcultures. For example, Gregory (1983) believes that many organizations are multicultural, composed of different occupational, divisional and ethnic groups, which approach organizational interactions with their own meanings and senses of priorities. Potter (1989) has criticized the way that the cultural concept has been formulated, arguing that it gives insufficient recognition to deviance, plurality and change.

Therefore, even though most definitions of organizational culture consider a basic aspect of the concept to be that cognitions and behavioural manifestations are commonly shared by organizational members, it has been acknowledged that within organizations different subgroups may develop their own cultures. In a review of the literature on organizational subcultures, Boisnier and Chatman (2003) argue that organizations may have both an overall strong culture and different subcultures at the same time. They distinguish between pivotal and peripheral values; pivotal values are strongly shared throughout the organization, whereas peripheral values are held by specific organizational units. Therefore, subcultures may incorporate the pivotal organizational values as well as their own peripheral values which make them distinct.

Subcultures can be independent, compatible or in conflict with each other (Martin & Siehl, 1983). In the case of conflicting subgroup cultures, the criterion of sharedness concerns the extent to which cognitions and actions are shared by subgroup rather than organizational members. At this point we should note that there are also scholars who have proposed that values and beliefs of organizational members which are not shared and create ambiguities are part of cultural communities, and they need to be studied to grasp a deep understanding of organizational culture (Meyerson, 1991). Culture differences rooted in occupational, gender, ethnic or hierarchical differentials reflect the priorities set by various social groups in the organization, and they can potentially be key contextual influences when facing, for example, conflict within work groups (see Chapter 3) or work group creativity (see Chapter 4).

The way organizational culture is defined is closely related to the different theoretical perspectives that examine the phenomenon in question. Smircich (1983) suggests that organizational culture has been developed in organizational studies either as a critical variable or as a root metaphor. On one hand, when culture is conceptualized as a critical variable it is considered as something the organization has and it is treated as an independent or dependent variable. On the other hand, there are theoretical approaches that define culture as something the organization is and present culture as a root metaphor of the organization. For example, the metaphors of machine and organism have been extensively used to understand the organization as instruments for task accomplishment and organisms striving for survival, respectively.

In conclusion, the definitions of organizational culture refer to the basic assumptions, meanings, values and beliefs that members of a specific organization share, the social norms that dictate how one is expected to behave as a member of the organization and the organizational practices that characterize the way the organization operates.

These commonly shared cognitions, behavioural patterns and practices are developed in order to give identity to the group, facilitate the confrontation of problems and promote intra-group understanding. However, it has been well argued that culture may include conflict and ambiguity as well as that which is commonly shared (Martin, 2002).

Case study

Understanding the organizational culture of Disneyland

Disneyland is part of Walt Disney Enterprises and has been a consistent money maker since 1955 when it first opened its gates in Anaheim, California. The corporation is self-presented to be 'The Happiest Place on Earth' certainly occupying an enviable position in the world of entertainment and commerce. Its product seems to be emotion, 'laughter and well-being', and top managers at Disneyland describe their job as doing business in the 'happiness trade'. However, the happiness trade is an interactive one since employees at the bottom of the organization are mostly the ones who provide laughter and happiness. They seem (more or less) eager to greet the guests, pack the trams, push the buttons, deliver the food, dump the garbage, and, overall try hard to meet and perhaps exceed customer expectations. False moves, rude words, careless disregard, detected insincerity can all undermine the enterprise of happiness. Disneyland, the smile factory, has its rules, regulations and procedures that ensure employees are dressed properly, behave kindly, and entertain the park's guests.

The rides and attractions in the park are run by ride operators who comprise the largest category of hourly workers on the payroll. During the summer months, they number close to four thousand. They are a well-screened group of employees. There is, among insiders and outsiders alike, a rather fixed view about how the standard-make Disneyland ride operator looks like. Single, white males and females in their early twenties, without facial blemish, of above average weight and below average weight, with straight teeth, conservative

(cont'd)

grooming and a chin-up, shoulder-back posture; all these attributes are typical features of ride operators. In case operators are ethnic minorities, they tend to be close copies of the standard model Disneylander. So, to get a job at Disneyland and keep it you need to conform to a rather explicit set of appearance as well as behavioural rules. These rules are written down in a manual and ride operators are expected to frequently refer to it to check on how they should look and behave towards guests.

After being selected to work for Disneyland a newcomer attends a 40-hour training programme, most of which takes place on the rides. In the classroom, however, newly hired ride operators are given a thorough introduction to the philosophy of Disneyland, its values, rules, procedures, and practices. Language is also a central feature of this apprenticeship programme and new employees are taught the corporation's jargon. Customers at Disneyland are, for example, never referred to as customers or clients; they are always called 'guests'. There are no rides, only 'attractions' and Disneyland itself is a 'Park' not an amusement centre. Emphasis is placed on the articulation, as well as absorption, of particular values the Disneyland management believes to be central to the organization's functioning. These values range from common held business beliefs such as 'the customer is king' to more tailored values as for example 'everyone is a child at heart when at Disneyland'. Appearance standards are also learned and gone over in the classroom as for example keeping uniforms fresh, wearing all uniforms' accessories, and polishing one's shoes. Facial hair and long hair is banned for men as are glasses and earrings, while women should refrain from wearing fancy jewellery, teasing their hair or apply heavy makeup. Newly hired employees are repeatedly told that if they are happy and cheerful at work, so, too, will be the guests. It's important that they have a wide smile on their face and exercise common courtesy to the people who visit the park.

Of course socialization in Disneyland takes place by formal, as well as informal, processes and newcomers quickly learn to recognize symbols of status. The ride and area an employee is assigned provides rewards and benefits beyond those of wages. Most employee status, however, goes to those whose jobs require higher degrees of special skill, relative freedom from constant and direct supervision, and provide the opportunity to direct customer wishes and behavior rather than to merely respond to them as spontaneously expressed. Employees very quickly also learn that supervisors are not only there to help them, but to monitor whether they violate set procedures or park policies. Much of the supervisory monitoring are directed at activities ride operators consider trivial such as taking a long break, not wearing part of one's official uniform or rushing the ride. Violation of such codes is often subjected to instant and harsh discipline, and employees may even get fired because of violating such rules.

(cont'd)

(1) Explain how personnel selection, training and performance appraisal is used to maintain and promote the Disneyland culture.

(2) Are socialization processes in Disneyland effective in facilitating the smooth operation of everyday activities?

(3) Give examples of the dressing code and 'people skills' that Disneyland front-line employees are expected to exhibit while 'on stage'.

Source: Adapted from Van Maanen (1991).

The manifestation of culture at various levels of awareness

Organizational culture researchers in their attempt to formulate the concept of culture have tried to identify the various ways that culture is manifested. Schein (1990, 1992) suggests that organizational culture has three levels, as follows: basic assumptions, values and artefacts/creations. The three levels of culture interact with each other and there is a clear hierarchical structure based on the issue of awareness. Basic assumptions are considered to be unconscious, values are characterized by a greater level of awareness and, finally, artefacts/creations are visible. Artefacts and creations are the constructed environment of the organization, its architecture, technology, office layout, manner of dress, visible or audible behaviour patterns and public documents, such as charts and stories. The second level of organizational culture contains organizational values – that is, what 'ought' to be done. According to Schein (1990, 1992), values are considered to be more difficult to identify in comparison to artefacts and creations. The third level of culture, namely basic assumptions, is the most important one in order to deeply understand a culture. Basic assumptions are invisible because they are taken for granted and organizational members are not aware of holding them. Therefore, basic assumptions exist and act at an unconscious level, which constitutes their main difference to values, as values are assumed to operate on a higher level of awareness. In fact, basic assumptions are values that are taken for granted and gradually drop out of consciousness. For example, basic assumptions may concern the dilemma on how we best approach reality, either by collecting hard-evidence business data or by reaching decision-makers' consensus. Another example of basic assumptions concerns lay theories about the essence of human nature describing people (at work) either as achievement-oriented and self-actualizing or lazy and self-indulgent.

Martin and Siehl (1983) suggested that besides the three levels of culture described by Schein there is a fourth one – that is, management practices.

This level contains the familiar management tasks, such as personnel selection, training, performance appraisal and allocation of rewards. Management practices may or may not include artefacts. For example, a training programme for new employees may be an occasion for telling organizational stories and concluding with a ceremony. In general, artefacts and management practices express values, while underlying those values are even deeper assumptions that rest at a preconscious level.

Although the relevant literature has described a number of levels at which an organizational culture is manifested, researchers usually choose to study culture by focusing on one of these levels. For example, Schein (1992) aims primarily at investigating and uncovering the basic assumptions that are unconsciously leading the behaviour of group members, while Martin and her colleagues (Martin & Siehl, 1983; Martin, Feldman, Hatch, & Sitkin, 1983) have examined organizational values as manifested in patterned sequences of events, namely stories (see Table 5.1). Moreover, Cooke and his associates (Cooke & Rousseau, 1988; Cooke & Szumal, 1993, 2000) have studied another level of culture, namely the behaviours it takes to fit in and get ahead, which are indicative of the social norms attached to the group. Finally, Trice and Beyer (1984, 1993) have focused on rites, rituals and ceremonies that take place within organizational settings.

In an attempt to incorporate all the levels of culture described in the existing literature, Rousseau (1990) developed a model of the structure of organizational culture. The various levels are organized from readily accessible to difficult to assess (Box 5.3). At the perimeter, material artefacts reflect the physical manifestations and products of cultural activity (e.g., logos and badges). At the next level, patterns of activity, such as decision-making, coordination and communication mechanisms, are observable to outsiders and help the organization to carry out everyday functioning activities. Social (behavioural) norms that refer to members' beliefs regarding acceptable and unacceptable behaviour are the third level of culture, and values that reflect priorities or preferences for specific outcomes are the fourth level. Finally, basic assumptions comprise the centre of the cultural model and require researcher–member interaction in order to be assessed.

Finally, Martin (2002) distinguishes between ideational and materialistic approaches to the study of culture and therefore presents a grouping of the levels of culture in terms of either cognitions and meanings, or material conditions. According to the ideational perspective, culture is conceptualized in terms of meanings or understandings while materialistic manifestations of culture such as physical layout, dressing code and pay practices are not part of the cultural superstructure. On the other hand, advocates of a materialistic approach to the study of culture argue that an exclusive emphasis on the ideational elements of culture can possibly lead to one ignoring the vastly different material conditions that are related to working at different levels of an organization's hierarchy, different departments or job positions.

Table 5.1 Organizational cultures as manifested in the content of stories (Martin et al., 1983)

Common story types that frequently occur in a wide variety of organizational contexts	Story example
1. What do I do when a higher status person breaks a rule? In the rule-breaking stories there are two starring characters, a high-status manager and a low-status employee. Four events occur in a fixed sequence. First, the high-status person does something that draws attention to his/her authority. Second, the high-status person breaks a company rule. Third, the subordinate challenges him/her, pointing out the infraction. Finally, the high-status person either does or does not comply.	The job of a young woman at IBM was to make sure that people entering security areas wore the correct clearance identification. Once Thomas Watson Jr., the intimidating chairman of IBM's board, approached the doorway to an area where she was on guard, wearing an orange badge acceptable elsewhere in the plant, but not a green badge, which alone permitted entrance at her door. 'I was trembling in my uniform' she recalled. 'I'm sorry' I said to him. I knew who he was all right. "You cannot enter. Your admittance is not recognized." That's what we were supposed to say'. The men accompanying Watson were stricken: the moment held unpredictable possibilities. 'Don't you know who he is?' someone hissed. Watson raised his hand for silence, while one of the party strode off and returned with the appropriate badge (Rogers, 1969, as cited in Martin et al., 1983).
2. Is the big boss human? The key role in these stories is played by a high status organizational member (i.e., founder or president). Three events occur. First, the status credentials of the 'big boss' are established. Second, the central character is given the opportunity to engage in a status equalization act. Third, the character does or does not put aside his or her high status temporarily by exhibiting human qualities.	'Country Club Repairman' Charles Brown was the CEO at Illinois Bell during the late 1960s. A strike has crippled the organization, as craftspeople refused to work for several months. On the weekends, 'Charlie,' as he was known, would start repairing telephones. One weekend, the country club where he belonged called with a complaint about a broken phone. Without even changing his clothes he went out and fixed the country club phone. People reacted with glee and teasing (Kleinfield, 1981 as cited in Martin et al., 1983).
3. Can the little person rise to the top? These stories concern the fit between an employee's abilities and his/her status in the organization. In one version of the story, the central role is filled by a low-status employee who deserves promotion and is rewarded with a rapid rise through the hierarchy. There are also other versions of this story in which a deserving low-status employee remains unrewarded or an undeserving low-status employee is promoted.	'The legend of Richard Deupree' At the age of 12 Deupree had left school to work as an insurance agency's office boy out of economic necessity. In 1905 he was hired by P&G as an office boy at the Treasury Department and he was soon promoted to the cashier's cage. It was there that he caught the attention of Thomas H. Beck, head of what was then P&G's newly organized Bulk Soap Sales Division. Beck was struck by Deupree's pleasant nature. 'You're the first cashier I've known who ever smiled when paying out money,' he said. Beck remembered the amiable young man when his division needed another salesman. From this point on, Deupree's rise was rapid, and by 1917 he was appointed as P&G General Sales Manager (Schisgall, 1981 as cited in Martin et al., 1983).

THE CONCEPT OF ORGANIZATIONAL CULTURE   107

4. How will the boss react to mistakes?

In this type of story there are two character types: the mistake maker and one or more superiors.

These stories begin at the point when the superior learns that a mistake has been made. A confrontation ensues. In one version of the story, the mistake maker is graciously forgiven. In the other version, it is clear that mistakes are considered dangerous and mistake makers are not forgiven easily, if at all.

A former employee of a large firm lost a deal to a competing firm. The Chairman of the company was most unforgiving. After the initial blow-up, the Chairman continued to chew him out whenever the opportunity presented itself. At each monthly meeting, the Chairman would recall, in some subtle way, the lost deal. The Chairman was never critical if someone paid too much for a property, but he never forgave anyone for losing a deal (Metz, 1975 as cited in Martin et al., 1983).

Box 5.3   The manifestation of organizational culture at different levels of awareness and accessibility (after Rousseau, 1990)

Levels of awareness (and accessibility)

Hierarchical structure of various forms of organizational culture based on different levels of awareness and accessibility

Artefacts

Patterns of activity

Behavioural norms

Values

Basic assumptions

The elements of organizational culture

Besides the various ways that organizational cultures are manifested it is also important to talk about the content of culture. There are a number of theoretical models presenting the *dimensions* of organizational culture, such as the competing values model (Quinn, 1988), the circumplex-based behavioural norms model (Cooke & Rousseau, 1988; Cooke & Szumal, 2000) and Denison and Mishra's (1995) theory of organizational culture and effectiveness. Early work on organizational culture suggested that organizations fall into a handful of *categories* or *types* of culture, such as the *macho* culture or the *role* culture. On the basis, however, of subsequent theoretical and empirical advancements showing that more complex configurations of organizational cultural attributes exist than that suggested by the culture categories approach, a dimensional approach to the study of culture has been pursued. Indeed, more recent work on organizational culture advocates a profile analysis in the assessment of an organization's culture that enables us to examine complex configurations of cultural dimensions.

Table 5.2   Dimensions of organizational culture found in the relevant literature and grouped in terms of content similarity

Models	Dimensions				
Quinn (1988)	Support orientation	Innovation orientation	Goal orientation	Rules orientation	
Xenikou and Furnham (1996)	Positive social relations at work	Openness to change in a cooperative culture	Task-oriented organizational growth	Bureaucracy	Negativism/resistance to new ideas
Cooke and Lafferty (1989)	Satisfaction needs (Humanistic-encouraging, Affiliative)	Satisfaction needs (Self-Actualizing)	Satisfaction needs (Achievement)	Security needs (Conventional, approval, avoidance, dependent)	Security needs (Competitive, power, oppositional, Perfectionistic)
O'Reilly et al. (1991)	Respect for people Team orientation	Innovation	Outcome orientation	Attention to detail Stability	Aggressiveness
Hofstede et al. (1990)	Employee oriented versus job oriented Parochial versus professional	Pragmatic versus normative	Process versus results oriented	Loose versus tight control Open versus closed system	
Denison and Mishra (1995)	Involvement	Adaptation	Mission		
Van den Berg and Wilderom (2004)	Human resource orientation Interdepartmental coordination	External orientation	Improvement orientation	Autonomy	

Theories of the content of organizational culture which have had a strong impact in the field, as well as elective models derived from empirical studies, are presented and grouped, in terms of content similarity, in Table 5.2. However, one has to note that theory and research on the dimensions of culture is rather limited mainly because organizational culture has been considered by many culture researchers to be a unique attribute of a given organization that is not similar or comparable to cultures developed by other organizations (Barney, 1986).

The competing values model (Quinn, 1988; Figure 5.1) proposes that organizations can be described on the basis of four culture orientations that are not mutually exclusive but reflect supposedly competing demands set on organizations. Effective organizations manage to balance competing demands and accomplish their coexistence, which in turn has a positive impact on the life quality of their employees (Quinn & Spreitzer, 1991). The four culture orientations are as follows: the human relations, the open systems, the internal process and the rational goal orientation. The *human relations model* or *support orientation* involves cooperation, participation, individual development and personal consideration. The *open systems model* or *innovation orientation* concerns openness to change, adaptation to business environment, customer focus and experimentation. The *internal process model* or *rules orientation* concerns organizational values referring to the importance of rules and procedures, information management, stability and control. Finally, the *rational goal model* or *goal orientation* is characterized by goal setting, the accomplishment of objectives, productivity, accountability and effectiveness. In a recent meta-analytic study of the competing values model Hartnell, Ou, and Kinicki (2011) argue that there is mixed

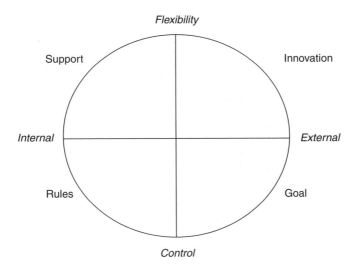

Figure 5.1   The competing values model of organizational culture (after Quinn, 1988)

support for the framework's nomological validity, and more emphasis should be placed on the interactive effect of the four culture orientations on effectiveness criteria.

The model of behavioural norms describes a set of *constructive* and *defensive behavioural norms* that operate within organizations and are related to organizational effectiveness and employees' satisfaction (Cooke & Rousseau, 1988; Cooke & Szumal, 1993; Cooke & Szumal, 2000; Simosi & Xenikou, 2010; Xenikou & Simosi, 2006). Constructive behavioural styles lead to high levels of organizational effectiveness and job satisfaction, whereas defensive behavioural styles are associated with low organizational effectiveness and employee satisfaction. There are four constructive styles, namely, achievement, affiliative, humanistic/encouraging and self-actualizing; these styles refer to goal accomplishment, productivity, social support, personal relations at work, cooperation, participation in decision-making, personal freedom and individual development. On the other hand, there are eight defensive styles divided into two general categories. The aggressive/defensive styles include: competitive, power, oppositional, and perfectionistic. The passive/defensive styles are: approval, conventional, dependent, and avoidance. The defensive styles are embedded in social environments that promote tough competition, respect for authority, negativism and destructive criticism, avoidance of conflict and confrontation, dependence on superiors and lack of empowerment (Figure 5.2).

In another model relating organizational culture to performance, Denison and Mishra (1995) have identified four culture traits and developed a theory

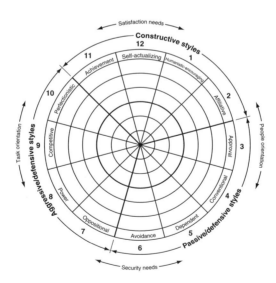

Figure 5.2   The Organizational Culture Inventory (OCI) circumplex (research and development by Cooke, and Lafferty; © 1973–2012 by Human Synergistics International; used by permission)

concerning the relation of those culture traits to organizational effectiveness. The four culture traits are *involvement, consistency, adaptation* and *mission*. Involvement concerns participation in decision-making and other organizational practices that promote employees' identification with the organization they work for. Consistency reflects the internal integration of the organization and, specifically, the degree to which organizational members have a common way to perceive and behave in regard to various organizational matters. Therefore, consistency does not refer to the elements of culture but to culture strength and for this reason we have excluded it from Table 5.2. Adaptation signifies the organization's tendency to pay attention to its external environment such as customers, competitors and government, and to promote necessary changes in order to be successful. Finally, mission concerns the general objectives and broad goals set by top management and the business philosophy that guide and coordinate organizational departments and divisions. These four culture traits were empirically found to distinguish effective and ineffective organizations across major regions of the world (Fey & Denison, 2003; Denison, Haaland, & Goelzer, 2004).

Similarly, Hofstede, Neuijen, Ohayv, and Sanders (1990) addressed the research question regarding the independent dimensions that can be used to measure organizational culture. They found that organizations differ as far as their practices are concerned rather than the values they endorse. Furthermore, this study showed that organizational practices were represented by six separate dimensions, which are the following:

1. *Process-oriented* versus *results-oriented* opposes a concern with means to a concern with goals.
2. *Employee-oriented* versus *job-oriented* opposes a concern for people to a concern for getting the job done.
3. *Parorchial* versus *professional* opposing organizations whose employees derive their identity largely from the organization to organizations in which people identify with their type of job.
4. *Open* versus *closed system* orientation describes an organization's communication climate – that is, the degree to which organizational members are expected to be open in their dealings with each other or closed and secretive.
5. *Loose* versus *tight control* orientation refers to the amount of internal structuring in the organization. It appears that tight formal control system is associated with strict unwritten codes in terms of dress and dignified behaviour.
6. *Normative* versus *pragmatic orientation* deals with the notion of 'customer orientation'. Pragmatic organizations are market-driven, whereas normative organizations perceive their interaction with the outside world as the implementation of inviolable rules.

Another study that investigated the content of organizational culture was conducted by O'Reilly, Chatman, and Caldwell (1991). Seven defining attributes of organizational cultures were found in this study. Organizational culture is regarded as a pattern of values that concern the following content themes: innovation, stability, respect for people, outcome orientation, attention to detail, team orientation and aggressiveness. 'Innovation' reflects the importance given to experimentation, the development of new opportunities and risk taking. 'Stability' concerns the degree to which the organization acts in a predictable way, and rules are well formulated and followed. 'Respect for people' is based on the values of fairness and tolerance, and 'outcome orientation characterizes organizations that place a high value on achievement, efficiency and cultivating high expectations for performance. 'Attention to detail' refers to the importance given to employees being analytical, precise and careful in doing their job and 'team orientation' reflects the values and norms that promote collaboration and concern for people. Finally, 'aggressiveness' is the set of values that encourage competition and aggressive behaviour as a means to accomplishment and success. Even though many of the attributes of culture identified by O'Reilly et al. resemble the dimensions of culture as described by other researchers, it seems that there is lack of a coherent theoretical framework.

Van den Berg and Wilderom (2004) have argued that the content of organizational culture needs to be systematically described to stimulate the accumulation of empirical findings on the culture construct. They have defined organizational culture as shared perceptions of organizational work practices and proposed that five dimensions cover the broad scope of culture. These aspects of culture or 'culture domains' are as follows: autonomy, external orientation, interdepartmental coordination, human resource orientation and improvement orientation. 'Autonomy' pertains to the degree to which employees have decision latitude at the job level. 'External orientation' refers to whether an organization is open to its dealings with the external environment in which it operates. 'Interdepartmental coordination' concerns communication between different departments and divisions, as well as the degree to which collaboration is accomplished between various organizational units. The fourth dimension, 'human resource orientation', involves an emphasis on employees and their individual needs. The final dimension is an 'improvement orientation' and reflects an organization's ambition to achieve even better organizational results.

In an attempt to explore the content of organizational culture, Xenikou and Furnham (1996) factor analyzed the subscales of four questionnaire measures of organizational culture, which focus on the assessment of either behavioural norms or organizational values. The factor analysis clearly suggested five identifiable themes or dimensions of culture as follows:

1. openness to change in a cooperative culture;
2. task-oriented organizational growth;
3. the human factor in a bureaucratic culture;
4. negativism and resistance to new ideas;
5. positive social relations in the workplace.

These findings seem to be supportive of Quinn's (1988) competing values model (see Figure 5.1). Quinn's model is circumplex – that is, the circle presented in Figure 5.1 can be read from right to left and vice versa. The neighbouring cultural orientations include values that to a certain extent share some common elements. For example, the innovation orientation shares some common characteristics with the support and the goal orientation, respectively. The first and the second culture themes proposed by Xenikou and Furnham (1996) empirically support these theoretical suggestions. The dimension of 'openness to change in a cooperative culture' shows that innovation and support share some common characteristics: innovation and openness to change are promoted by cooperation and social support. Moreover, the dimension of 'task-oriented organizational growth' reflects Quinn's theoretical proposition that innovation and organizational improvement are related to goal orientation and achievement. The third factor which emerged from Xenikou and Furnham's research resembles the rules orientation, that is an emphasis on rules and procedures, while the fourth factor, negativism and resistance to new ideas, indicates that besides innovation one needs to pay attention to negativism to new ideas as a separate construct. Lack of innovation does not necessarily signify negativism and resistance to new ideas; the fact that organizational members might not be expected to experiment and look for new ways to do their job does not necessarily imply that they have strong feelings against innovation and change. Finally, positive social relations in the workplace resembles Quinn's support orientation that refers to whether organizational members are supportive and willing to help each other at work.

Although research and theory development on the elements of organizational culture is rather limited primarily on the grounds of culture being considered as a unique attribute of organizations, there is theoretical and empirical work on the thematic dimensions of organizational culture that sheds light on this issue. It seems that a handful of organizational culture dimensions have repeatedly emerged as themes of organizational cultures, and uniqueness as an attribute of organizational culture is severely challenged (see the 'uniqueness paradox'; Martin et al., 1983). In any case, it is important that research comparing cultures or assessing congruence between cultures and individual employees uses a complete list of values (or any other manifestation of culture) that can define culture since omitting salient values may distort results (Adkins & Caldwell, 2004).

The use of qualitative and quantitative methods

Early studies of organizational culture used almost exclusively a qualitative methodology to unravel the essence and functions of culture in organizational settings as is clearly demonstrated by Glick (1985), who attempted to clarify the difference between the concepts of organizational culture and climate. Glick suggests that climate research tends to be nomothetic, using quantitative techniques to describe phenomena, whereas culture research is primarily idiographic, employing qualitative methods to explain dynamic processes.

The preference of culture researchers for qualitative methods can be attributed to the fact that the concept of organizational culture was displaced from anthropology, where the study of culture relies heavily on qualitative methods. Geertz (1973), who is one of the most influential cultural anthropologists, considers culture to be the meaning of symbols representing webs of significance. He, therefore, suggests that the analysis of culture is not an experimental science in search of law but an interpretive one in search of meaning. In the case of organizational culture, researchers should focus on how organizational members interpret their experiences, how these interpretations influence their behaviour and how they arrive at shared interpretations, meanings and knowledge (Van Muijen, 1998).

The exclusive use of qualitative methods was primarily grounded on two theoretical issues:

1. The unconscious quality of culture that prescribes an idiographic rather than a positivistic methodology.
2. The uniqueness of a particular organization's culture such that an outsider cannot form a priori questions or measures.

Advocates of qualitative methods have suggested that their choice is based on the presumed inaccessibility, depth or unconscious quality of culture. For example, Schein (1992) suggests that the most important level of organizational culture is basic assumptions. Basic assumptions exist at a preconscious level and can be traced through a complex interactive process of joint enquiry between a specific culture's insiders and outsiders.

The second point regarding the justification of the exclusive usage of qualitative methodology refers to the possible uniqueness of an organization's culture such that an outsider cannot form a priori questions or measures. Smircich (1982), for example, conceptualizes organizational culture as a particular set of meanings that provides a group with a distinctive character. This, in turn, leads to the formulation of a social reality unique to members of a group and, as such, makes it impossible for standardized measures to unravel cultural processes.

However, even though there are good reasons for using qualitative methods in investigating organizational culture, the exclusive use of qualitative methodology can be bought at a cost since the data collected cannot be the basis for systematic comparisons. Some important questions in the study of culture, such as sharedness of belief systems, can be adequately addressed with the usage of quantitative rather than qualitative methods. Quantitative methods can also provide the necessary empirical basis to compare and contrast the cultures of different organizations, as well as the subcultures of the same organization.

Theorists of organizational culture have suggested that a combination of research methods is preferred to the exclusive usage of qualitative or quantitative methodologies. At an early stage of research a qualitative approach may be required to acquire knowledge about a particular organization (see Box 5.4), while at a later stage quantitative research can be conducted to enable systematic comparisons of the collected data (e.g. Hofstede, 2001; Hofstede et al., 1990; Siehl & Martin, 1988).

Box 5.4   A checklist of questions for conducting in-depth interviews to unravel organizational culture (Hofstede, 2001; Hofstede et al., 1990)

In-depth interviews with organizational informants can provide rich data on the manifestations of an organization's culture as reflected in symbols, heroes, rituals and values. A checklist of questions for such interviews is as follows:

- What terms are only used by insiders?
- What are famous words here? (to identify organizational symbols)
- What things are important here to get on?
- Are there, according to you, people who are of great importance to the organization? (to identify organizational heroes)
- What events are celebrated in the organization?
- What are some of the important rules – written and unwritten – that apply here?
- How are, according to you, important decisions made? (to identify organizational rituals)
- What do people especially like to see here?
- What are the greatest mistakes one can make here?
- What is the most negative (positive) image in the outside world about this organization that you can think of? (to identify organizational values)

Finally, Rousseau (1990) argues that different research methods should be used in the organization culture research depending on the level of culture to be examined. As the levels of culture become more conscious (values, behavioural norms) or observable (artefacts), these are accessible by both structural and non-standardized assessments. In contrast, assumptions unconsciously held are difficult to assess without interactive probing because members' fears and defences are elusive psychodynamics difficult to elicit without interaction.

The relationship between organizational culture and organizational climate

The growth of interest in the concept of organizational culture in the late 1970s and early 1980s led naturally to theoretical attempts at clarifying the similarities and differences between the two concepts. Glick (1985), for example, distinguished culture from climate on conceptual grounds and argued that these differences have implications for measurement. More recently, Verbeke, Volgering, and Hessels (1998) after examining a great number of definitions of organizational climate and culture have suggested that there are two separate core concepts that characterize these terms. Organizational climate is the way people perceive and describe the characteristics of their working environment, and organizational culture reflects the way things are done in an organization. In other words, climate is a concept that reflects how members perceive and come to describe their organization according to specific characteristics, while culture reveals that something is commonly learned by organizational members and it shapes the way things are done. However, one may criticize such a conceptual distinction between the two constructs since the review of numerous definitions of organizational culture presented at the beginning of this chapter reveals that shared perceptions, values, beliefs and cognitions in general are basic components of defining organizational culture.

According to Reichers and Schneider (1990), climate is widely defined as shared perceptions of organizational policies, practices and procedures, both formal and informal. On the other hand, culture refers either to something the organization is or something the organization has. The first conceptualization of culture as something the organization is promotes the study of culture within a native-view paradigm (emic approach) that focuses on asking respondents to make sense of and interpret their own behaviour.

The second theoretical approach applies an external-view paradigm (etic approach) in which the researcher provides the conceptual framework for the study of organizational culture. Reichers and Schneider argue that the second approach to culture, that is the etic paradigm, is conceptually similar to the concept of climate. Specifically, within the etic paradigm to the study of organizational culture, culture is defined as a set of shared cognitions about the organization and its problems, goals and practices. Climate researchers have also acknowledged the importance of shared perceptions (meanings) and have wrestled extensively to operationalize how perception is shared.

Furthermore, Reichers and Schneider suggest that even though there is a high degree of conceptual overlap between the two concepts, culture can be distinguished from climate because it exists at a higher level of abstraction, and some of its levels involve unconscious processes (i.e., basic assumptions). Climate, on the other hand, does not relate to unconscious processes and, therefore, can be seen as a manifestation of the unconscious aspects of culture.

Similarly, Denison (1996) argues that culture and climate overlap and, more specifically, that culture encompasses climate. Moreover, Martin (2002) points out that climate researchers tend to investigate the beliefs, values and basic assumptions of organizational members, as well as the informal practices (behavioural norms) that are promoted within a working environment, while avoiding the study of cultural forms such as stories, physical arrangements, jargon and rituals. Since climate researchers focus on a subset of the possible manifestations of culture the concepts of climate and culture are considered to be closely related only in the case that one takes an integration perspective to culture, which assumes consistency between the various cultural manifestations (e.g., values, practices, stories, artefacts). If a differentiation or fragmentation perspective to culture is adopted then climate and culture are conceptually quite different because in these perspectives inconsistency across a variety of manifestations of culture is allowed for.

More recently, there is an attempt to sharply distinguish climate from culture by suggesting that climate is a property of individual employees and concerns their individual perceptions of their work environment – that can be aggregated to some group level (i.e., work group or department). On the other hand, organizational culture is defined as system values and norms that are often viewed as products of group dynamics – that is, interaction among system members (James et al., 2008). Nevertheless, climate research has paid a lot of attention to the extent to which perceptions of organizational members are shared and, therefore social interaction is certainly of great interest to researchers working on climate.

In conclusion, although both organizational culture and climate emerged in order for organizational theorists to explain the effect of the social environment on human behaviour within organizations, the two concepts have to a large extent developed separately. One of the reasons for this isolation is the fact that climate and culture researchers tend to use different research methods in studying organizations. Climate research is primarily 'nomothetic' using quantitative methods, whereas culture research is primarily idiographic employing a qualitative methodology. However, there has been a systematic attempt to promote a theoretical and empirical basis for the study of organizational culture that combines quantitative and qualitative methods (Hofstede et al., 1990; Siehl & Martin, 1988). In light of these theoretical and research advances, climate can be viewed as an aspect of culture that is more accessible than other levels of organizational culture, such as basic assumptions.

Summary

Organizational culture has been defined in many different ways, such as organizational members' shared perception of the social norms regarding expected behaviour or belief systems that influence organizational action. Most definitions of organizational culture refer to the thoughts, beliefs, values or attitudes of organizational members, as well as the behavioural norms and behaviours related to these cognitions either in rational or irrational ways. The cultures of organizations are considered to be manifested in various levels, which are more or less accessible to outsiders, as well as insiders. For example, basic assumptions are held at a preconscious level and therefore are more difficult to be unravelled in comparison to values and behavioural norms that are characterized by a greater level of awareness.

Besides the forms in which an organization's culture is manifested, it is important to investigate the content of a culture. Are there thematic dimensions on which one can describe the cultures of different organizations in different industry sectors? Early organizational culture research advocated against such an attempt primarily on the grounds of the presumed uniqueness of each organization's culture. More recently, theoretical, as well as empirical, research on the content of organizational culture has shown that there are a limited number of culture orientations that can be utilized in our effort to describe and compare organizational cultures. It seems that goal or achievement orientation, support or humanistic orientation and adaptation or innovation are the central themes of the concept of organizational culture.

The introduction of the organizational culture construct in the early 1980s as a new explanatory device of the complexities of organizational life was accompanied by the pessimistic expectation that culture would prove to be another fad of the business literature. However, there has been a hot debate for almost three decades on the nature of the concept, the appropriateness of qualitative and quantitative methods as tools to unravel it, and the culture's relationship to the construct of organizational climate (just to name a few), which show that organizational culture has been proven conceptually and empirically useful in our efforts to understand organizations.

Questions

1. Given the numerous definitions of organizational culture, which are the core conceptual issues on the nature of organizational culture that most researchers would agree upon?

2. Describe the elements or levels of culture by presenting the various theoretical approaches that exist. In your experience, which are the most accessible elements of culture?

3. Is organizational culture a unique attribute of an organization? Does uniqueness of culture relate to competitive advantage and, if yes, how?

4. Can the content of organizational culture be described in reference to a number of organizational culture dimensions? Give examples to distinguish cultural dimensions from the levels of culture.

5. Can organizational cultures be 'measured' quantitatively or can they only be described by the use of a qualitative methodology?

6. Is a combination of qualitative and quantitative methods possible, as well as fruitful, in our efforts to unravel the dynamics of cultures? Critically assess the combination of qualitative and qualitative methods in studies of organizational culture.

7. Which is the conceptual relation between organizational climate and culture?

References

Adkins, B., & Caldwell, D. (2004). Firm or subgroup culture: where does fitting in matter most. *Journal of Organizational Behavior*, **25**, 969–978.

Barney, J. B. (1986). Organizational culture: Can it be a source of sustained competitive advantage? *Academy of Management Review*, **11**, 656–665.

Boisnier, A., & Chatman, J. A. (2003). The role of subcultures in agile organizations. In R. S. Peterson and E. A. Mannix (eds.), *Leading and Managing People in the Dynamic Organization* (pp. 87–112). Mahwah, NJ: Lawrence Erlbaum.

Carroll, D. T. (1983). A disappointing search for excellence. *Harvard Business Review*, **61**, 78–88.

Cooke, R. A., & Lafferty, J. C. (1989). *Organizational Culture Inventory* (r), Plymouth, MI: Human Synergistics.

Cooke, R. A., & Rousseau, D. M. (1988). Behavioral norms and expectations: A quantitative approach to the assessment of organizational culture. *Group and Organization Studies*, **13**, 245–273.

Cooke, R. A., & Szumal, J. L. (1993). Measuring normative beliefs and shared behavioral expectations in organizations: The reliability and validity of the Organizational Culture Inventory. *Psychological Reports*, **72**, 1299–1330.

Cooke, R. A., & Szumal, J. L. (2000). Using the Organizational Culture Inventory to understand operating cultures in organizations. In N. M. Ashkanasy, C. P. M. Wilderom, & M. F. Peterson (eds.), *Organizational Culture and Climate* (pp. 147–62). Thousand Oaks, CA: Sage.

Deal, T., & Kennedy, A. (1982). *Corporate Cultures: The Rites and Rituals of Corporate Life*. Reading, MA: Addison-Wesley.

Denison, D. R. (1996). What is the difference between organizational culture and organizational climate? A native's point of view on a decade of paradigm wars. *Academy of Management Review*, **21**, 619–654.

Denison, D. R., & Mishra, A. K. (1995). Toward a theory of organizational culture and effectiveness. *Organization Science*, **6**, 204–222.

Denison, D. R., Haaland, S., & Goelzer, P. (2004). Corporate culture and organizational effectiveness: Is Asia different from the rest of the world? *Organizational Dynamics*, **33**, 98–109.

Fey, C. F., & Denison, D. R. (2003). Organizational culture and effectiveness: Can American theory applied in Russia? *Organization Science*, **14**, 686–706.

Geertz, C. (1973). *The Interpretation of Cultures*. New York: Basic Books.

Glick, W. H. (1985). Conceptualizing and measuring organizational and psychological climate: Pitfalls in multilevel research. *Academy of Management Review*, **10**, 601–616.

Gordon, G. G. (1985). The relationship of corporate culture to industry sector and corporate performance. In H. R. Kilman, M. J. Saxton, & R. Serpa (eds.), *Gaining Control of the Corporate Culture* (pp. 103–125). San Francisco: Jossey-Bass.

Gregory, K. L. (1983). Native-view paradigms: Multiple cultures and culture conflicts in organizations. *Administrative Science Quarterly*, **28**, 359–376.

Hampden-Turner, C. (1990). *Corporate Culture: From Vicious to Virtuous Circles*. London: The Random Century.

Handy, C. (1986). *Understanding Organizations*. Harmondsworth: Penguin Books.

Harrison, R. (1972). Understanding your organization's character. *Harvard Business Review*, May–June, pp. 119–128.

Hartnell, C. A., Ou, A. Y., & Kinicki, A. (2011). Organizational culture and organizational effectiveness: A meta-analytic investigation of the competing values framework's theoretical suppositions. *Journal of Applied Psychology*, doi: 10.1037/a0021987.

Hitt, M. A., & Ireland, R. D. (1987). Peters and Waterman revisited: The unended quest for excellence. *Academy of Management Executive*, **1**, 91–98.

Hofstede, G. (2001). *Culture's Consequences: Comparing Values, Behaviours, Institutions, and Organizations Across Nations* (2nd edition). Thousand Oaks, CA: Sage.

Hofstede, G., Neuijen, B., Ohayv, D. D., & Sanders, G. (1990). Measuring organizational cultures: A qualitative and quantitative study across twenty cases. *Administrative Science Quarterly*, **35**, 286–316.

James, L. R., Choi, C. C., Ko, E.-H., E., McNeil, P. K., Minton, M. K., Wright, M. A., & Kim, K. (2008). Organizational and psychological climate: A review of theory and research. *European Journal of Work and Organizational Psychology*, **17**, 5–32.

Kroeber, A., & Kluckholm, C. (1952). Culture: A critical review of concepts and definitions. *Peabody Museum of American Archaeology and Ethnicology*, **47**, 1–60.

Lorsch, J. W. (1985). Strategic myopia: Cultures as an invisible barrier to change. In H. R. Kilman, M. J. Saxton, & R. Serpa (eds.), *Gaining Control of the Corporate Culture* (pp. 84–102). San Francisco: Jossey-Bass.

Margulies, N., & Raia, A. (1978). *Conceptual foundations of organizational development*. New York: McGraw/Hill.

Martin, H. J. (1985). Managing specialized corporate cultures. In H. R. Kilman, M. J. Saxton, & R. Serpa (eds.), *Gaining Control of the Corporate Culture* (pp. 148–162). San Francisco: Jossey-Bass.

Martin, J. M. (2002). *Organizational Culture: Mapping the Terrain*. Thousand Oaks, CA: Sage.

Martin, J., Feldman, M. S., Hatch, M. J., & Sitkin, S. B. (1983). The uniqueness paradox in organizational stories. *Administrative Science Quarterly*, **28**, 438–453.

Martin, H. J., & Siehl, C. (1983). Organizational culture and counterculture: An uneasy symbiosis. *Organizational Dynamics*, Autumn, 52–64.

Meyerson, D. (1991). 'Normal' ambiguity? A glimpse of an occupational culture. In P. Frost, L. Moore, M. Louis, C. Lundberg, & J. Martin (eds.), *Reframing Organizational Culture* (pp. 131–144). Newbury Park, CA: Sage.

O'Reilly, C. A., Chatman, J., & Caldwell, D. F. (1991). People and organizational culture: A profile comparison approach to assessing person-organization fit. *Academy of Management Journal*, **34**, 487–516.

Peters, T. J., & Waterman, R. H. (1982). *In Research of Excellence: Lessons from America's Best-Run Companies*. New York: Harper and Row.

Potter, C. C. (1989). What is culture: And can it be useful for organizational change agents? *Leadership and Organizational Development Journal*, **10**, 17–24.

Quinn, R. E. (1988). *Beyond Rational Management*. San Francisco: Jossey-Bass.

Quinn, R. E., & Spreitzer, G. M. (1991). The psychometrics of the competing values culture instrument and an analysis of the impact of organizational culture on quality of life. *Research in Organizational Change and Development*, **5**, 115–142.

Reichers, A. E., & Schneider, B. (1990). Climate and culture: An evolution of constructs. In B. Schneider (ed.), *Organizational Climate and Culture* (pp. 5–39). San Francisco: Jossey-Bass.

Reynolds, P. D. (1986). Organizational culture as related to industry, position and performance: A preliminary report. *Journal of Management Studies*, **23**, 333–345.

Rousseau, D. (1990). Quantitative assessment of organizational culture: The case for multiple methods. In B. Schneider (ed.), *Organizational Climate and Culture* (pp. 153–192). San Francisco: Jossey-Bass.

Schein, E. H. (1990). Organizational culture. *American Psychologist*, **45**, 109–119.

Schein, E. H. (1992). *Organizational Culture and Leadership* (2nd edition). San Francisco: Jossey-Bass.

Schwartz, H. M., & Davis, S. M. (1981). Matching corporate culture and business strategy. *Organizational Dynamics*, Summer, pp. 30–48.

Siehl, C., & Martin, J. (1988). Mixing qualitative and quantitative methods. In M. O. Jones, M. D. Moore, & R. C. Snyder, *Inside Organizations: Understanding the Human Dimension*. Newbury Park, CA: Sage.

Simosi, M., & Xenikou, A. (2010). The role of organizational culture in the relationship between leadership and organizational commitment: An empirical study in a Greek organization. *International Journal of Human Resource Management*, 21, 1598–1616.

Smircich, L. (1982). Organizations as shared meanings. In L. R. Pondy, P. Frost, G. Morgan, & T. C. Dandringe (eds.), *Organizational Symbolism*. Greenwich CI: JAI Press.

Smircich, L. (1983). Concepts of culture and organizational analysis. *Administrative Science Quarterly*, 28, 339–358.

Trice, H. M., & Beyer, J. M. (1984). Studying organizational cultures through rites and ceremonials. *Academy of Management Review*, 9, 653–669.

Trice, H. M., & Beyer, J. M. (1993). *The Cultures of Work Organizations*. Englewood cliffs, NJ: Prentice-Hall.

Van den Berg, P. T., & Wilderom, C. P. M. (2004). Defining, measuring, and comparing organizational cultures. *Applied Psychology: An International Review*, 53, 570–582.

Van Maanen, J. (1991). The smile factory: Work at Disneyland. In P. J. Frost, L. F. Moore, M. R. Louis, C. C. Lundberg, & J. Martin (eds.), *Reframing Organizational Culture* (pp. 58–76). Newbury Park, CA: Sage.

Van Muijen, J. J. (1998). Organizational culture. In P. J. D. Drenth, H. Thierry, & C. De Wolff (eds.), *Handbook of Work and Organizational Psychology* (pp. 113–131). Hove, UK: Psychology Press.

Verbeke, W., Volgering, M., & Hessels, M. (1998). Exploring the conceptual expansion within the field of organizational behaviour: Organizational climate and organizational culture. *Journal of Management Studies*, 35, 303–329.

Williams, A., Dodson, P., & Walters, M. (1989). *Changing Culture: New Organizational Approaches*. London: IPM.

Xenikou, A., & Furnham, A. (1996). A correlational and factor analytic study of four questionnaire measures of organisational culture. *Human Relations*, 49, 349–371.

Xenikou, A., & Simosi, M. (2006). Organizational culture and transformational leadership as predictors of business unit performance. *Journal of Managerial Psychology*, 21, 566–579.

Leadership and Organizational Culture

6

Chapter outline

Introduction
Schein's theoretical account of organizational culture and leadership
    Founders and the creation of culture
    Leadership and the maintenance or change of culture
Trice and Beyer's approach to cultural leadership
    Cultural innovation
    Cultural maintenance
Transformational leadership and organizational culture
Leadership and national culture
Leadership, organizational culture and performance
Summary
Questions

Chapter objectives

The main objectives are to:

- approach the dynamic formation of organizational culture by examining the developmental stages organizations go through;
- analyse the role of founders and leaders in the development of organizational culture, and emphasize social interaction between leaders and other organizational members as the basis for cultural maintenance and change;
- describe the various mechanisms that leaders have at their disposal to influence cultural maintenance and change;

(cont'd)

- understand and explain the limitations set by organization cultures on the emergence of leadership behaviours;
- introduce the theory of transformational leadership and explore its links with societal and organizational cultures.

Introduction

The major organizational leadership research traditions involve trait theories, behavioural style approaches, contingency theories, participative leadership and decision theories and transformational/charismatic leadership approaches. In these theoretical and research perspectives, emphasis is traditionally put either on the traits and behaviours that differentiate effective versus ineffective leaders or on the organizational circumstances under which specific leadership behavioural patterns are most effective (Blake & Mouton, 1985; Fiedler, 1967; Fleishman & Harris, 1962; House & Mitchell, 1974; Likert, 1961; Vroom & Jago, 1988; Vroom & Yetton, 1973; for a review, see Furnham, 2005). Even though the contingency approach acknowledges that the abilities and qualities required in a leader depend to a large extent on the social aspects of a leader's context, this research tradition has been criticized on the grounds that the situational factors that have been examined are micro- rather than macro-level contextual factors. For example, situational variables under study include the dyadic relationship between a leader and his/her followers or task structure, while organizational culture, formal structure or environmental conditions are rather neglected.

In broad terms the thinking about leadership over the past 80 years has gone through four phases. It started with the 'trait' or 'great-man' approach but faltered because there was little agreement and ever less data on what the fundamental traits were and how they operated. After the Second World War the trait approach was replaced by the 'style' approach as researchers tried to specify and categorize the particular leadership styles used and their impacts. This, in turn, was replaced by the situational approach which emphasized that the emergence and success of leaders was essentially a function of the context in which they worked. From the 1980s the transformational–transactional distinction led researchers to focus on when, how and why good leaders are different from mere managers. The last 20 years have seen the field split with an interest in different types of leadership from servant leadership to self-destructive leadership. What remains is the tension between those who look at intrapersonal – as opposed to interpersonal explanations – and those that emphasize external social, economic and political forces within and outside organizations and how they shape behaviour.

There are a number of researchers who have argued that there is a constant interplay between organizational culture and leadership (e.g., Bass & Avolio, 1993; Schein, 1992; Trice & Beyer, 1993; Waldman & Yammarino, 1999). Organizational cultures are often considered to be the creation of their entrepreneurial founders. Founders and their successors' leadership shape a culture of shared values and assumptions restricted by the founder's personal beliefs. The success or failure of an organization depends on the relevance of the founder's philosophical beliefs to the current opportunities and constraints confronting the organization. However, culture affects leadership as much as leadership affects culture. Both can enhance or destroy the other. For example, a strong organizational culture with values and internal guides for more autonomy at lower hierarchical levels can prevent top administration from increasing its personal power at the expense of middle- or lower-level administration. Culture pre- and proscribes leadership style. More recently, there is accumulated empirical evidence suggesting that organizational culture mediates the relation of leadership with important organizational outcomes, such as performance, commitment and innovation (Ogbonna & Harris, 2000; Sarros et al., 2008; Simosi & Xenikou, 2010; Xenikou & Simosi, 2006).

The most extensive and thorough theoretical examination of the relationship between organizational culture and leadership has been put forward by Schein (1992), who suggested that the developmental stage of an organization is a crucial variable in our attempt to understand the interconnection between leadership and culture. Another notable theoretical account has been articulated by Trice and Beyer (1993). These authors put emphasis on a cultural approach to leadership that refers to how leaders influence the development and expression of culture in their organizations. They suggest that leadership involves both an instrumental aspect that refers to how leaders influence the accomplishment of work, and a cultural aspect that indicates the degree to which leaders affect shared philosophies and practices within an organization.

Schein's theoretical account of organizational culture and leadership

In this approach to leadership and culture, the links between the two concepts are examined in relation to the developmental phases an organization goes through. In the founding stage the creation of culture is considered to be primarily in the hands of organizational leaders. As the organization matures then organizational structure, systems and practices are taken for granted and culture becomes more the cause rather than the effect of leadership processes. Leaders, however, do have at their disposal a considerable number of mechanisms to create or change culture depending on the developmental stage of their organization.

Founders and the creation of culture

The role that founders play in the creation of organizational cultures has been extensively discussed by Schein (1992) in his book *Organizational Culture and*

Leadership. Organizations are created by one or more individuals who perceive that the coordinated action of a number of people can accomplish something that the individual action cannot. This process as it usually takes place in a typical business organization follows four steps:

1. An individual, namely the founder, has an idea.
2. The founder brings in other people and creates a core group that believes that the idea is a good one, workable and worth the investment of time, money and energy.
3. The founding group take action by raising funds, obtaining patents and locating space.
4. Other people are selected to join the group, which will develop assumptions about how to do things to survive and grow.

Founders usually have a major impact on how the group deals with problems of external adaptation and internal integration in the early time of its existence. Founders not only have a high level of self-confidence and determination but also, because they had the original idea, hold strong beliefs about how to fulfil it. In addition, founders are normally characterized by strong assumptions about the nature of the world and how organizations should be managed. For example, a founder's beliefs about human nature – that is, whether employees are intrinsically motivated to work hard and do their job effectively or are by essence lazy and seek to avoid hard work and responsibilities – can have a profound impact on the creation of an organizational culture. The new organization needs a number of ideas to put in trial about how to function effectively and accomplish its objectives. These initial ideas are often taught by the founder and if they prove to be successful become – through a learning experience – the taken for granted appropriate ways of thinking and acting. It is the leaders' values, motives, personality and abilities that determine how they shape the early organization. Culture can, therefore, be seen as the behavioural manifestations of the preferences, priorities and plans of the founder (see case study at the end of the chapter).

Leaders as founders of organizations initiate the culture formation process by imposing their assumptions and values on the new group. There are a number of mechanisms that become involved as founders and other leaders teach their assumptions to the emerging group. A way for leaders to get their message across is by charisma – that is, by communicating their assumptions and values in an attractive, clear and vivid manner. However, charismatic leaders are considered to be rather rare and therefore one needs to look for other mechanisms that enable leaders to create a culture.

There are six primary embedding mechanisms that founders and other powerful figures can possibly use to communicate their values (see Box 6.1). One of the most powerful mechanisms concerns what leaders pay attention to, measure and control on a systematic basis. If leaders are aware of this mechanism, then being systematic in paying attention to certain things becomes a powerful way of communicating values and priorities. In short, what gets measured gets managed and vice versa. The second mechanism refers to how leaders react to critical incidents and organizational crises. When an organization faces a crisis, then the way management deals with it reveals the organization's basic underlying assumptions and possibly creates new values. Crises are especially significant in culture creation and transmission because the increased emotional involvement during this period facilitates learning. For example, as many organizations face crisis of shrinking sales and excess inventories, the strategies their leaders implement to react to these problems unravel the importance they place on employees. The third mechanism concerns observed criteria by which leaders allocate scarce resources. How budgets are created in organizations is another process that reveals leaders' assumptions and beliefs about organizational life. The budgeting and resource allocation processes can, for example, show whether centralized decision-making is preferred to the entrepreneurial bottom-up system in setting organizational goals and objectives.

Box 6.1   Mechanisms that founders and other leaders use to communicate, establish and reinforce their values and assumptions at the early stages of organizational development (Schein, 1992)

Primary embedding mechanisms

- what leaders systematically pay attention to, measure and control;
- how leaders react to critical incidents and organizational crises;
- how leaders allocate scarce resources;
- observed criteria for allocating rewards and status;
- observed criteria by which leaders recruit, select, promote, retire and excommunicate organizational members;
- role modelling, teaching and coaching.

Secondary articulation and reinforcement mechanisms

(these mechanisms become primary ones in reinforcing the culture in mature organizations)

- organization design and structure;
- organizational systems and procedures;
- organizational rites and rituals;
- design of physical space and buildings;
- stories and legends;
- formal statements of organizational philosophy.

The fourth cultural embedding mechanism involves deliberate role modelling, teaching and coaching. Founders and leaders of organizations seem to know that their own visible behaviour has a great value for communicating assumptions and values to organizational members. Leaders act as role models in either formal or informal occasions. For example, leaders might grab the opportunity of a welcoming ceremony for newcomers to outline their philosophies or might set the example when observed informally in an everyday activity. Another mechanism for embedding culture employed by leaders is the observed criteria for allocating rewards and status. Actual organizational practices of positive and negative reinforcement constitute a powerful devise for leaders to communicate their priorities and values. Both the nature of the behaviour rewarded and punished, and the nature of the rewards and punishments themselves convey the message. The final mechanism concerns observed criteria by which leaders recruit, select, promote, retire and excommunicate organizational members. This cultural embedding mechanism is subtle as it operates unconsciously in most organizations; founders and leaders tend to find attractive and hire individuals who resemble the values, assumptions and behavioural styles of the existing members. Basic assumptions are further reinforced through criteria for promotion, early retirement or excommunication.

Moreover, a number of secondary articulation and reinforcement mechanisms exist (see also Box 6.1):

- *Organization design and structure.* The beliefs leaders have about how to organize for maximum effectiveness are reflected on the design and structure of the organization.

- *Organizational systems and procedures.* Founders and leaders have the opportunity to reinforce their assumptions by building systems and routines within organizations.

- *Organizational rites and rituals.* Rites and rituals can also be used as strong reinforces of a leader's ideology.

- *Design of physical space and buildings.* The physical environment may reflect the philosophy and style of the leader if they are explicitly managed to do so.

- *Stories and legends.* Leaders cannot always control what stories are told by organizational members, but they can certainly reinforce stories that they feel good about and perhaps can even launch stories that carry desired messages.

- *Formal statements of organizational philosophy.* Formal statements represent a way for the leader to publicly articulate his philosophy of how the organization should operate. However, formal statements cannot be seen as a way of defining organizational culture since formal statements and culture might be quite divergent.

These mechanisms are labelled secondary because they are effective only if they are consistent with the primary culture-creating mechanisms. When they are consistent with the primary mechanisms, they tend to formalize what is being informally taught at the outset. It is important to note that these secondary mechanisms can become primary ones in perpetuating the assumptions in a mature organization.

The explicit design of the organization, as partly manifested in the organizational structure, and the periodic reorganizations provide ample opportunities for the founders and other leaders to embed their beliefs. Organizational systems and procedures are the most visible parts of an organization's everyday functioning and lend predictability to the organizational world. Depending on the nature of the organization those processes and procedures maybe carefully organized and prescribed. Because of different legal requirements and regulations organizations in certain sectors maybe strikingly more formal than in other areas. As employees seek a kind of stability to reduce anxiety, founders and leaders have the opportunity to reinforce their assumptions by building systems and routines around them. Founders and other powerful figures can also use rites and rituals to reinforce behaviours that they consider to be important.

However, one should be careful when interpreting those rituals not to overestimate the degree to which they convey important messages. The design of the physical space and the buildings might symbolize the assumptions of early leaders, as far as they intend to do so. As a group develops some of its history becomes embodied in stories, myths and legends. Stories that carry desired messages can be reinforced by leaders in order to embed their values into the group. Founders and leaders do choose formal statements of philosophy to explicitly express their values and priorities about organizational functioning, and thus influence the way members think and behave. Most of us, however, recognize that there is often a striking difference between what an organization likes to say and think about itself, and how it really behaves.

Leadership and the maintenance or change of culture

In the founding stage culture embedding is essentially a socialization process in the hands of the founders and the leaders directly selected by them, but in more mature organizations the founder (or the team of founders) does not lead the corporation any longer. The general managers do not have the same leadership options as founders and owners since they are more vulnerable to removal by their boards of directors. As the organization matures and stays successful for a period of time, its structures, processes and practices come to be taken for granted. At this stage the culture defines leadership more than leadership creates culture; in other words, culture becomes more of a cause than an effect.

As organizations grow they undergo a process of differentiation, which facilitates the creation of subcultures in the divisions, departments and other fairly stable subgroups of the organization. Differentiation can take place in terms of a number of variables, such as functional lines, geographies, hierarchical levels, products, markets and technologies. The content of these subcultures reflects the basic internal and external tasks the group has to fulfil. Therefore, during organizational midlife leaders are responsible for coordinating and integrating different subcultures in order for the organization to function effectively. Leaders should aim to encourage the evolution of common goals, common language and common procedures for solving problems. Indeed many have argued that once organizations have reached at a particular stage of growth (and size) they split into multiple cultures. Thus the culture of the finance department is strikingly different from the culture of human resources. When workgroups consist of organizational members coming from different departments, task and personal conflicts may arise as a result of variations in value priorities and everyday practices (see Chapter 3) which can turn out to be beneficial if leaders effectively manage conflict and its resolution.

As far as culture change is concerned, the role a leader plays depends on the evolutionary stage of the organization. For example, when the organization is in the growth stage the tools leaders have in their hands to embed culture can also be used to change culture. In mature organizations, however, culture has stabilized and leaders find that the embedding mechanisms are not effective in attempting to change culture. Before describing the mechanisms for culture change related to an organization's developmental stage, it should be noted that there are three fundamental elements underlying any change in a human system bearing considerable similarity to the elements proposed by Lewin (1951). The first element is called 'unfreezing' and refers to a state of disequilibrium caused by disconfirming data, which cannot be denied and therefore lead to anxiety and guilt. For unfreezing to take place it is essential that people feel psychologically safe in the sense that the problem can be solved without loss of identity or integrity. The second element is 'cognitive restructuring', which involves a learning process either through trial and error or through the imitation of a role model. The essence of the learning process is usually a cognitive redefinition of the core concepts in the assumption set. Finally, 'refreezing' takes place, which is the necessity for the new cognition and behavioural patterns to be reinforced by producing once again confirming data. Confirming data are provided by sources external to the organization such as the customers and financial bodies, as well as by internal sources such as organizational members. The learning process that started at the second phase can at this point terminate since the group works effectively.

As already mentioned, there are different possibilities for culture change depending on the developmental phase the organization goes through. In the founding and early growth only an external crisis of survival such as a sharp drop in growth rate or loss of sales can unfreeze the newly embedded culture. If the organization is not under high external pressure and the founder is running the corporation, the culture evolves in small increments by continuing to assimilate what works best over the years. As the organization evolves it becomes differentiated and diversified, it grows in complexity and subcultures are created. In this process the basic assumptions may be retained, but the form in which they appear may change and, therefore, create new behavioural patterns that in turn influence the original basic assumptions. Often when founders stay on for too long they tend to be too change aversive and lead their organization to decay.

A second mechanism of culture change operating in the growth phase is called by Schein (1992) 'self-guided evolution through organizational therapy'. Members of an organization can collectively gain insight of the basic beliefs underlying their group's functioning by collectively examining their culture. Once organizational members have understood the values and beliefs that collectively guide their behaviour, then they are in a position to cognitively redefine the elements that are perceived to be dysfunctional. Therefore, organizational 'therapy' that operates by creating self-insight permits cognitive redefinition to take place. Finally, founders and leaders can achieve culture change by managing 'evolution through hybrids'. This mechanism of change is employed when the external environment demands a deep change of organizational culture. A gradual and incremental change can be achieved through the systematic promotion of insiders whose own assumptions are better adapted to the external demands. Leaders can select for key jobs those organizational members who best represent the new set of assumptions that they want to enhance.

In the midlife stage of an organization's evolution the most important elements of the culture have become embedded in the organization's structure and processes. During this stage the organization has developed into different departments and divisions, and subcultures have emerged. A leader can possibly change the organization's culture by systematically promoting people from selected subcultures. They will inevitably show the leader's values, temperament and motivation. This mechanism is an extension of the promotion of hybrids that is used for culture change in the early stage of organizational growth; it is however a stronger change mechanism in the midlife period because at this stage preservation of the total culture is not as important as for the growing organization. A second mechanism refers to change through organizational development that primarily concerns the coordination and integration of different groups in the organization working with different set of assumptions. Programmes of organizational development involve the creation of a temporary parallel learning system in which some part of the organization learns and puts into test the new assumptions. The final change mechanism in the organizational midlife stage is 'technological seduction'. New technology can be utilized by leaders to 'seduce' organizational members into new ways of thinking and behaving that can potentially replace the existing set of basic assumptions. The creation of some common concepts and language can be facilitated by the diffusion of technological innovation leading to the formulation of novel shared assumptions within the organization.

During the last stage of organizational growth – that is, maturity and possible decline – there are five mechanisms that leaders initiate in their attempts to change the culture of their organizations. Cultural change can be initiated by the infusion of outsiders so that the composition of the organization's dominant groups is altered. Outsiders can be placed at the management team, including the position of the CEO, and at jobs below the top management level in order to facilitate the diffusion of change to the whole organization. The second mechanism of change concerns the usage of scandals and the explosion of myths. Scandals and myths cannot cause culture change, but they can be powerful disconfirming data facilitating the unfreezing of the system. The third mechanism is called 'coercive persuasion' and refers to providing information to organizational members on organizational ineffectiveness and at the same time making sure that members find it very difficult to leave the organization. This situation usually leads members to undergo a cognitive redefinition of their assumptions and eventually learn new ways of thinking and doing things. The fourth mechanism is labelled 'turnarounds' and is a combination of many of the previously discussed mechanisms coordinated into a single programme by a talented manager or team of change agents. Two fundamentally different leadership models have been described for managing turnarounds. In the 'strong vision model', the leader has a clear vision of where the organization should head at and how to get there, while in the 'fuzzy vision model', the leader states forcefully that the organization has to change but relies on the organization to develop the vision and the ways to accomplish it. The final change mechanism concerns the process of reorganization and rebirth, which is a traumatic process and is rarely used as a deliberate strategy (see Box 6.2). Change at this level sometimes results from mergers and acquisitions if the new owners completely restructure the organization and fire the key supporters of the old culture.

Schein's work has offered a great deal towards the understanding of organizational life by following a holistic approach in studying leadership and organizational culture. However, the use of a holistic approach and the obscurity of the subject probably led to the theoretical account being rather static, complex and abstract, and therefore, to some extent, difficult to test (see Hatch, 1993 for a critique).

Box 6.2   Different tools in leaders' hands and opportunities for culture change depending on the developmental stages of an organization (Schein, 1992)

Founding and early growth

- external crisis of survival
- self-guided evolution through organizational therapy
- evolution through hybrids

Midlife stage

- systematically promoting people from selected subcultures
- change through organizational development
- technological seduction

Box 6.2   (cont'd)

Last stage

- infusion of outsiders
- usage of scandals and the explosion of myths
- coercive persuasion
- turnarounds
- reorganization and rebirth

Trice and Beyer's approach to cultural leadership

Trice and Beyer (1993) have suggested that leadership may be conceptualized as both instrumental and cultural. Cultural leadership involves the extent to which a leader shapes ideologies and expressive behaviours. They focus on the consequences of leadership and suggest that 'cultural leadership' concerns both cultural innovation and maintenance. Cultural innovation occurs when leaders create new sets of shared beliefs, values and norms within a social group, whereas cultural maintenance entails the continuance and reinforcement of existing sets of shared ideologies and practices. We should note that cultural innovation refers both to creating a totally new culture or changing an existing one. Therefore, cultural leadership involves originating new cultures, changing old cultures, as well as maintaining already existing ones.

Cultural innovation

Organizational cultures are created when leaders set 'social processes' – such as persuasion and social influence – in motion to achieve their vision of a new organization. A leader's vision provides the substance of the organizational culture that is being created. Personal charisma can possibly be a route to the creation of culture but there are ample examples of effective culture creation that lack the distinctive features of charisma. However, Trice and Beyer suggest that organizations do not necessarily build their cultures around the philosophy of their founders since not all founders are successful in winning over others to their way of thinking. It is acknowledged that organizational cultures may instead form around the values of other leaders or subgroups within the organization. Therefore, this is a more social or group-based model in comparison to Schein's theoretical approach to leadership and culture.

As far as cultural change is concerned, Trice and Beyer (1993) argue that change in organizations can be initiated either by top management or by organizational members in other positions. Designated leaders, who might be newcomers to the organization or part of the existing top management team, normally undertake cultural change. The second kind of change is more revolutionary in nature since it involves emergent leaders, who might overturn existing designated leaders in their efforts to bring about cultural change. There are three groups of cultural change leadership found in the literature, namely turnaround leadership, transformational leadership and emergent cultural change leaders.

Turnaround leadership entails crisis situations in which leaders propose radical visions with persistence, persuade others to follow their visions and finally their philosophies are validated by success. A leader, however, can change an organization even though it is not in a crisis. Leaders who see benefits and undertake major changes in their organizations before the organization experiences a crisis are transformational leaders. Finally, an emergent leader can create cultural change from within the organization. This phenomenon is rather rare and it takes a charismatic person with a radical vision and enormous persuasiveness.

All three types of culture change leadership focus on leaders' ability to persuade others of their powerful vision. Therefore, turnaround, transformational and emergent cultural change leadership might not be distinct enough constructs to represent different types of culture change leadership.

Cultural maintenance

The importance of a leader's role in maintaining a culture has been systematically underestimated. The literature on leadership and organizational culture has emphasized the impact that leaders may have on creating or changing rather than reinforcing and integrating existing cultures. Even for charismatic leadership to have lasting impacts, it is essential that the vision and practices of the charismatic leader are routinized by some sort of administrative processes. Organizations should cultivate embodiment leadership that will carry forward new or transformed cultures and keep them vital. Thus, proscriptive and prescriptive processes are activated that ensure desirable and culturally acceptable behaviours are followed.

An important role for cultural leadership is to preserve and embody existing cultures. In particular, a leader is in a position to sustain the commitments of the organization, to implement its mission and stabilize the organization's shared ideologies. 'Embodiment leaders' can be institutional, group or heroic leaders. The term 'institutional leadership' refers to leaders refining the mission and goals of an organization, and promoting the shared ideologies held by its members. The term applies primarily to formally designated leaders who embody their organizations' cultures. The leader acts as a representative of the group's most cherished principles and values that comprise the core of its culture and identity. Institutional leaders often are those whose behaviour helps towards the institutionalization of practices that have been launched by previous leaders. For example, a policy of open and informal communication between top management and other organizational members can be encouraged by a leader and then be institutionalized by his/her successors.

Another form of cultural leadership that embodies culture is 'group leadership' – that is, informal leaders emerging in small-group settings. Emergent leaders tend to be conformists to the prevailing cultures in their groups, rather than reformers. Leaders of small groups are often cultural leaders because their efforts are directed towards the reinforcement of existing group norms and practices.

Finally, 'heroic leadership' refers to the fact that heroes may embody culture to the degree that others are influenced by their examples. Heroes symbolize the priority placed on certain ideas and behaviours, and act as role models for organizational members.

Culture maintenance is also achieved by leadership that integrates cultures. Organizations normally have various subcultures that may be compatible to the dominant culture or in conflict with it (Martin & Siehl, 1983; see also Chapter 3). There is a need for leadership in certain circumstances to integrate the differences within the organization or between the organization and its environment. 'Consensus leadership' refers to top managers who pull together diverse interests from within and outside the organization to ensure that the organization operates smoothly. Consensus leaders negotiate among groups with different values and interests, and aim to incorporate the groups into decision-making and action. While consensus leaders operate at the top of organizations, other levels of integration leadership are essential in dealing with conflicts at the lower ranks of an organization. 'Transaction leaders' rely on conventional social exchange processes to confront conflicting interests and values among different members and groups of the organization. Transactional leaders balance and coordinate diverse value systems to achieve coordinated effort; often the rewards and punishments they administer are non-material and symbolic, such as positive and negative feedback, praise, reprimand, public recognition and public disgrace (see Box 6.3).

The perspective of Trice and Beyer (1993) on cultural leadership has received rather limited empirical examination possibly because research, in general, on organizational culture has not dealt adequately with the tension between the usage of qualitative and quantitative research methods. The understanding of cultural innovation and maintenance can profoundly benefit from the investigation of the socio-psychological mechanisms that underlie the interaction between leaders and other organizational members.

Box 6.3   Cultural leadership in creating, maintaining and changing organizational cultures (Trice and Beyer, 1993)

Creation or change of culture

The leader (designated or emergent)

- cultivates shared values and norms within a social group;
- promotes a powerful vision;
- sets social influence and persuasion in motion;
- exploits crisis situations if they emerge.

Box 6.3   (cont'd)

Maintenance of culture

The leader (designated or emergent)

- sustains the commitments of the organization;
- implements its mission;
- stabilize the organization's shared ideologies;
- integrates organizational subcultures.

In sum, founders and small groups (i.e., the board including the leader) play a profound role in the creation of organizational cultures, and mature organizational cultures, in turn, have an impact on various aspects of organizational behaviour including leadership and group functioning. Founders and other leaders are considered to have distinct ideologies and visions dictating how the organization should integrate its internal forces and adapt to environmental demands in order to be successful. A rather recent approach to organizational leadership, namely the transformational/charismatic perspective, has extensively investigated the leadership process in terms of the transformational and transactional relationships that emerge between leaders and followers. Transformational leadership is characterized by the leader's motivation to change the organization's cultural framework, while transactional leadership is based on the acceptance, at least partly, of the existing culture value priorities and practices.

Transformational leadership and organizational culture

To understand leadership in business organizations Bass and his colleagues (Avolio, Bass, & Jung, 1999; Bass, 1985, 1999; Hater & Bass, 1988; Waldman, Bass, & Yammarino, 1990; Yammarino, Spangler, & Bass, 1993) have suggested that the terms of transformational and transactional leadership, first introduced by Burns (1978), can be of great importance. The transactional leader recognizes what it is that subordinates want to get from their work and tries to see that they do get it, as far as their performance is high. Subordinates' effort is exchanged for rewards and promises of rewards. The transactional leader is responsive to the subordinates' immediate self-interests if they can be met by their getting the job done. The leader clarifies the role and task requirements for the subordinate reaching the desired outcomes. This gives the subordinate sufficient confidence to exert the required effort. They also recognize what the subordinate needs and clarify how these needs will be satisfied if the necessary effort is expended by the subordinate. Transactional leaders pursue a cost–benefit economic exchange to meet subordinates' current material and psychic needs in return for contracted services rendered by the subordinates. The leader provides a sense of direction to the subordinates, while not questioning the main goals of the organization.

Transformational leadership, on the other hand, recognizes the existing needs in subordinates but tends to go further, seeking to arouse and satisfy higher needs. Transformational leaders raise our level of consciousness about the importance and value of designated outcomes. Employees transcend their own self-interests for the sake of the team, organization or larger society. In doing so, transformational leadership may result ultimately in higher levels of satisfaction, commitment and effectiveness. Transformational leaders are charismatic in the sense that they are perceived by their subordinates as self-confident, competent, energetic and optimistic about the future. They are able to arouse in their subordinates faith and trust in the leader's motives and competence. Subordinates tend to be emotionally involved with the leader and get inspired by the leader's behaviour. Transformational leaders offer individual consideration for each of their subordinates as they are interested in the followers' needs, ambitions and individual growth. They also provide the subordinate with intellectual stimulation concerning new ways to think about problems or to do things. They reframe the situation and provide creative insight to deal with environmental changes.

Bass and his colleagues, in contrast to Burns (1978), have proposed that leaders tend to exhibit a variety of patterns of transformational and transactional leadership, and that most leaders do both but in different amounts (Box 6.4).

Box 6.4 Attributes of transformational and transactional leadership

Transformational leadership

- Show personal integrity, self-confidence, competence and optimism for the future
- Articulate a clear and persuasive vision
- Inspires subordinates to adopt goals and values consistent with the leader's vision
- Arouses emotional attachment to the leader
- Provides intellectual stimulation and creative inputs to solving problems
- Reframes the situation and deals with changes creatively

Transactional leadership

- Clarifies the task and role requirements of each subordinate and offers direction
- Recognizes what subordinates want to get from their work
- Rewards effort expenditure and accomplishment of set goals and objectives
- Criticizes negative work behaviours
- Punishes unreasonably low performance by withholding desired outcomes
- Pursue a cost–benefit exchange in dealing with the subordinates

As far as the effect of transformational and transactional leadership on culture is concerned, Bass (1985) suggested that transactional leadership works primarily within the culture as it exists, whereas transformational leadership aims at changing at least some elements of organizational culture. However, a mixture of both transactional and transformational leadership is needed for organizational cultures to maintain or gain a sustainable advantage (Bass, 1999). Company founders often are transformational leaders shaping company policies, norms and values that dominate its culture. The personality and the talents of the founders are reflected in the organization that develops. The set of values the founder articulates, their personal assumptions and vision of the future, become embedded in the emerging organizational culture. But the transformational leader who firmly establishes the corporate culture can be far removed in time from the company founder (see Box 6.5).

Box 6.5   The Bell System

Alexander Graham Bell displayed his telephone in 1876 and started the Bell Telephone Company soon after, but Theodore N. Vail, starting 30 years later, endowed the Bell System with its organizational culture for the three-quarters of the century which ended in 1984 with the break-up of AT&T into seven independent companies. His policy slogan which was at the heart of the system was, 'One policy, one system, universal service'. He sought government regulation for his company, which he conceived to be a natural monopoly that must put the public interest ahead of profits. Public utilities giving good service at fair rates should not have to compete in the marketplace against unfair rates. This approach set into place everything in 'Ma Bell' from secure managerial career planning to common and preferred stocks provided to widows and orphans. This plan worked well up to the point that a new interconnect industry emerged and competition was legislated by the courts.

Research on the relation between transformational leadership and various organizational outcomes has shown that transformational leadership is empirically associated with organizational commitment (Bono & Judge, 2003; Bycio et al., 1995; Simosi & Xenikou, 2010; Walumbwa, Wang, Lawer, & Shi, 2004), employee satisfaction (Bycio, Hackett, & Allen, 1995; Podsakoff, MacKenzie, Moorman, & Fetter, 1990), leader effectiveness (Bycio et al., 1995; Hater & Bass, 1988; Lowe, Kroeck, & Sivasubramaniam, 1996) and organizational citizenship behaviours (Podsakoff, MacKenzie, Paine, & Bachrach, 2000). A number of scholars have pointed out that theory and research on transformational and charismatic leadership have neglected the effect that contextual factors have on the emergence, operation and effectiveness of leadership in organizational settings (Beyer, 1999; Bommer, Rubin, & Baldwin, 2004; Pawar & Eastman, 1997; Pillai & Meindl, 1998; Shamir & Howell, 1999; Yulk, 1999).

There are, thus, a rather limited number of conceptual and empirical studies that have examined the emergence of transformational and charismatic leadership as a function of various contextual factors such as organizational life cycle (Baliga & Hunt, 1988; Shamir & Howell, 1999), organizational structure (Pawar & Eastman, 1997), organizational culture (Pawar & Eastman, 1997; Shamir & Howell, 1999), national culture (Singer & Singer, 1990), the congruence between organizational main goals and dominant social values (Shamir & Howell, 1999; Shamir, House, & Arthur, 1993), managerial peer influence (Bommer et al., 2004) and organizational tasks and technology (Shamir & Howell, 1999).

As far as organizational culture is concerned, Pawar and Eastman (1997) argued that organizational receptivity to transformational leadership is influenced by the mode of organizational governance; organizations with a clan (supportive, with community ties) culture are expected to be more receptive to transformational leadership than organizations with either market or bureaucratic cultures. Shamir and Howell (1999) suggested that the probability of the emergence and effectiveness of charismatic leadership depends on the type of organizational culture, where a clan mode of governance and an adaptive culture is conducive to charismatic leadership, as well as the congruence between the dominant societal values and the values represented in main organizational goals. In other words, organizational culture and its congruence with societal values have an impact on the emergence and effectiveness of charismatic leadership. In similar lines, Block (2003) found that employees who rated their immediate supervisor high in transformational leadership were more likely to perceive the culture of their organization as involving, integrating, adaptive and having a clear mission.

Moreover, Waldman and Yammarino (1999) proposed that there is a reciprocal causation between charismatic leadership in senior managers and adaptive organizational cultures; adaptive cultures tend to precede or allow for the emergence of charismatic leaders, and a charismatic leader is in a position to have an impact on organizational culture. In contrast, nonadaptive cultures are averse to change, innovation and risk-taking, and therefore prevent the emergence of charismatic leadership. In another investigation of the link between leadership and organizational culture, Sarros, Cooper, & Santora (2002) showed that cultures with an emphasis on supportiveness were best predicted by transformational leadership style, while cultures with an emphasis on rewards were best predicted by a mixture of transactional and transformational leadership styles. Finally, Pillai and Meindl (1998) found that the presence of collectivistic values in work groups and a heightened sense of community are associated with charismatic leadership.

Bass and Avolio (1993) have proposed that transformational/transactional leadership and organizational culture are so well interconnected that it is possible to describe an 'ideal' transactional organizational culture and an 'ideal' transformational organizational culture (Box 6.6). They further explained that organizations are likely to have cultures that are characterized by both styles of leadership. A transactional culture focuses on everything in terms of explicit and implicit contractual relationships. All job assignments are explicitly spelled out along with conditions of employment, disciplinary codes and benefit structures. Stories, rites, jargon and values in the transactional culture depend on setting a price on everything. The organization is a marketplace comprised of individuals, whose reward is contingent on their performance. Management-by-exception is often actively practiced. Employees work as independently as possible from their colleagues and little identification of the employees with the organization is observed. Innovation and risk-taking are not encouraged in this type of organizational culture.

On the other hand, in a transformational culture there is a sense of purpose and commitments are long-term. Leaders and followers share mutual interests and a sense of interdependence and shared fate. A transformational culture like leadership can build on or augment the transactional culture of the organization. The inclusion of assumptions, values and norms that are transformationally based does not preclude individuals pursuing their own goals and rewards. Leaders and followers go beyond their self-interests or expected rewards for the good of the team and the organization. Organizations are effective when they move in the direction of more transformational qualities in their cultures, while also maintaining a base of effective transactional qualities. In a highly innovative and satisfying organizational culture it is likely to see transformational leaders who believe that people are trustworthy and purposeful and that complex problems are handled at the lowest level possible. Leaders who build such cultures and articulate them to followers typically exhibit a sense of vision and purpose. They foster a culture of creative change and growth rather than a culture which maintains the status quo.

Box 6.6   Attributes of the 'prototypical' transformational and transactional organizational cultures (OCs)

Ideal transformational OC

- creates a sense of interdependence and close ties;
- does not inhibit individuals from pursuing their own goals and interests;
- encourages members to go beyond their self-interests;
- exhibits a sense of vision and purpose;
- promotes creative change and growth.

Ideal transactional OC

- encourages employees to work independently from their colleagues;
- allocates rewards on the basis of individual effort expenditure and performance;
- controls and punishes negative work-related behaviours;
- promotes a metaphor of the organization as a 'marketplace' where one gets what he/she deserves;
- does not promote innovation and risk-taking.

Although an essential aspect of transformational leadership is the cultural changes that it sets off, there is scare theoretical and empirical research on the interplay between transformational leadership and organizational culture partly because both are difficult to define. A question that has received some attention is how culture can affect organizational receptivity to transformational leadership. It has been suggested that an adaptive and innovative culture is expected to be more receptive to the social process of transformational leadership rather than a culture focused on the preservation of the status quo.

Leadership and national culture

Organizations to some extent reflect the values and practices of the wider society within which they operate. According to Hofstede (2001), the national environment partly influences the cultures of organizations, but certainly national cultures and organizational cultures are not identical. He argues that the perception of an effective leader fairly depends on the values of the national culture in which the leader is situated. For example, in a masculine culture, the effective leader is decisive, assertive and aggressive (aggression in a masculine culture is considered a positive trait). Therefore, in organizations that operate in masculine cultures, such as Japan and Austria, leaders are effective as much as they are characterized as dynamic, competitive, resilient and tough. On the other hand, effective organizational leaders in feminine cultures (i.e., Norway and Sweden) are less visible and place a high value on consensus. Similarly, Trompenaars and Hampden-Turner (2004) suggest that in cultures of North America and Northwest Europe leaders are expected to have the power to direct the organization according to their plans, whereas organizational leaders in East Asia are thought to be effective even if they are fatalists and see their role as trying to deal with the uncontrollable elements of the external environment.

A line of research that has examined the effect of culture, defined at a societal level, on perceptions of effective leadership concern culturally endorsed implicit theories of leadership. Lord and Maher (1991) suggest that leadership can be recognized based on the fit between the perceiver's beliefs of what 'leaders' should be and the observed attributes and behaviours of an individual acting as a leader. In other words, people develop implicit leadership theories (ILTs) – that is, assumptions about how leaders behave in general and what is expected of them. ILTs are cognitive schemata or prototypes containing the attributes that distinguish a leader from a nonleader (or a successful leader from an average leader). These cognitive structures are activated when followers interact with a person in a leadership position. It is likely for individuals to behave as followers when their leadership prototypes match the perceived characteristics of the leader (Brodbeck et al., 2000). Under these conditions the leader is seen to be powerful and influential. As far as the content of these prototypes is concerned, Offermann, Kennedy, & Wirtz (1994) found that ILTs comprise eight distinct traits: six prototypic traits (sensitivity, dedication, charisma, attractiveness, intelligence and strength) and two anti-prototypic traits (tyranny and masculinity) (Box 6.7).

Box 6.7   Prototypic and anti-prototypic leadership traits proposed by implicit leadership theories

Prototypic traits

- *Sensitivity* concerns the extent to which a leader offers help to his followers, shows understanding and is sincere in his dealings with them.
- *Dedication* refers to a leader's motivation and enthusiasm regarding the accomplishment of goals and objectives.
- *Charisma* reflects a leader's quality to be extraordinary and to possess a number of attributes that are considered to make a person special.
- *Attractiveness* is the degree to which the leader is attractive to his followers.
- *Intelligence* refers to the leader's education, as well as his intellectual abilities and skills.
- *Strength* is the degree to which a leader is dynamic, strong and energetic.

Anti-prototypic traits

- *Tyranny* concerns leader's attributes such as selfishness, social domination and manipulation.
- *Masculinity* reflects the manifestation of stereotypically male characteristics, such as aggression and independence, by the leader

---

An important question concerning leadership perception is whether culture has an impact on the formulation of the preferred leadership traits contained in ILTs. Different groups may consider effective leadership to be associated with different leadership attributes (Hunt, Boal, & Sorenson, 1990). Culturally endorsed implicit theories of leadership (CLTs) refer to the different leadership prototypes shared by people belonging to various cultural groups. The Global Leadership and Organizational Behaviour Effectiveness Research Programme (GLOBE) is a cross-cultural research project, which aims at investigating whether there are leader attributes and behaviours and organizational practices, which are (1) nation or culture specific and (2) universally accepted and effective across cultures (Brodbeck et al., 2000; Den Hartog et al. 1997, 1999; House et al., 1999; Koopman et al., 1999).

There are leader attributes that are universally endorsed as contributing to effective leadership, as well as attributes that are universally seen as impediments to outstanding leadership; moreover, the existence of culturally contingent attributes of effective leadership has been empirically supported (Den Hartog et al., 1999). In specific, most of the universally positively endorsed attributes are components of charismatic/transformational and team-oriented leadership styles such as trustworthy, just, honest, encouraging, confidence-building, positive, dynamic, excellence-oriented, communicative and effective in team building. On the other hand, attributes such as being a loner, noncooperative, ruthless, nonexplicit, irritable and dictatorial were found to be universally viewed as ineffective or impediments to outstanding leadership. Finally, there was evidence showing that being individualistic, ambitious, status conscious and cunning were culturally contingent leadership attributes.

Of course the universal endorsement of an attribute as contributing to effective leadership does not preclude cultural differences in the enactment of such an attribute (Den Hartog et al., 1999). Charismatic/transformational leadership was found to be universally endorsed but the behaviours indicative of this trait were different in different cultures; for example the communication of a charismatic leader vision range from the quiet, soft-spoken manner of Ghandi to the more 'macho' oratory of J. F. Kennedy.

Moreover, Dorfman et al. (1997) examined the similarities and differences in effective leadership processes between Asian (i.e., Japan, South Korea and Taiwan) and Western countries (i.e., Mexico and the United States). The results indicated that leader supportiveness, contingent reward and charismatic leadership showed universally positive impacts in all five countries, whereas participativeness, directiveness and contingent punishment had positive impacts in only two countries. The impact of contingent punishment was the most unique among leader behaviours as it had a desirable effect only in the United States, but equivocal or undesirable effects in the other countries.

There is also empirical evidence that preferred leadership varies by culture within Europe (Brodbeck et al., 2000; Koopman et al., 1999). Following the distinction between North/West and South/East parts of Europe, Koopman et al. showed that there are 'cultural contingent' leadership attributes and behaviours within Europe, namely participative leadership, humane leadership, autonomous leadership and narcissistic leadership. Attributes such as authoritative style, diplomacy, face saving, procedural, administrative competence and status consciousness are more strongly endorsed by middle managers from the South/East part of Europe, who also describe their societal cultures as higher on power distance and lower on achievement and future orientation. In addition, charismatic/value-based leadership and team-oriented leadership were endorsed as contributing to effective leadership by all European countries included in their research.

Similarly, Brodbeck et al. found that leadership concepts vary as a function of cultural differences in Europe, and identified leadership prototypicality dimensions that describe differences between European countries and regions. For example, it was shown that 'interpersonal directness' and 'proximity' were more strongly associated with superior leadership in the Nordic countries (e.g., Finland, Norway) than in the near-east (e.g., Greece, Turkey) or central European countries. Germanic countries (e.g., Austria, Germany), on the other hand, placed a high value on the leadership attributes of 'autonomy' as a prerequisite for outstanding leadership.

In sum, it has been shown that there are leader attributes that are universally perceived as contributing or hindering effective leadership such as the transformational or the dictatorial leadership style, respectively. In addition, research has demonstrated that culturally endorsed implicit theories of leadership do exist, advocating for the effect of societal culture on the perception of leadership effectiveness in organizational settings.

Leadership, organizational culture and performance

Even though the contingency models of leadership have examined how situational variables moderate the relationship between leadership and effectiveness, the influence of organizational or societal culture as a key moderator variable of the relationship between leadership and effectiveness has been neglected. Bjerke (1999) argues that although the importance of the social context on the effectiveness of leadership styles is taken into account by the contingency theories, the definition of social contexts in this approach is rather restrained to a limited number of variables and does not consider the informal social networks within organizations. The norms, values and assumptions that operate mainly through the informal network of the organization have not been systematically examined as moderators of the relationship between leadership and effectiveness.

Lim (1995) suggested that culture might be the filter through which other important variables such as leadership influence organizational performance. Sapienza (1985) has shown that organizational culture as shared beliefs can influence what managers perceive and how they respond to environmental stimuli. Moreover, Smith and Vecchio (1997) suggested that organizational culture moderates the reciprocal influence of environment and strategy formulation. Strategy is built on the beliefs the top management holds about the organization and its business environment, whereas organizational culture filters the perspectives of its members and affects their ability to ask the right questions.

Researchers have examined the links between leadership, organizational culture and performance, and found that the form of organizational culture mediates the relationship between leadership style and performance (Ogbonna & Harris, 2000; Xenikou & Simosi, 2006). Ogbonna and Harris showed that supportive and participative leadership were positively linked to performance through innovative and competitive forms of organizational culture. Similarly, Xenikou and Simosi showed that transformational leadership and a humanistic cultural orientation had an indirect positive impact on business unit performance via achievement cultural orientation. In other words, transformational leadership traits seems to stimulate goal setting, task accomplishment and an achievement orientation, which, in turn, has a positive effect on performance.

Hennessey (1998) showed that organizational culture facilitated or hampered the 'reinvention of government' – that is, a change of the federal government away from complacency and entitlement towards initiative and empowerment, in nine federal offices of the United States. The findings also indicated that leaders influenced the reinvention of the government and organizational performance measures, most likely via organizational culture.

In conclusion, when leadership is seen as a social process that involves leaders, followers and certain social situations, it seems that an adequate analysis of leadership requires identifying not only the leader but also the relevant group of followers, and how the situation affects the social process of leadership. There are some preliminary findings that support the theoretical point that organizational culture might be the filter through which leadership influences various organizational outcomes. On the basis of these findings, future research should more thoroughly investigate the hypotheses that leadership influences organizational effectiveness to some extent via its effect on culture, and that culture affects organizational receptivity to various leadership styles.

Summary

Entrepreneurial founders are considered to be the people who play a key role in the creation of organizational cultures. They often have strong values and a vision of how their corporation should deal with problems of internal integration and external adaptation. The founder's philosophical beliefs influence the selection of organizational members, as well as the strategy, structure and managerial practices of the new organization. As the organization evolves it is of interest to consider the processes through which organizational culture is maintained or changed. An essential aspect of leadership is to influence the shared ideologies that people hold, and therefore leaders put effort into the maintenance and change of organizational cultures. The various mechanisms leaders employ to produce cultural maintenance or change such as the communication of existing values or new ideologies are thoroughly presented. However, it seems that leadership affects culture as much as culture affects leadership.

The relationship between transformational leadership and organizational culture is examined since one of the main attributes of transformational leadership concerns a leader's motivation to induce cultural change. It has been suggested that in a highly innovative and satisfying organizational culture we are likely to see transformational leaders who build on assumptions such as 'people are trustworthy' and 'everyone has a unique contribution to make'. Moreover, the effect of societal culture on the perceptions of effective leadership is investigated within the approach of culturally endorsed implicit theories of leadership. An important issue in this domain is whether there are cultural differences in the perception of leadership qualities that are related to effectiveness. Finally, some preliminary findings are reviewed that show leadership to influence various organizational outcomes via its effect on organizational culture.

Questions

1. How does the culture of an organization originate?
2. By which mechanisms do founders and other leaders of an organization teach their assumptions to the group?

3. How does culture change in the growth phase of an organization?

4. Does organizational culture affect organizational receptivity to transformational leadership?

5. Are there any leader attributes that make a leader being perceived as effective across cultures?

6. Do different cultural groups have variant conceptions of what leadership in organizations should entail?

Case study

How leaders create organizational cultures?

The Jones Food Company

Founder Jones operated a grocery store with his wife following some basic attitudes toward customers that his parents, particularly his mother, had taught him. His mother was the person who helped him form the vision that he could succeed in building a thriving enterprise that would bring him and his family a fortune.

Jones was the main ideological force in his company and continued to impose his assumptions until his death in his late seventies. He believed that his main objective was to supply high-quality products to customers in a clean and attractive surrounding. The customers' needs were the primary consideration in all major decisions that he made. Jones displayed trust in his customers by giving them credit and taking products back if there was the slightest complaint. He kept his store absolutely spotless to inspire customer confidence in his products. Ultimately, he built a large chain of supermarkets, department stores and other related businesses that were for many decades the dominant force in the marketplace.

Jones believed that close supervision of subordinates is a necessary condition for a business to be successful. He used to visit his stores unexpectedly, inspect every detail and teach his employees the basic principles he endorsed. These assumptions became one of the core themes in his philosophy of management and he expected his store managers to be always around to set the example for employees and teach them the right way to do things.

Most of the founding group in his company consisted of Jones's three brothers and a manager who was not a family member and was recruited early to become one of the main culture creators and carriers. He shared Jones's basic assumptions about how to best run a business; he was the person who set up formal systems to ensure that those assumptions were the basis of everyday business operation. After Jones' death, this manager continued to communicate the theory of 'visible management' and set a personal example by following the same close supervision policies that Jones had used.

(cont'd)

Jones thought that one could win in the marketplace only by being highly innovative and technically in the forefront. He always encouraged his managers to try new approaches and travelled to conventions and other businesses where new technological innovations were displayed. As a result, his company was one of the first to introduce the bar code technology. Jones also brought in a variety of human resource consultants and started selection and development programmes through assessment centres long before other companies. If things worked Jones encouraged their adoption; if they did not, he ordered them to be dropped. Measuring results and solving problems were major principles in how he ran his company.

Even though Jones was very interested in developing good managers, he treated several members of his family favourably by giving them key managerial positions when they did not have the necessary management experience. If they performed poorly Jones would have a good manager to support them; in the case that their performance remained poor, they would be removed but with various face-saving excuses.

Jones's assumptions about how things should be done were reinforced by the market as his business was successful. The company grew and prospered and the founder felt confidence that his assumptions were right. However, there was a basic inconsistency in the way Jones believed that employees, and particularly managers, should be treated. On the one hand, he was concerned with hiring and keeping the best managers and often employed human resource consultants to ensure that this was the case. On the other hand, he made his managers feel uncertain about their career development as they saw him treating his family members in a favourable way. Although Jones wanted open communication and a high level of trust among the members of his organization, he actually believed and in some indirect ways communicated that family members were more trustworthy. Jones did not perceive his own conflicts and inconsistencies and failed to understand why some of his best people left the company to work for other firms.

(1) Identify and describe the basic assumptions of how to best run a business that founder Jones held.

(2) By which practices did he impose those assumptions on his managers and workforce in general?

(3) Pinpoint the inconsistencies in Jones' belief system and practices regarding the way he treated his managers.

(4) Would you expect that those inconsistencies could form the basis for the creation of a counterculture?

Source: Adapted from Schein (1992).

References

Avolio, B. J., Bass, B. M., & Jung, D. I. (1999). Re-examining the components of transformational and transactional leadership using the multifactor leadership questionnaire. *Journal of Occupational and Organizational Psychology*, 72, 441–462.

Baliga, B. R., & Hunt, J. G. (1988). An organizational life cycle approach to leadership. In J. G. Hunt, B. R. Baliga, H. P. Dachler, & C. A. Schriesheim (eds.), *Emerging Leadership Vistas* (pp. 129–149). Lexington, MA: Lexington Books.

Bass, B. M. (1985). *Leadership and Performance Beyond Expectations*. New York: Free Press.

Bass, B. M. (1999). Two decades of research and development in transformational leadership. *European Journal of Work and Organizational Psychology*, 8, 9–32.

Bass, B. M., & Avolio, B. J. (1993). Transformational leadership and organizational culture. *Public Administration Quarterly*, 17, 112–121.

Beyer, J. M. (1999). Taming and promoting charisma to change organizations. *Leadership Quarterly*, 10, 307–330.

Bjerke, B. (1999). *Business Leadership and Culture: National Management Styles in the Global Economy*. Cheltenham: Edward Elgar.

Blake, R., & Mouton, J. (1985). *The Managerial Grid*. Houston: Gulf.

Block, L. (2003). The leadership-culture connection: An exploratory investigation. *Leadership and Organization Development Journal*, 24, 318–334.

Bommer, W. H., Rubin, R. S., & Baldwin, T. T. (2004). Setting the stage for effective leadership: Antecedents of transformational leadership behaviour. *Leadership Quarterly*, 15, 195–210.

Bono, J. E., & Judge, T. A. (2003). Self-concordance: Towards understanding the motivational effects of transformational leaders. *Academy of Management Journal*, 46, 554–571.

Brodbeck, F. C., Frese, M., Akerblom, S., Audia, G, Bakacsi, G., et al. (2000). Cultural variation of leadership prototypes across 22 European countries. *Journal of Occupational and Organizational Psychology*, 73, 1–29.

Burns, J. M. (1978). *Leadership*. New York: Harper and Row.

Bycio, P., Hackett, R. D., & Allen, J. S. (1995). Further assessments of Bass's (1985) conceptualisation of transactional and transformational leadership. *Journal of Applied Psychology*, 80, 468–478.

Den Hartog, D., Koopman, P., Thierry, H., Wilderom, C., Maczynski, J., & Jarmuz, S. (1997). Dutch and Polish perceptions of leadership and culture: The GLOBE project. *European Journal of Work and Organizational Psychology*, 6, 387–413.

Den Hartog, D. N., House, R. J., Hanges, P.J., Ruiz-Quintanilla, S. A., Dorfman, P. W., & associates (1999). Culture specific and cross-culturally generalizable implicit leadership theories: Are attributes of charismatic/transformational leadership universally endorsed? *Leadership Quarterly*, 10, 219–256.

Dorfman, P. W., Howell, J. P., Hibino, S., Lee, J. K., Tate, U., & Bautista, A. (1997). Leadership in Western and Asian countries: Commonalities and differences in effective leadership processes across cultures. *Leadership Quarterly*, 8, 233–274.

Fiedler, F. (1967). *A Theory of Leadership Effectiveness*. New York: McGraw-Hill.

Fleishman, E., & Harris, E. (1962). Patterns of leadership behaviour related to employee grievances and turnover. *Personnel Psychology*, 15, 43–56.

Furnham, A. (2005). *The Psychology of Behaviour at Work*. Hove, East Sussex: Psychology Press.

Hatch, M. J. (1993). The dynamics of organizational culture. *Academy of Management Review*, 18, 657–693.

Hater, J. J., & Bass, B. M. (1988). Superiors' evaluations and subordinates' perceptions of transformational and transactional leadership. *Journal of Applied Psychology*, 73, 695–702.

Hennessey, J. T. (1998). Reinventing government: Does leadership make the difference? *Public Administration Review*, 58, 522–532.

Hofstede, G. (2001). *Culture's Consequences: Comparing Values, Behaviors, Institutions, and Organizations Across Nations.* Thousand Oaks: Sage.

House, R. J., Hanges, P. J., Ruiz-Quintanilla, S. A., Dorfman, P. W., Javidan, M., Dickson, M. W., Gupta, V., et al. (1999). Cultural influences on leadership and organizations: Project GLOBE. In W. H. Mobley, M. J. Gessner, & V. Arnold (eds.), *Advances in Global Leadership* (pp. 171–233). Stamford, CT: JAI Press.

House, R., & Mitchell, T. (1974). Path-goal theory of leadership. *Journal of Contemporary Business*, 3, 81–99.

Hunt, J. G., Boal, K. B., & Sorenson, R. L. (1990). Top management leadership: Inside the black box. *Leadership Quarterly*, 1, 41–65.

Koopman, P. L., Den Hartog, D. N., Konrad, E., & associates (1999). National culture and leadership profiles in Europe: Some results from the GLOBE study. *European Journal of Work and Organizational Psychology*, 8, 503–520.

Lewin, K. (1951). *Field Theory in Social Science.* New York: Harper and Row.

Likert, R. (1961). *New Patterns in Management.* New York: McGraw-Hill.

Lim, B. (1995). Examining the organizational culture and organizational performance link. *Leadership and Organization development Journal*, 16, 16–21.

Lord, R. G., & Maher, K. J. (1991). *Leadership and Information Processing.* Boston: Routledge.

Lowe, K. B., Kroeck, K. G., & Sivasubramaniam, N. (1996). Effectiveness correlates of transformational and transactional leadership: A meta-analytic review of the MLQ literature. *Leadership Quarterly*, 7, 385–425.

Martin, H. J., & Siehl, C. (1983). Organizational culture and counterculture: An uneasy symbiosis. *Organizational Dynamics*, Autumn, 52–64.

Offermann, L. R., Kennedy, J. K., Jr., & Wirtz, P. W. (1994). Implicit leadership theories: Content, structure and generalizability. *Leadership Quarterly*, 5, 43–58.

Ogbonna, E., & Harris, L. C. (2000). Leadership style, organizational culture and performance: Empirical evidence from UK companies. *International Journal of Human Resource Management*, 11, 766–788.

Pawar, B. S., & Eastman, K. K. (1997). The nature and implications of contextual influences on transformational leadership: A conceptual examination. *Academy of Management Review*, 22, 80–109.

Pillai, R., & Meindl, J. R. (1998). Context and charisma: A 'meso' level examination of the relationship of organic structure, collectivism and crisis to charismatic leadership. *Journal of Management*, 24, 643–671.

Podsakoff, P. M., MacKenzie, S. B., Moorman, R. H., & Fetter, R. (1990). Transformational leader behaviours and their effects on the follower's trust in leader, satisfaction and organizational citizenship behaviours. *Leadership Quarterly*, 1, 107–142.

Podsakoff, P. M., MacKenzie, S. B., Paine, J. B., & Bachrach, D. G. (2000). Organizational citizenship behaviours: A critical review of the theoretical and empirical literature and suggestions for future research. *Journal of Management*, 26, 513–565.

Sapienza, A. M. (1985). Believing is seeing: How culture influences the decisions top managers make. In R. H. Kilman, M. J. Saxton, R. Serpa, et al. (eds.), *Gaining Control of the Corporate Culture* (pp. 66–83). San Francisco: Jossey-Bass.

Sarros, J. C., Gray, J., & Desten, I. L. (2002). Leadership and its impact on organizational culture. *International Journal of Business Studies*, 10, 1–26.

Sarros, J. C., Cooper, B. K., & Santora, J. C. (2008). Building a climate for innovation through transformational leadership and organizational culture. *Journal of Leadership and Organizational Studies*, **15**, 145–158.

Schein, E. H. (1992). *Organizational Culture and Leadership*. San Francisco: Jossey-Bass.

Simosi, M., & Xenikou, A. (2010). The role of organizational culture in the relationship between leadership and organizational commitment: An empirical study in a Greek organization. *International Journal of Human Resource Management*, **21**, 1598–1616.

Singer, M. S., & Singer, A. E. (1990). Situational constraints on transformational versus transactional leadership behaviour, subordinates' leadership preference, and satisfaction. *The Journal of Social Psychology*, **130**, 385–396.

Shamir, B., & Howell, J. M. (1999). Organizational and contextual influences on the emergence and effectiveness of charismatic leadership. *Leadership Quarterly*, **10**, 257–283.

Shamir, B., House, R. J., & Arthur, M. B. (1993). The motivational effects of charismatic leadership: A self-concept based theory. *Organization Science*, **4**, 577–594.

Smith, C. G., & Vecchio, R. P. (1997). Organizational culture and strategic leadership: Issues in the management of strategic change. In R. P. Vecchio (ed.), *Leadership: Understanding the Dynamics of Power and Influence in Organizations* (pp. 484–501). Notre Dame, IN: University of Notre Dame Press.

Trice, H. M., & Beyer, J. M. (1993). *The Cultures of Work Organizations*. Englewood Cliffs, NJ: Prentice-Hall.

Trompenaars, F., & Hampden-Turner, C. (2004). *Managing People Across Cultures*. Chichester: Capstone.

Vroom, V., & Jago, A. (1988). *The New Leadership: Managing Participation in Organizations*. Englewood Cliffs, NJ: Prentice-Hall.

Vroom, V., & Yetton, P. (1973). *Leadership and Decision-Making*. Pittsburg, PA: University of Pittsburg Press.

Waldman, D. A., & Yammarino, F. J. (1999). CEO charismatic leadership: Levels-of-management and levels-of-analysis effects. *Academy of Management Review*, **24**, 266–285.

Waldman, D. A., Bass, B. M., & Yammarino, F. J. (1990). Adding to contingent-reward behaviour: The augmenting effect of charismatic leadership. *Group and Organization Studies*, **15**, 381–394.

Walumbwa, F. O., Wang, P., Lawer, J. J., & Shi, K. (2004). The role of collective efficacy in the relations between transformational leadership and work outcomes. *Journal of Occupational and Organizational Psychology*, **77**, 515–530.

Xenikou, A., & Simosi, M. (2006). Organizational culture and transformational leadership as predictors of business unit performance. *Journal of Managerial Psychology*, **21**, 566–579.

Yammarino, F. J., Spangler, W. D., & Bass, B. M. (1993). Transformational leadership and performance: A longitudinal investigation. *Leadership Quarterly*, **4**, 81–102.

Yulk, G. (1999). An evaluation of conceptual weaknesses in transformational and charismatic leadership theories. *Leadership Quarterly*, **10**, 285–305.

Organizational Culture and Performance

7

Chapter objectives

The main objectives are to:

- understand the strong culture hypothesis and go through the empirical findings that have tested it;

- explore the different culture contexts in which organizational performance is to thrive;

- investigate the relationship among culture dimensions and organizational effectiveness outcomes;

(cont'd)

- analyse the role of achievement, humanistic and adaptability culture dimensions in promoting organizational performance;
- examine the implications that person–organization fit have on organizational efficiency.

Introduction

During the 1980s the term 'organizational culture' was increasingly used in the popular business literature, as well as in academic studies of organizational behaviour, mainly because the culture of an organization was considered to have an impact on organizational effectiveness beyond the effect of business environment, corporate structure and other formal organizational processes. Business consultants and academics in their attempt to solve the puzzle of Japanese companies' success proposed this new explanatory variable.

The central question that was put forward at the time was whether excellent organizations are characterized by a set of cultural attributes that distinguish them from underachieving ones. There was also a debate on whether strong cultures – often defined as cultures widely shared by organizational members – interact with these 'positive' cultural attributes to produce a profound effect on organizational performance. Later on, a contingency approach to the study of the culture–performance link argued that the value systems of 'excellent' organizations in different industry sectors might not be the same. It may be necessary for companies in different competitive environments to develop more (or less) flexible structures. Strategy and industry can and should be included in the examination of the influence of organizational culture on performance.

More recently, researchers have pointed out that performance has been primarily examined in terms of financial and economic factors while neglecting other important aspects of it, such as employee satisfaction and customer or suppliers' demands. The examination of organizational performance solely on the basis of financial and economic indices shows a short-term orientation, which inevitably has a detrimental effect on overall performance. A stakeholder perspective in studying organizational life advocates in favour of considering various social groups that coact within the organization, as well as those social groups outside the organization that interact with organizational members, as important factors in determining the link between organizational culture and performance.

The strong culture hypothesis

The strong culture hypothesis proposes that appropriate cultural traits enhance organizational performance in proportion to the strength of their manifestation (Calori & Sarnin, 1991; Deal & Kennedy, 1982; Denison, 1990;

Denison & Mishra, 1995; Denison, Haaland, & Goelzer, 2004; Gordon & DiTomaso, 1992; Smart & John, 1996; Sorensen, 2002; Wiener, 1988). In other words, organizational culture has a more profound influence on organizational outcomes when the organization has a strong culture.

However, culture strength has been defined in many different ways; strong cultures are considered to be homogeneous, widely shared, greatly enforced, cohesive or fully articulated. Therefore, it seems that culture strength is a multidimensional construct consisting of a number of elements, which should be taken into account when we examine the relation between culture strength and performance.

Saffold (1988) has argued that the strength of culture has not been defined precisely in the research literature and suggested that the study of high-performance cultures might be advanced if one takes into account the following measures of culture's impact:

- *Cultural dispersion* is defined by the degree to which cultural characteristics are dispersed throughout an organization.
- *Sociological penetration* is the degree to which cultural manifestations are shared across different groups or subcultures within the organization.
- *Psychological penetration* occurs when members of the organization or subculture deeply internalise the values, meanings and assumptions of the cultural paradigm. Members strongly bonded to the culture are 'patriots' who will exert considerable effort to further the organization's goals.
- *Historical penetration* develops when a particular cultural paradigm remains stable over a long period of time.
- *Artefactual penetration* occurs when intangible elements of the cultural paradigm become embodied in visible cultural artefacts.

Moreover, we can assess the power of the cultural paradigm itself to act as an influence on behaviour by using the following measures of cultural potency:

- *Elemental coherence* is the degree to which elements of the cultural paradigm are mutually coherent. Does the organization possess a coherent set of values or are there conflicts? Lack of coherence among elements renders the culture's impact less predictable.
- *Symbolic potency* refers to whether a symbol becomes more potent with age or whether it fades, losing its capacity to communicate and mobilize.
- *Strategic fit* measures the fit of the culture with internal personnel and capabilities, as well as its compatibility with external demands.
- *Alloplasticity* concerns the extent to which a culture is able to incorporate new elements. Alloplastic cultures can adapt rapidly without undue trauma, thus enhancing their performance, whereas more rigid cultures suffer impaired ability to compete.

This may be a useful and analytic description of culture's impact, but the empirical research conducted to examine the culture–performance link has not taken into account all the measures of culture's impact as proposed by Saffold possibly because of the description's complexity.

Culture strength has been operationalized primarily in terms of how intensively and widely organizational culture is shared by organizational members, as well as whether the elements of a given culture are internally consistent. However, research investigating the effect of culture strength on organizational effectiveness might benefit by paying closer attention to Saffold's conceptual advancements. In particular, the notion of sociological penetration can possibly be of great interest since organizational studies on the culture–performance link have been criticized for ignoring the existence of subcultures. Culture strength can be operationalized in terms of consensus among organizational members on core assumptions, values and practices at the level of the whole organization, as well as at the level of various meaningful groups within the organization. Research to date on the culture–performance link has measured culture strength primarily in terms of how widely shared culture is throughout the organization without thus examining the degree of agreement among different organizational groups, which might be the source of various subcultures.

An early theoretical account of the relationship between organizational culture – defined as a value system – and effectiveness has been put forward by Wiener (1988). As a variable, organizational value systems are considered to span a continuum from weak, in which key values are not intensively and widely shared by members, to strong, in which they are. Two measures of value system strength were proposed, namely, an intensity measure and a breadth measure. Intensity reflects the degree to which members agree with the value system as a whole (i.e., the system's intensity), whereas breadth refers to the relative number of members who do not hold the organization's central values (i.e., the extent to which values are shared). Culture orientation is expected to influence organizational effectiveness in proportion to the strength of culture; that is, an appropriate culture orientation accompanied by a strong value system is more likely to contribute to higher levels of effectiveness. He also presented a typology of value systems that can be used to classify organizations on the grounds of (1) focusing on being primarily functional or superior in comparison to other organizations and (2) resulting from tradition or charismatic leadership. An intensively and widely shared organizational value system that focuses on functionality and is rooted in tradition is described as the organizational culture leading to high performance. However, even useful typologies are simplified representations of the complexity of real life, and therefore it seems difficul to fit organizations into the typology described above.

Denison and his associates (Denison, 1990; Denison & Mishra, 1995; Denison et al., 2004) have developed and empirically tested a different model of the cultural traits that are related to effectiveness and performance. They

	Internal integration	External adaptation
Flexibility/change	Involvement	Adaptability
Stability	Consistency	Mission

Figure 7.1   Four organizational culture traits presented by Denison and his colleagues

have introduced four primary traits that one needs to consider when examining the culture–performance link, namely involvement, consistency, adaptability and mission (Figure 7.1). The concept of culture strength is represented in this model by the trait called 'consistency' or 'normative integration'. Consistency refers to the collective definition of behaviours, systems and meanings in an integrated way that requires individual conformity and internalization of organizational values. High consistency provides integration of organizational members and coordination of their actions. However, organizations that appear to be highly cohesive might have to deal with the negative effects of resistance to change and low adaptability.

In a number of case studies conducted by Denison and Mishra the qualitative data supported the hypothesis that consistency is associated with effectiveness. In addition, survey measures of the cultural traits were obtained and compared to a set of effectiveness measures of profitability, quality, sales growth, employee satisfaction and overall effectiveness. The results showed that the cultural trait of consistency was a predictor of organizational effectiveness measured in terms of profitability.

However, in a different study Denison showed that consistency was associated with better short-term performance, whereas it was not related to long-term performance. This was a comparative study in a sample of 34 firms over a five-year period alongside a number of case studies based primarily on historical data. An explanation of this finding offered by Denison was that a strong culture, through implicit coordination, helps to achieve short-term performance, but over the long run such a culture tends to restrict the variety of options available to an organization. Since variety is needed to react to changes in the external environment, a highly consistent, strong culture may inhibit adaptation. Therefore, a strong culture is an asset to an organization in the short term, but over the longer term, particularly when an organization's environment changes rapidly, that consistency can impair an organization's ability to change. New bases for consistency must be continually reformulated in response to changes in the external environment, and these must build on the variety that already exists in the organization.

In a field study of five French companies Calori and Sarnin (1991) examined the relation between strength of corporate culture and economic performance. The results showed that a strong culture defined in terms of homogeneity and intensity was linked with high growth in the short run (a three-year period). They suggested that this finding should be interpreted with caution because the sample firms were single-business companies. Multi-business (diversified) companies might need more heterogeneous cultures to succeed in different businesses. Moreover, the economic performance of the sample companies was examined through a short period of time; short-term economic performance has been shown in the relevant literature to be predicted by culture strength, whereas long-term economic performance is either not related or negatively related to economic performance.

The relation between organizational culture and long-term economic performance was studied in four studies carried out by Kotter and Heskett (1992). They proposed that strong cultures are related to excellent performance since in strong corporate cultures almost all managers share a set of relatively consistent values and methods of doing business, and new employees adopt these values very quickly. Cultural strength is considered to relate to performance through its impact on goal alignment, motivation and control. In an organization with a strong culture, members tend to share goals and coordinate their behaviour towards the same direction. Strong cultures seem to create an unusual level of motivation in employees since shared values and behaviours make people feel good about working for an organization and increase their commitment and loyalty. Finally, strong cultures provide needed structure and controls without having to rely on a stifling formal bureaucracy that can inhibit motivation and innovation.

Kotter and Hesket collected data from 207 firms from 22 different US industries. Six hundred managers working in these firms completed a survey questionnaire, and culture strength indices were constructed for almost all of these firms. Moreover, a number of interviews were conducted with employees from 7 out of the 207 firms, which supported the validity of the strength indices. The findings showed that there was a modest positive relationship between strength of corporate culture and long-term economic performance. Therefore, it seems quite possible that a firm has a strong culture and weak performance or a weak culture and excellent performance. The authors suggest that this finding can be explained by the fact that strong cultures can include dysfunctional elements, as well as functional ones. It is, therefore, necessary that we examine the content of culture in addition to its strength to be able to predict economic performance on the basis of cultural differences.

A strong culture can become arrogant, internally focused, politicized and bureaucratic; in an increasingly competitive and rapidly changing world that kind of culture undermines economic performance. A second interesting question concerning these findings is why some firms with weak cultures are able to perform well. The authors suggest that by closely examining their data set they found that these companies had 'monopolistic market positions', which led to excellent performance.

On similar lines, Smart and John (1996) showed that the interaction of culture type and culture strength was predictive of the differential performance of four-year American colleges and universities. They examined the relation of dominant culture type and culture strength on organizational effectiveness. Following Quinn's (1988) competing values model, four culture types were identified – namely, human relations (supportive) culture, open systems (innovative) culture, bureaucratic (rules) culture and market (goal-oriented) culture. Culture strength was defined as the degree of congruence between espoused values and beliefs, and organizational practices. The findings showed that culture type had a main effect on effectiveness suggesting that culture type is predictive of organizational performance. However, the interaction of culture type and culture strength was also significant. Further analysis of the interaction effect showed that the differences among the strong culture types were more pronounced than among the weak culture types. Supportive and innovative cultures were related to higher performance in comparison to market culture, which in turn was related to higher performance compared to bureaucratic cultures. For weak cultures these findings were in the same direction but less profound.

The relationship of culture strength and cultural values with organizational performance was also investigated by Gordon and DiTomaso (1992), who operationalized culture strength as the consistency of responses to survey items across participants. Their results showed that both a strong culture regardless of content and a substantive value placed on adaptability were associated with better corporate performance in the insurance industry. They noted that the explanation of how consistency alone enhances performance is not clear. A possible explanation they offered is that management has a common orientation in various situations given that they have a consistent perception of company's behaviour. An organization where individual managers act according to their own preferences rather than a widely accepted pattern may suffer both from missing important opportunities and from failing to develop selected opportunities in an orchestrated, powerful manner. However, even though it is important that organizational culture ensures alignment of values and processes, this may possibly reduce organizational creativity and innovation, which, in turn, are necessary factors for organizational success.

Finally, Sorensen (2002) studied the relationship between the strength of corporate culture, organizational learning processes and performance reliability in a sample of large, publicly held firms. The findings showed that strong cultures in general led to reductions in performance variability, which is

Table 7.1   Summary findings on the relation between culture strength and organizational performance

Findings	Studies
Strength of culture is positively related to short-term performance	Calori and Sarnin (1991) Denison (1990)
Strength of culture is positively related to long-term performance	Kotter and Heskett (1992)
Strength of culture interacts with culture type to predict performance	Kotter and Heskett (1992) Smart and John (1996)
Strength of culture and adaptability to external environment are predictors of performance	Gordon and DiTomaso (1992) Sorensen (2002)

beneficial to organizational functioning. However, the results also demonstrated that strong-culture firms have more reliable performance in relatively stable environments, whereas the reliability benefits of strong cultures disappeared in volatile environments.

Thus, it is a sound finding that culture strength is associated with short-term economic performance. This finding has been interpreted as an indication that cohesiveness and homogeneity among organizational members are conducive to smooth and coordinated organizational functioning, and promote higher levels of motivation and effort expenditure. However, group homogeneity can possibly have negative effects on effectiveness in the longer run because it can lead to low adaptability and resistance to necessary changes (see Table 7.1). Research needs to pay more attention to the conceptualization and operationalization of culture strength as it can be a potentially rich source of new directions in the study of culture–performance link.

Dimensions of culture related to performance

The proposition that strong cultures contribute to organizational effectiveness is closely related to whether there are certain cultural dimensions that account for improvements in performance. Research on the culture–performance link has shown that both culture strength, as well as culture content, affect organizational performance. There are also research findings that demonstrate a joint effect of culture strength and culture orientation on organizational effectiveness; that is, culture profiles have a stronger effect on effectiveness under the condition of high culture strength (Gordon & DiTomaso, 1992; Smart & John, 1996). Before examining the empirical work conducted on the cultural profiles that enhance organizational performance, some early and mainly theoretical, models of the culture–performance link are presented.

Some early models

Wilkins and Ouchi (1983) were among the first theorists who explored the relationship between culture and organizational performance in depth. They proposed the notion of a 'clan culture' that was defined as a distinct or idiosyncratic culture of an organization. The development of a clan culture was considered as rather infrequent because it requires long history and stable membership, absence of institutional alternatives and intensive attraction among organizational members. Organizational members come to share a rather complex understanding of their world, which is largely taken for granted and which they label with a special language. Because these socially acquired understandings are largely assumed, the patterned language and activities of such a community are 'thick' with meaning.

Besides the clan culture Wilkins and Ouchi suggested that there are two other forms of organizational governance, the 'market' and the 'bureaucracy'. Organization, or cooperative action, necessarily involves interdependent exchange between individuals in which each party gives something of value (e.g. labour) and receives something in return (e.g. money). How can a perception of equity be achieved among self-interested parties who are rational? A market form of governance resolves this social problem with a price mechanism in competitive situations. Contracts are made between parties who, because of competition, will offer a 'fair' price and fulfil their commitments. Bureaucracy deals with the social problem of governing transactions by providing employees with wages in exchange for submitting to supervision. The clan addresses the social problem of exchange quite differently; by socializing parties to the exchange in such a way that, though self-interested, they see their objectives in the exchange as being congruent and not mutually exclusive. The use of the term 'goal congruence' is intended to convey the idea that clan members tend to believe that in the long run they will be dealt with equitably. If members of the organization believe that others would intentionally attempt to seek personal ends, at the expense of the collective good, then cooperation and tolerance of short-run inequities would disappear. This belief changes the assumption that joint effort is the best way to achieve individual self-interest.

As far as the relation between organizational culture and efficiency is concerned, Wilkins and Ouchi (1983) proposed that the clan will be more efficient under conditions of ambiguity, complexity and interdependence of transactions. Bureaucratic or market forms will be more efficient than clan forms where the level of complexity or uncertainty is relatively low or moderate.

However, one can argue back that since clan culture is an idiosyncratic culture resulting from stable membership, long history and intensive attraction among group members, it may be prone to groupthink and therefore inhibit efficient operation under complex and ambiguous conditions. A clan culture seems to imply the lack of diversity among organizational members, which may be a source of low creativity and adaptability to a changing environment.

In an early approach to culture and productivity, Akin and Hoplain (1986) suggested a 'culture of productivity' that consists of employees' perceptions of the workplace conditions that are conducive to productivity. In this perspective culture does not cause productivity but rather consists of the fundamental structures and processes perceived by employees to constitute productivity. Akin and Hopelain by using ethnography found that the culture of productivity has five elements:

1. *Types of people* refer to the worker characteristics considered necessary to do the job well, such as willingness to work hard and identification with the job.

2. *Teamwork* is essential to productivity and in particular, effective teamwork results from strong team identity, trust and support among team members, and status determined by knowledge of the job and performance.

3. *Work structure* involves a sound understanding of the skills required to accomplish the job, autonomy in choosing the activities and skills necessary to complete a job; productive workers see themselves as 'designing the job' rather than just performing a routine.

4. The *person in charge* is not necessarily the person employees formally report to, but rather the person for whom people are willing to work hard. The 'person in charge' supports accomplishment and mediates the relationship between workgroup members and the management or customers.

5. *The management* conveys two fundamental messages: a clearly expressed desire for productivity and support for the accomplishment of organizational objectives.

Aiken and Hopelain's approach to culture and effectiveness has narrowly defined effectiveness in terms of productivity, neglecting the role of employee satisfaction in making an organization function properly and successfully. They seem to underestimate the importance of human relations and individualized consideration for running a high-performance organization as they focus on job design, skills and achievement.

In an influential paper, Barney (1986) suggested that under a relatively narrow set of conditions a firm's culture is a source of sustained competitive advantage. This set of conditions are the following: first, the culture must enable the corporation to do things and behave in ways that lead to high sales, low costs, or in other ways add financial value to the firm; second, the culture must have attributes that are not common to the cultures of a large number of other companies; and third, such a culture must be imperfectly imitable. Overall, a culture that adds economic value to the corporation and at the same time is rare and difficult to imitate is expected to be a source of competitive advantage. A corporation that has a valuable, rare and imperfectly imitable culture enjoys a sustained competitive advantage that reflects its culture. Such a corporation obtains positive financial results; few other corporations will be in a position to obtain these same benefits, while those corporations that do not enjoy them cannot engage in activities that will make it possible to obtain them.

Barney notes that a change in the economic or competitive conditions can lead a valuable culture to become an economic liability. Moreover, it is possible that several companies in an industry can obtain sustained superior financial performance based on different competitive advantages resulting from different cultural attributes. But it is not possible for a large number of firms to obtain such performance on the basis of a single type of organizational culture. If a large number of corporations were instructed in how to modify their cultures to obtain economically valuable attributes, then culture would cease to give any one corporation a competitive advantage. A corporation's culture can hold promise for sustained financial performance for some companies precisely because culture is difficult to describe and to change.

Finally, a theoretical model of organizational value systems and effectiveness was presented by Wiener (1988). In this model a typology of value systems based on two value dimensions, namely, the focus and the source of values, is articulated. Any given value can be assessed, in terms of the focus of its content, as primarily functional or elitist. 'Functional values' concern the mode of conduct of organizational members, focusing in particular on goals, functions and style of operations. They deal with issues such as product quality, customer service, or innovation. 'Elitist' refers to values concerning the status, superiority and importance of the organization itself, particularly in relation to other institutions. Thus, elitist values are comparative in nature, reflecting a kind of corporate nationalism: we are the best.

As far as the source of values is concerned, any given core organizational value can be derived primarily from organizational tradition or charismatic leadership. When values are rooted in tradition, similar values are transmitted from one generation of organizational membership to the next. Such values are relatively independent of the potential influence of individuals or situations. Traditional values are more likely to lend stability and predictability to organizational functioning. When values are anchored in a charismatic leader, their internalization by members is determined to a great extent by members' personal identification with the leader. Such values potentially are less stable and permanent than traditional ones.

Value systems that are classified both as functional and traditional are most likely to contribute to the development of proper values and, consequently, to organizational effectiveness. This value system is considered more likely to encourage two elements that are necessary for the effective setting of corporate polices and strategies: (1) broad organizational participation embedded in the realities of day-to-day business conduct and (2) patient, hard-to-copy, step-by-step changes rather than trendy strategic leaps. Largely functional and traditionally rooted values, such as the importance of quality, cooperation, effort, shared obligations and loyalty, seem very likely, under most conditions, to contribute to organizational effectiveness. An elitist and charismatic value system is least likely to result in long-term organizational success. This organizational value system is likely to produce group dynamics that are highly susceptible to groupthink, with the illusion of invulnerability and self-rightfulness. The functional-charismatic value system has the potential to produce effective organizational outcomes. Consistent with the temporary character of charismatic value systems in general, a functional-charismatic system would tend to be a transitional phase, ultimately involving into a functional-traditional one. Finally, the elitist-traditional value system sustains a stable, long-term, elitist dimension. When organizations perpetuate an elitist, club-like value system, they do so to serve specific organizational purposes such as satisfying the needs of customers.

The early approaches to the culture–performance link were either theoretical or based solely on qualitative research methodologies. These approaches explored a set of cultural themes and their association with effectiveness, such as cooperation, goal congruence, teamwork, trust and support, task achievement, organizational objectives, goal orientation and innovation. Following these early models of culture–performance link, a considerable number of comparative studies more systematically investigated the relation between organizational culture and effectiveness.

Denison's theory of organizational culture and effectiveness

Denison and his colleagues (Denison, 1984, 1990; Denison & Mishra, 1995; Denison et al., 2004; Fey & Denison, 2003) have provided the most systematic investigation of the culture–performance link to date. They have constructed and tested a theory comprising of four cultural traits that are positively related to organizational effectiveness. According to this model, high levels of involvement and consistency appear to characterize effective organizations. High involvement creates a sense of ownership and responsibility. Out of this ownership grows a greater commitment to the organization and a growing capacity to operate under conditions of autonomy. Increasing the input of organizational members is also seen as increasing the quality of decisions and their implementation. However, the model suggests that involvement can lapse into insularity and have a limited, or even negative, impact on effectiveness.

The second cultural trait identified by Denison and his colleagues as a predictor of organizational effectiveness is 'consistency' or 'normative integration'. Consistency, as already explained in a previous section of this chapter, concerns the collective definition of behaviours and meanings in an integrated way by the members of a given organization. The cultural trait of consistency provides coordination of organizational members' actions, as well as group cohesiveness. But, it is also possible that highly cohesive organizations find adapting to new environmental challenges a very difficult task.

Involvement and consistency take as their primary focus the 'internal integration' of the organization. These two concepts alone cannot capture the relation between culture and organizational effectiveness because culture is one of the primary means an organization is linked to its environment. Cases in which cultural integration becomes detached from the external environment often develop into insular bureaucracies and fail to be adaptable. Therefore, the third cultural trait related to effectiveness is 'adaptability' or the capacity for internal change in response to external conditions. The adaptability hypothesis proposes that an effective organization should develop values and norms that support its ability to receive signals from its environment and translate these into internal cognitive, behavioural and structural changes.

Finally, the 'mission' of an organization is the fourth cultural trait associated with effectiveness. The mission principle was based on the observation that several organizations were effective because they pursued a mission combining economic and noneconomic objectives, which provided meaning and direction to organizational members. The mission principle differs from the adaptability principle in that it emphasizes the stability of an organization's main goal and de-emphasizes its capacity for adaptability and change.

The four traits are organized into a framework based on two contrasts: that between internal integration and external adaptation, and that between change and stability (Figure 7.1). Involvement and consistency have as their focus the dynamics of internal integration, whereas mission and adaptability address the dynamics of external adaptation. The framework recognizes the inherent interdependence and contradiction of these traits. In line with Quinn's (1988) propositions, it is acknowledged that the balancing of competing demands distinguishes excellent managers and organizations from their more mediocre counterparts.

Denison (1990) and Denison and Mishra (1995) provided empirical evidence supporting their model's main theoretical propositions. Denison examined the relation between the four cultural traits and effectiveness by carrying out a comparative study in a sample of 34 firms over a five-year period and a number of case studies. The comparative study showed that involvement and participation contributed to organizational effectiveness. More specifically, it was found that companies with high levels of participation in decision-making were better performers over the longer run, even though they did not show high performance initially. On the other hand, a measure of involvement concerned with the emphasis on human resources is a better predictor of short-term performance rather than long-term performance. The findings on consistency showed that consistency was a predictor of short-term rather than long-term performance.

As far as adaptability is concerned, the evidence provided by Denison (1990) that adaptability affects performance is limited. The findings showed that internal flexibility as an aspect of adaptability is positively related to organizational effectiveness. However, this study did not provide data on the link between effectiveness and another important aspect of adaptability, namely, an organization's capability to perceive the changing conditions in the external environment and translate them into internal changes. Perhaps there is a curvilinear relation between effectiveness and adaptation to changing environmental conditions – that is, moderate levels of adaptability to environmental changes are the best predictors of effectiveness. Finally, the data showed that there was a positive impact of organizational mission on effectiveness. A clear vision seems to offer a strong sense of direction to organizational members, which in turn contributes to higher performance. In other words, important ideals can serve to tie an organization together in a way that is highly functional.

Denison and Mishra (1995) conducted another study examining the linkage between the four cultural traits and effectiveness. The authors presented a number of case studies where the qualitative data supported the four cultural hypotheses. In addition, survey measures of the four traits were obtained, which were correlated with profitability, quality, sales growth, employee satisfaction and overall effectiveness. The findings indicated that each of the four cultural traits was significantly associated with a wide range of both subjective and objective measures of organizational effectiveness. In particular, the stability traits of mission and consistency were useful predictors of profitability, while the flexibility traits of involvement and adaptability were more potent predictors of growth. However, it should be noted that the correlations between the four cultural traits and the objective criteria were size dependent (the correlations were significant in the case of large organizations but not of small ones), but the correlations between the four traits and subjective criteria were not size dependent. They interpret these differences in two alternative ways:

1. Culture and effectiveness are more closely linked in larger firms as the coordinating effects of culture are more important in larger and more complex systems.
2. The subjective measures of effectiveness are better suited for the comparison of a disparate set of firms than are the objective measures.

The four traits of organizational culture were expanded to include three subdimensions for each trait, for a total of 12 dimensions (Denison et al., 2004; Fey & Denison, 2003; Table 7.2). Involvement comprises of empowerment, team orientation and capability development; consistency comprises of core values, coordination/integration and agreement; adaptability contains customer focus, creating change and organizational learning; and finally, mission comprises of strategic direction/intent, goals and objectives and vision. They examined whether there are cross-cultural differences in the relationship between organizational culture and effectiveness. Denison et al. found that the link between organizational culture and effectiveness appears to follow a very similar pattern across major regions of the world including Asia, Europe/Middle East/Africa and North America, while Fey and Denison showed the validity of the model in predicting organizational effectiveness in the Russian national context. The cultural factors identified by the model distinguished effective and ineffective organizations in all the regions of the world they examined. However, they suggest that even though these results support that the identified cultural traits are linked to effectiveness it is probable that these traits have different meanings and

Table 7.2   Organizational culture traits and their subdimensions as modelled by Denison and his colleagues

Organizational culture traits	Trait subdimensions	
Involvement	1.	Empowerment
	2.	Team orientation
	3.	Capability development
Consistency	1.	Core values
	2.	Coordination/integration
	3.	Agreement
Adaptability	1.	Customer focus
	2.	Creating change
	3.	Organizational learning
Mission	1.	Strategic direction/intent
	2.	Goals and objectives
	3.	Vision

are expressed in different ways in various national contexts. Finally, the mission, involvement and adaptability traits were found to be significantly correlated with organizational performance in Hong Kong (Chan, Shaffer, & Snape, 2004).

The theory of Denison and his colleagues can be criticized on methodological grounds and, in particular, on the lack of validation for the measurement of organizational culture. In accordance with all empirical studies on the culture–performance link to date (Wilderom, Glunk, & Maslowski, 2000), Denison and his colleagues have not put a lot of effort into validating the measurement of the four cultural traits. Since organizational culture has not been precisely defined and there is not a widely accepted measurement of the organizational culture concept (actually some would argue that culture cannot be measured at all), it is essential that researchers provide validation data for the measures that they are using. Another point of criticism can be raised with regard to the nature of the cultural trait of consistency. The theory suggests that consistency refers to the shared cognitions among organizational members, as well as the coordinated action resulting from these widely shared meanings. One has to note thus that consistency is considered to result from internalization of organizational values and conformity to social norms. However, treating the mechanisms of internalization of values and conformity interchangeably can be rather obscuring when one attempts to unravel the relation between culture and performance. Finally, the effect of each of the four cultural traits on effectiveness has been examined independently, whereas there are theoretical reasons to believe that an interplay between the cultural traits takes place. For example, Denison has suggested that the positive effect of an organization's mission on effectiveness can possibly be explained by important ideals binding an organization together – that is, creating consistency, in a way that is highly functional.

In sum, the theory of organizational culture and effectiveness put forward by Denison and his colleagues identifies four cultural traits that are related to organizational performance. These four cultural traits concern employees' involvement and participation in decisions affecting their job, consistency and integration of organizational members, adaptability to changes in business environments and organizational mission comprising of strategy, objectives and vision. The relation of these cultural dimensions to organizational performance has been empirically demonstrated in a number of studies involving a large sample of organizations from different industry sectors and regions of the world.

The centrality of humanistic and achievement orientations

The empirical work on the culture–performance link has employed a great variety of theoretical models concerning the dimensions of organizational culture, which makes it difficult to directly compare the existing findings and conclude on whether there are specific cultural dimensions that have been shown to affect effectiveness. Yet a thorough study of the theoretical models and the empirical findings can lead one to argue that there are a number of culture themes that are constantly found to be related to organizational effectiveness. We shall first review the models and the research findings and then make an attempt to integrate them in order to identify the recurring themes of culture that have been shown to relate to effectiveness.

Cooke and Rousseau (1988) presented a circumplex model depicting the dimensions of organizational culture and their relation to effectiveness (see Chapter 5). They suggested that efficient organizations are characterized by constructive organizational norms that promote achievement, self-actualization and development, empowerment, creativity, risk-taking, participation in decision-making, constructive interpersonal relations and social support. On the other hand, inefficient organizations cultivate normative beliefs that encourage seeking of approval and avoidance of conflict, sticking to rules and procedures (conventionality), conformity, nonparticipative decision-making (dependence), avoidance of failure, deconstructive criticism, hierarchical power, competition and perfectionism. Rousseau (1990) investigated whether group norms – that is, beliefs regarding appropriate and inappropriate behaviour in a social setting – are related to organizational performance in 32 charity organizations. The results showed that fund-raising performance was negatively related to group norms putting emphasis on conventionality, approval and dependence. Moreover, there were positive but nonsignificant correlations between achievement, self-actualization, participation and social support, and constructive interpersonal relations on the one hand, and success in fund-raising performance on the other. Constructive cultural norms were also shown to be positively associated with individual, as well as organizational, performance drivers such as job satisfaction, quality of products, and quality of customer service (Balthazard, Cooke, & Potter, 2006).

Petty, Beadles, Lowery, Chapman, & Connell (1995) studying 12 service units of a firm in the electric utility industry found an organizational culture that emphasizes teamwork to be more conducive to organizational effectiveness compared to a culture that does not promote cooperation. Cooperative behaviours such as sharing information/resources, helping others with their work, seeking ways to help the work group meet its goals, making sacrifices for the good of the group, and being rewarded for working as a team were shown to influence organizational performance. On similar lines, Nahm, Vonderembse, & Koufteros (2004) found that a customer orientation led to a set of managerial beliefs that are collaborative and integrating, which, in turn, support time-based manufacturing practice and high performance. The importance of the cultural element of cooperation for firm performance was highlighted by Van Dyck, Frese, Baer, & Sonnentag's (2005) finding that an error management culture is conducive to performance – that is, communicating about errors, sharing error knowledge and helping in error situations were shown to be related to objective indicators of firm performance such as return on assets and firm goal achievement.

As already mentioned, Smart and John (1996) studied organizational culture and effectiveness in American colleges and universities and found that there was a main effect of culture type on organizational performance, as well as a significant interaction between culture type and culture strength. Supportive and innovative strong cultures were related to higher performance in comparison with market (goal-oriented) culture, which in turn was related to higher performance compared with bureaucratic culture. Similarly, Hartnell, Ou, and Kinicki (2011) in a meta-analysis of the relation between culture types and organizational effectiveness found that supportive (clan) cultures were more strongly associated with product and service quality, as well as positive employee attitudes, compared with market and innovation (adhocracy) cultures. On the other hand, they found that market cultures had a significantly stronger relation with financial effectiveness criteria and innovation in comparison with supportive and innovative cultures. In another study, Berson, Oreg, & Dvir (2008) showed that CEO values were indirectly related to firm's performance via organizational culture. More specifically, they found that CEO values of self-direction, benevolence and security were related to sales growth, employee satisfaction and organizational efficiency via innovation, supportive and bureaucratic cultures.

An exploratory model concerning how an organization's culture visible aspects, such as organizational structure/purpose, task organization, organizational values, climate, and worker attitudes and goals, may affect organizational performance was put forward by Marcoulides and Heck (1993). Their results showed that all the variables included as comprising organizational culture had a direct or indirect effect on the level of organizational performance. Task organization was shown to have a strong direct effect on performance. The most important contributors to task organization were personnel selection methods, the quality of methods used to evaluate employee performance, and the criteria and practices for remuneration. Of secondary importance to performance outcomes were decision-making practices, mentoring and providing opportunities for interesting and challenging work. Therefore, these results are supportive of the importance of recruiting, evaluating and compensating employees to enhance performance. Moreover, organizational values such as risk-taking, safety in the workplace, productivity and efficiency, rapid response to market opportunities, and the creation of new outputs were shown to strongly predict the attitudes of employees, which in turn had a direct effect on organizational performance.

Huselid, Jackson, and Schuler (1997) examined whether human resource management (HRM) activities were associated with organizational performance. They distinguished between technical HRM activities, such as, recruiting, selection, performance appraisal, training and the administration of compensation and benefits, and strategic HRM activities, such as, empowerment, team-based designs and development of talent for the long term. The findings showed that strategic HRM effectiveness was significantly associated with firm performance, but technical HRM effectiveness was not associated with firm performance. The fact that technical HPM activities were shown not to be related to performance was explained as an indication that technical HRM activities are widespread employed and therefore cannot be a source of competitive advantage.

Finally, the joint effect of transformational leadership and organizational culture on performance was investigated by Xenikou and Simosi (2006). The results showed that the achievement and adaptability culture orientations directly predicted organizational performance. On the other hand, a humanistic culture orientation has an indirect positive impact on performance via achievement orientation.

The review of the previously presented literature (Table 7.3) has revealed that two general cultural themes have been identified and empirically tested as predictors of organizational effectiveness. The first of these traits concerns a 'humanistic orientation' and it reflects the 'human relations movement' in the workplace. Humanistic orientation is characterized by cooperation among organizational members, emphasis put on teamwork, employees' self-actualization and empowerment, development of people's creative potential, participation in decision-making, constructive interpersonal relations and social support. The second cultural trait concerns an 'achievement orientation' and involves assumptions, values and practices on task organization, goal setting, organizational objectives, experimentation, and an emphasis put on organizational efficiency. Finally, there is research on the culture–performance link that has put emphasis on a set of contingency factors that moderate

Table 7.3   Studies in culture–performance link and their results on the relation between organizational culture dimensions and performance

	Dimensions of organizational culture related to performance		
Study	Positively related	Negatively related	Not related
Rousseau (1990)	1. Achievement 2. Self-actualization 3. Participation 4. Constructive interpersonal relations*	1. Conventionality 2. Approval 3. Dependence	
Petty et al. (1995)	1. Teamwork 2. Cooperation		
Marcoulides and Heck (1993)	1. Task organization 2. Decision-making practices 3. Mentoring 4. Opportunities for challenging work		
Smart and John (1996)	1. Supportive orientation 2. Innovative orientation 3. Goal orientation	1. Bureaucratic orientation	
Huselid et al. (1997)	Strategic HRM activities: 1. Empowerment 2. Team-based deigns 3. Individual development		Technical HRM activities: 1. Recruiting 2. Selection 3. Performance appraisal 4. Training 5. Rewards system
Nahm et al. (2004)	1. Customer orientation 2. Collaborative beliefs 3. Time-based manufacturing practice		
Van Dyck et al. (2005)	1. Error management culture		
Balthazard et al. (2006)	1. Achievement 2. Self-actualization 3. Participation 4. Constructive interpersonal relations		

Xenikou and Simosi (2006)	1. Achievement
	2. Adaptability
Berson et al. (2008)	1. Supportive
	2. Innovation
	3. Bureaucratic
Hartnell et al. (2011)	1. Supportive orientation
	2. Innovative orientation
	3. Goal orientation

*The correlations between achievement, self-actualization, participation and constructive interpersonal relations and performance were positive but nonsignificant.

the relation between culture traits and effectiveness. This literature, which is presented in the following section of the chapter, has identified a third cultural theme as an important predictor of organizational performance, namely adaptability.

The contingency approach to the culture–performance link

There are organizational culture researchers who have questioned whether cultural dimensions are conducive to effectiveness irrespective of other organizational factors and conditions in the business environment. A contingency approach to the relation between culture and organizational effectiveness has identified variables such as competitive environment, strategy and diversity of a business portfolio as moderators of the culture–performance link (Calori & Sarnin, 1991; Chow & Liu, 2009; Gordon, 1985, 1991; Gordon & DiTomaso, 1992; Kotter & Heskett, 1992; Panayotopoulou, Bourantas, & Papalexandris, 2003; Schwartz & Davis, 1981).

Kotter and Heskett (1992) put forward the so-called 'performance question': what kind of corporate cultures enhance long-term economic performance? From their perspective the content of a culture is as important, if not more important, as its strength. Further, they suggested that there is not a generically good cultural content and that a culture contributes to performance when there is a good fit between an organization's culture and its external environment. To test this perspective they selected a group of 22 companies from an original sample of 207. All companies had relatively strong cultures – in terms of shared values that are consistent with organizational practices – but 12 of them significantly outperformed the other matched group of ten. Seventy-five industry analysts were asked to rate on a seven-point scale the degree to which the culture of an organization fits its environment (7 = superb fit, 1 = terrible fit). The results showed that the higher-performing organizations received higher scores on the culture–environment fit in comparison with the lower performers.

In addition, interviews with current and former managers of four organizations included in the sample, as well as interviews with managers who did not work for any of those organizations, uncovered little disagreement with the ratings of the industry analysts.

They further analysed the interview data to examine whether a changing environment can undermine a good fit, resulting in low long-term economic performance. They found that the theme of tougher competition helping to create culture/environment mismatches is pervasive in the case of the lower performing organizations. On the other hand, the better performers successfully adapted to changes in the external environment, despite having reasonably strong cultures.

Therefore, the content of a given culture and in particular the culture–environment fit is associated with performance in a relatively stable external environment. However, the culture–environment fit cannot explain differential success at adapting to external changes and, by implication, differences in long-term performance. Kotter and Heskett argue that only cultures which help an organization to anticipate and adapt to external changes contribute to superior performance over long periods of time. By analysing the interviews of executives and employees of twenty-two companies from their original sample, they found that in organizations with more adaptive cultures, the cultural ideal is that managers throughout the hierarchy should provide leadership to initiate change in strategies and tactics whenever necessary to satisfy the legitimate interests of customers, employees and stockholders. Kotter and Heskett's notion of an adaptive culture is similar to the cultural trait of adaptability suggested by Denison and Mishra (1995), as well as Quinn's (1988) open systems model or innovation orientation.

Gordon (1985, 1991) suggested that different industries have developed distinct cultural patterns to suit their business demands. The characteristics of the industry and the marketplace define the broad outlines of an appropriate culture. Gordon (1985) examined the top management perceptions of how their companies operate and found that high-performing utilities (i.e., electric, gas and local telephone companies) held different cultural profiles from that of high-performing dynamic-market companies (i.e., manufacturers of high technology products). Successful utilities were oriented towards a high degree of interdependence – that is, (1) units were encouraged to operate in a coordinated manner and (2) upper management offered clear communication and support to employees. In addition, high-performing utilities promoted openness in dealing with conflicts and criticisms, clarity of performance expectations, and concern for the development of people. The most dominant value of the high-performing dynamic-marketplace companies was a drive to make the company bigger and different than it was previously. This tendency is reinforced at the individual level by emphasizing individual initiative, an open environment to its dealing with the marketplace and a bias towards action.

Gordon and DiTomaso (1992) assessed culture strength and the cultural values of adaptability and stability in 11 insurance companies by using a survey measure. They found that culture strength and adaptability were both predictive of performance in the insurance industry. In discussing these findings they put forward a contingency model of organizational culture and performance by suggesting that a combination of strong culture and culture appropriate for an industry is most powerful in predicting effectiveness. Similarly, Lee and Yu (2004) found that organizational culture was associated with performance among Singaporean companies and that there are industry dynamic attributes that characterize different industry sectors; for example, insurance companies were significantly more task oriented, manufacturing firms were more humanistic and hospitals were more team oriented.

Another set of contingency factors were proposed and tested in an exploratory field study by Calori and Sarnin (1991). The factors that they took into account when examining the culture–performance link were as follows:

- The diversity of the company's business portfolio (i.e., single business, related businesses and unrelated businesses).

- The competitive characteristics of the industries in which the company is involved (e.g., dynamic–turbulent industries versus mature–stable industries).

- The generic competitive strategy (e.g., differentiation versus low-cost strategy). Their sample consisted of five French companies with a single business involved in mature industries pursuing a differentiation strategy

The results showed that a company's growth performance was associated with a clear cultural profile consisting of the following values: personal fulfilment, listening to others, team spirit, responsibility, trust, openness to environment, adaptation, entrepreneurship, quality and consistency. On the other hand, very few values were related to profitability (i.e., openness to environment, participation in local activities and societal contribution). However, Calori and Sarnin's study suffers from methodological pitfalls – as their sample did not, for example, include companies from dynamic business environments or with low-cost strategies – and therefore their findings are questionable.

Finally, Panayotopoulou et al. (2003) explored the relationship between HRM orientation defined in terms of Quinn's competing values framework and organizational performance. They tested the moderating effects of business environment characteristics and competitive strategy on the link between HRM orientation and performance. The findings showed that in the dynamic business environment higher performance was positively related to the human relations and internal process models, and negatively related to HRM control. Therefore, the need for cooperation, communication and group commitment seem to increase in the case of rapid changes. The results also showed that the interaction between HRM orientation and corporate strategy was of great importance to achieve good external fit. Higher organizational performance was achieved either by combining a flexible HRM orientation with a differentiation strategy (e.g., by introducing novel products) or a control HRM orientation with a cost leadership strategy (i.e., emphasis on cost reduction). More recently, additional international research on the culture–performance link has demonstrated that matching human resource systems with organizational culture (Ngo & Loi, 2008), as well as business strategy (Chow & Liu, 2009) promotes organizational performance.

The contingency approach to the organizational culture–performance link has argued that organizational performance is a function of the fit between organizational culture and industry/organizational characteristics, such as competitive environment, corporate strategy and diversity of business portfolio (Table 7.4). Kotter and Heskett (1992) proposed that a good fit between an organization's culture and its environment is conducive to economic performance. Moreover, Gordon (1985, 1991) advocated that differences in the competitive environment – that is, stable versus dynamic marketplaces – affect which cultural traits are related to organizational efficiency. Organizations in dynamic business environments characterized by a culture that focuses on open communication with the marketplace, individual initiative and bias towards action are high-performance systems. On the other hand, stable marketplaces ask more for a culture of coordination and interdependence, concern for employees, clarity of performance expectations and openness in dealing with conflicts and criticisms.

One thus has to notice that there is a distinction between the notions of organization–environment fit and adaptability, which is particularly useful in examining the culture–performance link. A good organization–environment fit implies that an organization's culture is appropriate, and by implication functional, for the business environment in which the organization is situated. For example, in dynamic and fast-changing business environments a culture of risk-taking, experimentation and openness to environmental changes is appropriate. On the other hand, adaptability refers to an organization's ability to perceive

Table 7.4   Contingency factors of the culture–performance link identified in the research literature

Contingency factors	Studies
1. Competitive environment	Kotter and Heskett (1992) Gordon (1985, 1991) Gordon and DiTomaso (1992) Lee and Yu (2004) Calori and Sarnin (1991) Panayotopoulou et al. (2003)
2. Strategy	Calori and Sarnin (1991) Panayotopoulou et al. (2003) Chow and Liu (2009)
3. Diversity of business portfolio	Calori and Sarnin (1991)

the changes in the environmental demands, to accommodate its functions and systems to these changes, and to learn from its failures. Therefore, organizations need to pay close attention to culture–environment fit, as well as their culture's capability to change and adapt in accordance with environmental demands.

Person–organization fit and organizational performance

Besides the importance of culture–environment fit for organizational performance, another line of research has focused on the implications that person–organization fit has on organizational efficiency. Person–organization fit is conceptualized in terms of fit between employees' desired organizational cultures and their perception of the organizational culture of the organization they work for (O'Reilly, Chatman, & Caldwell, 1991). Individuals who strongly identify on the basis of value congruence with a collective identity and feel valued are more likely to be an active contributor to the organization.

Wilderom and Van den Berg (1998; as cited in Wilderom et al., 2000) looked into the relationship between average culture gap within organizations and their performances. The findings suggested that the gap between employees' preferred organizational practices and their perceptions of the organizations' practices is negatively related to organizational performance. They argue that organizations instead of striving for strong cultures should attempt to reduce the gap between employees' preferred organizational practices and perceived organizational practices of the organizations they work for. Actually, it has been shown that the socialization tactics employed by organizations can possibly influence employees' perceptions of cultural fit with the organization, organizational commitment and satisfaction (Cooper-Thomas, van Viaven, & Anderson, 2004). However, one should be careful not to differentiate culture gap from the strength of organizational culture, since culture gap can be seen as an element of culture strength (Saffold, 1988).

Moreover, there are findings showing that person–organization fit is associated with employees' task and contextual performance (Goodman & Svyantek, 1999). Task performance includes all the key activities that comprise a formal part of one's job; these activities are prescribed by the formal contract between the organization and the employee. Contextual performance (or organizational citizenship behaviours), on the other hand, involves organizational members' activities that augment organizational effectiveness while not being directly related to their chief task functions and duties. Goodman and Svyantek found that both perceptions of organizational culture and the discrepancy between employees' ideal organizational culture and perceptions of the actual culture were important predictors of contextual and task performance.

According to Sparrow (2001), there are a series of mental, emotional and attitudinal processes through which salient organizational behaviours linked to an effective culture are seen to influence performance. The most important of the mental, emotional and attitudinal states are trust and an effective psychological contract, perceived level of organizational support, fairness and justice, work motivation, job satisfaction and job involvement. Once these mental, emotional and attitudinal states are established in a positive direction, then employees begin to exhibit organization citizenship behaviours that generate effective performance. Research conducted by Coyle-Shapiro, Kessler, and Purcell (2004) showed that perceived organizational justice influenced the manifestation of organizational citizenship behaviours through its effect on mutual commitment – that is, perceptions of organizational support towards the individual employee and organizational commitment expressed as loyalty, identification with the organization and involvement. Finally, Major (2000) in a prescriptive model of organizational culture and effectiveness suggests that high performance is determined by the extent to which organizational expectations of employees, as well as employees' expectation of the organization, are mutually fulfilled.

The conceptualization of person–environment fit in terms of the notion of culture gap has generated research findings showing that organizational effectiveness is related to discrepancies in preferred cultures and perceived cultures. In addition, this line of research has addressed the culture–performance link at the individual or the group level of analysis, rather than the organizational level. Most research on the relation between organizational culture and effectiveness has operationalized effectiveness as financial and economic performance, while neglecting the performance of individual employees or workgroups (see Kopelman, Brief, & Guzzo, 1990 for an exception). Research on person–environment fit comes to fill in this gap by examining organizational citizenship behaviours, as well as task performance.

Some final considerations

Denison (1990) suggests that perhaps the most basic question as far as the relation between organizational culture and effectiveness is concerned, is 'effectiveness for whom?' This fundamental question implies a number of stakeholders who have legitimate interests that may be compatible, opposed or mutually exclusive. Stakeholders include employees, customers, suppliers, stockholders, financial institutions, regulatory agencies, or the general public. According to a stakeholder theory of the corporation (Donaldson & Preston, 1995), the corporation is a constellation of cooperative and competitive interests of various groups, and simultaneous attention should be given to the legitimate interests of all appropriate stakeholders. Siehl and Martin (1990) pointed out that one should consider the perspective of those organizational members, such as lower-level employees, who benefit less fully and directly, if at all, from an improvement in profitability.

Therefore, organizational effectiveness varies for different groups with a stake in the organization and constitutes a multidimensional construct. Organizational effectiveness includes the more conventional performance criteria, namely financial and economic performance, productivity, organizational growth, as well as indicators of work life quality, job satisfaction, customer satisfaction and contributions to the larger society. However, organizational effectiveness is traditionally measured by financial indicators, such as profitability and sales growth. Finally, it is worth noting that although stakeholder theory is primarily concerned with redefining the purpose of an organization as a vehicle for coordinating stakeholder interests, a stakeholder perspective to organizational analysis and management has been suggested to be conducive to economic performance (Donaldson & Preston, 1995).

Another essential issue that should be addressed by future research is the causal direction of the relationship between organizational culture and performance. The empirical findings have shown that there is an association between culture and performance, but there is little evidence to support the argument that organizational culture causes effectiveness and not the other way around. It is equally possible that high levels of organizational performance lead to the manifestation of certain cultural traits such as, support for the employees, risk-taking or experimentation, and group cohesiveness. For example, psychological research has shown that group success leads to higher levels of cohesiveness and attraction towards the group. Therefore, high-performing organizations may grow stronger cultures attracting members to the values and practices of the organization because of its successful course. To determine the causal direction of the culture–performance link, longitudinal research designs should be employed, in which the measurement of organizational culture precedes that of organizational efficiency.

Finally, the culture–performance link can be examined at the individual, as well as the group level of analysis. At the individual level, one can investigate the effect of organizational culture on organizational outcomes such as, individual productivity, job satisfaction, turnover, absenteeism and commitment (Cooke & Rousseau, 1988; Finegan, 2000; Kopelman et al., 1990). At the group level, organizational effectiveness can be operationalized in terms of group productivity, problem solving, quality of decision making or brainstorming and creativity (Turner, 2001). It would be a new and exciting research approach to the culture–performance link to explore the connection between organizational culture and effectiveness in terms of group outcomes such as, group problem solving and generation of innovative ideas.

Summary

The main objectives of this chapter were to examine if organizational culture affects performance and whether there are contingency factors that one should consider when investigating the culture–performance link. In a number of studies it has been demonstrated that culture strength and certain dimensions of culture are associated with effectiveness. In addition, the findings have shown that culture strength and cultural traits have a joint effect on organizational performance– that is, there is a stronger effect of specific culture traits on performance in the case of strong cultures. The review of the relevant literature identified two main dimensions of culture as predictors of effectiveness, namely a humanistic orientation and an achievement orientation. The humanistic orientation consists of cooperation, teamwork, involvement, participation in decisions, individual development, activation of creative potential, social support and constructive social relations. On the other hand, the achievement orientation focuses on values and practices concerning goal setting, task organization, efficiency, organizational objectives and performance feedback.

However, the contingency approach to the culture–performance link has argued that organizational and environmental factors, such as competitive environment and business strategy, should be considered when investigating the effect of cultural traits on effectiveness. Organizations are effective if their culture fits the business environment they are situated in. For example, dynamic and complex environments put more emphasis on innovation and novelty, while in stable and mature environments the quality of product or service is more important. Besides culture–environment fit another important variable is the cultural trait of adaptability. Adaptability refers to an organization's capacity to change in response to marketplace demands and to engage in a productive learning process when responding to these demands.

The vast majority of the empirical studies on the culture–performance link have operationalized organizational effectiveness in terms of financial and economic factors. However, future research might usefully examine effectiveness at the individual and the group level of analysis by looking at the effect of culture profiles on the productivity, problem solving and decision-making of individuals or groups at work. In addition, if ones take a stakeholder approach to organizational analysis it is essential that organizational effectiveness should be treated as a multidimensional construct, which includes the traditional financial and economic elements, as well as indicators of employees' satisfaction and quality of working life. Finally, a promising line of research concerns the concept of person–organization fit as the degree to which personal preferred cultural profiles match the perceived profiles of organizations. Person–organization fit has been shown to affect task performance and organizational citizenship behaviours.

Questions

1. Is there a link between organizational culture and organizational performance?
2. Is a strong culture related to better organizational performance?
3. What specific variables comprise an effective organizational culture?
4. What is the relationship between organizational culture and industry sectors?
5. Do we need a contingency approach to answer the question on the culture–performance link?
6. How can the notions of culture-environment fit and person–organization fit help us understand the relation between culture and effectiveness?

Case study

Understanding excellence in a Higher Education Organization via a culture perspective

AS-SS is a School of Social Sciences situated in a metropolitan city and is part of a large public university that has been operating for over 150 years. The university has many campuses located in different areas of the city, in particular four major campus and several smaller ones. AS-SS occupies a medium-sized campus located in the city centre; it specializes in Social Sciences comprising of different departments, such as the Department of Psychology, Economics and Sociology, covering a wide range of scientific disciplines. A large number of academic members of staff (around 500) and a considerable number of administrative personnel are employed by the school. AS-SS's mission, as communicated to the general public by formal documents and various scientific and educational activities, is to promote excellence in scientific research, education and practice by focusing on its people.

The link between AS-SS and the larger university is more of an official and administrative nature than of substance, since AS-SS is self-managed and totally independent in all aspects of its academic functioning.

Heads of the departments are often seen as consultative, humanistic, communicating frequently and openly with academic and administrative personnel. Decision-making is decentralized, primarily taking place in academic staff meetings, in which a wide spectrum of educational, research and administrative issues are efficiently handled. The divergent, and occasionally contrasting, opinions expressed by individual members of academic staff are respected and thoroughly processed, irrespective of differences in hierarchy. Academic, as well as administrative, personnel are empowered to control how their roles are performed; for example, employees have discretion in how they carry out their duties and handle problems that usually emerge at work.

Organizational members are expected to be supportive in their dealing with one another, the organization is managed in a participative and person-centred way, and an emphasis is put on cooperation and constructive interpersonal relations. AS-SS is characterized by an achievement culture placing a high value on goal setting, the accomplishment of objectives and the pursuit of a standard of excellence. There are, however, organizational rules and procedures that are followed to gain in stability and efficiency. People at AS-SS acknowledge that some degree of formality is at times necessary to deal with challenging and demanding situations.

Leadership in AS-SS focuses on promoting constructive and cooperative relations at work accompanied by goal setting and task accomplishment to gain in organizational excellence. An emphasis on innovation and creativity is reflected in the school's stated mission of doing first line scientific research, as well as offering a highly advanced technological environment to its members – that is, academics, students and administrative personnel. Despite the fact

(cont'd)

that leading people at AS-SS have a realistic vision of what types of culture enhance employee satisfaction and performance, and systematically work towards strengthening these cultural traits, there are tensions between different subcultures aiming at creating a power base for those who cultivate them.

A strong and influential minority of faculty members advocate for strategically reorienting the school to a community focus while putting less emphasis on the importance on the school's image as a research-oriented higher education institution. They argue that social sciences should be primarily concerned with the welfare of ordinary people rather than the advancement of bits and pieces of scientific knowledge of little relevance to the quality of people's lives. Contributions to the society can be channelled by establishing a permanent link between the school and the community as, for example, when opportunities for continuous adult education are given on an open basis and social services activities are organized by the school.

On the other hand, there is a strong culture within the school of academic excellence thought to be accomplished on the grounds of conducting high-rate scientific research published in prestigious international journals, and attracting funds for being able to do so. The tensions and conflicts occurring between the two subcultures are, for instance, well represented in the 'negotiation' of the performance criteria on which promotion and climbing the ladder of hierarchy are based. Should academic members of staff be promoted on the grounds of research output accomplishments or the impact they have made on improving the quality of people's lives? Even though the dilemmatic nature of this question is not a necessity, this is the way most often culture ideologies within the same organizational setting evolve, coexist and occasionally clash.

(1) Describe the cultural orientations that characterize AS-SS. Give examples illustrating the various culture traits that you identify.

(2) Are the culture profiles at AS-SS conducive to organizational performance?

(3) To which extent are the values and behavioural norms promoted within the school widely shared? Do you think that AS-SS's culture is a strong culture?

References

Akin, G., & Hoplain, D. (1986). Finding the culture of productivity. *Organizational Dynamics*, 7, 19–32.

Balthazard, P. A., Cooke, R. A., & Potter, R. E. (2006). Dysfunctional culture, dysfunctional organization: Capturing the behavioural norms that form organizational culture and drive performance. *Journal of Managerial Psychology*, 21, 709–732.

Barney, J. B. (1986). Organizational culture: Can it be a source of sustained competitive advantage? *Academy of Management Review*, 11, 656–665.

Berson, Y., Oreg, S., & Dvir, T. (2008). CEO values, organizational culture, and firm outcomes. *Journal of Organizational Behavior*, 29, 615–633.

Calori, R., & Sarnin, P. (1991). Corporate culture and economic performance: A French study. *Organization Studies*, 12, 49–74.

Chan, L. L. M., Shaffer, M. A., & Snape, E. (2004). In search of sustained competitive advantage: The impact of organizational culture, competitive strategy, and human resource management practices on firm performance. *International Journal of Human Resource Management*, 15, 17–35.

Chow, I. H. S., & Liu, S. S. (2009). The effect of aligning organizational culture and business strategy with HR systems on firm performance in Chinese enterprises. *International Journal of Human Resource Management*, 20, 2292–2310.

Cooke, R. A., & Rousseau, D. M. (1988). Behavioral norms and expectations: A quantitative approach to the assessment of organizational culture. *Group and Organization Studies*, 13, 245–273.

Cooper-Thomas, H. D., van Viaven, A., & Anderson, N. (2004). Changes in person-organization fit: The impact of socialization tactics on perceived and actual P-O fit. *European Journal of Work and Organizational Psychology*, 13, 52–78.

Coyle-Shapiro, J. A-M., Kessler, I., & Purcell, J. (2004). Exploring organizationally directed citizenship behaviour: Reciprocity or 'it's my job'? *Journal of Management Studies*, 41, 83–106.

Deal, T., & Kennedy, A. (1982). *Corporate Cultures: The Rites and Rituals of Corporate Life.* Reading, MA: Addison-Wesley.

Denison, D. R. (1990). *Corporate Culture and Organizational Effectiveness.* New York: Wiley.

Denison, D. R., & Mishra, A. K. (1995). Toward a theory of organizational culture and effectiveness. *Organization Science*, 6, 204–222.

Denison, D. R., Haaland, S., & Goelzer, P. (2004). Corporate culture and organizational effectiveness: Is Asia different from the rest of the world? *Organizational Dynamics*, 33, 98–109.

Donaldson, T., & Preston, L. E. (1995). The stakeholder theory of the corporation: Concepts, evidence, and implications. *Academy of Management Review*, 20, 65–91.

Fey, C. F., & Denison, D. R. (2003). Organizational culture and effectiveness: Can American theory be applied in Russia? *Organization Science*, 14, 686–706.

Finegan, J. E. (2000). The impact of person and organizational values on organizational commitment. *Journal of Occupational and Organizational Psychology*, 73, 149–169.

Goodman, S. A., & Svyantek, D. J. (1999). Person-organization fit and contextual performance: Do shared values matter? *Journal of Vocational Behavior*, 55, 254–275.

Gordon, G. G. (1985). The relationship of corporate culture to industry sector and corporate performance. In R. H. Kilman, M. J. Saxton, R. Serpa, and associates (eds.), *Gaining Control of the Corporate Culture* (pp. 103–125). San Francisco: Jossey-Bass.

Gordon, G. G. (1991). Industry determinants of organizational culture. *Academy of Management Review*, 16, 396–415.

Gordon, G. G., & DiTomaso, N. (1992). Predicting corporate performance from organizational culture. *Journal of Management Studies*, 29, 783–798.

Hartnell, C. A., Ou, A. Y., & Kinicki, A. (2011). Organizational culture and organizational effectiveness: A meta-analytic investigation of the competing values framework's theoretical suppositions. *Journal of Applied Psychology*, doi: 10.1037/a0021987.

Huselid, M. A., Jackson, S. E., & Schuler, R. S. (1997). Technical and strategic human resource management effectiveness as determinants of firm performance. *Academy of Management Journal*, 40, 171–188.

Kopelman, R. E., Brief, A. P., & Guzzo, R. A. (1990). The role of climate and culture in productivity. In B. Schneider (ed.), *Organizational Climate and Culture* (pp. 282–318). San Francisco: Jossey-Bass.

Kotter, J. P., & Heskett, J. L. (1992). *Corporate Culture and Performance*. New York: Free Press.

Lee, S. K. J., & Yu, K. (2004). Corporate culture and organizational performance. *Journal of Managerial Psychology*, **19**, 340–359.

Major, D. A. (2000). Effective newcomer socialization into high-performance organizational cultures. In N. M. Ashkanasy, C. P. M. Wilderom, and M. F. Peterson (eds.), *Organizational Culture and Climate* (pp. 355–367). Thousand Oaks, CA: Sage.

Marcoulides, G. A., & Heck, R. H. (1993). Organizational culture and performance: Proposing and testing a model. *Organization Science*, **4**, 209–225.

Nahm, A. Y., Vonderembse, M. A., & Koufteros, X. A. (2004). The impact of organizational culture on time-based manufacturing and performance. *Decision Sciences*, **35**, 579–607.

Ngo, H. Y., & Loi, R. (2008). Human resource flexibility, organizational culture, and firm performance: An investigation of multinational firms in Hong Kong. *International Journal of Human Resource Management*, **19**, 1654–1666.

O'Reilly, C. A., Chatman, J. A., & Caldwell, D. F. (1991). People and organizational culture: A profile comparison approach to assessing person-organization fit. *Academy of Management Journal*, **34**, 487–516.

Panayotopoulou, L., Bourantas, D., & Papalexandris, N. (2003). Strategic human resource management and its effects on firm performance: An implementation of the competing values framework. *International Journal of Human Resource Management*, **14**, 658–679.

Petty, M. M., Beadles, N. A., II, Lowery, C. M., Chapman, D. F., & Connell, D. W. (1995). Relationships between organizational culture and organizational performance. *Psychological Reports*, **76**, 483–492.

Quinn, R. E. (1988). *Beyond Rational Management: Mastering the Paradoxes and Competing Demands of High Performance*. San Francisco: Jossey-Bass.

Rousseau, D. M. (1990). Normative beliefs in fund-raising organizations: Linking culture to organizational performance and individual responses. *Group and Organization Studies*, **15**, 448–460.

Saffold, G. S., III (1988). Culture traits, strength, and organizational performance: Moving beyond 'strong' culture. *Academy of Management Review*, **13**, 546–558.

Siehl, C., & Martin, J. (1990). Organizational culture: A key to financial performance? In B. Schneider (ed.), *Organizational Climate and Culture* (pp. 241–281). San Francisco: Jossey-Bass.

Smart, J. C., & St. John, E. P. (1996). Organizational culture and effectiveness in higher education: A test of the 'culture type' and 'strong culture' hypotheses. *Educational Evaluation and Policy Analysis*, **18**, 219–241.

Sparrow, P. R. (2001). Developing diagnostics for high performance organizational cultures. In C.L. Cooper, S. Cartwright, P. C. Earley, et al. (eds.), *The International Handbook of Organizational Culture and Climate*. Chichester: Wiley.

Schwartz, H., & Davis, S. M. (1981). Matching corporate culture and business strategy. *Organizational Dynamics*, **10**, 30–48.

Sorensen, J. B. (2002). The strength of corporate culture and the reliability of firm perfprmance. *Administrative Science Quarterly*, **47**, 70–91.

Turner, M. E. (2001). *Groups at Work: Theory and Research*. Mahwah, NJ: Lawrence Erlbaum Associates.

Van Dyck, C., Frese, M., Baer, M., & Sonnentag, S. (2005). Organizational error management culture and its impact on performance: A two-study reputation. *Journal of Applied Psychology*, **90**, 1228–1240.

Wiener, Y. (1988). Forms of value systems: A focus on organizational effectiveness and cultural change and maintenance. *Academy of Management Review*, **13**, 534–545.

Wilderom, C. P. M., & Van den Berg, P. T. (1998, August). *A test of the leadership-culture–performance model within a large Dutch financial organization.* Paper presented at the annual meeting of the Academy of Management, San Diego, CA.

Wilderom, C. P. M., Glunk, U., & Maslowski, R. (2000). Organizational culture as a predictor of organizational performance. In N. M. Ashkanasy, C. P. M. Wilderom, and M. F. Peterson (eds.), *Organizational Culture and Climate* (pp. 193–209). Thousand Oaks, CA: Sage.

Wilkins, A. L., & Ouchi, W. G. (1983). Efficient cultures: Exploring the relationship between culture and organizational performance. *Administrative Science Quarterly*, **28**, 468–481.

Xenikou, A., & Simosi, M. (2006). Organizational culture and transformational leadership as predictors of business unit performance. *Journal of Managerial Psychology*, **21**, 566–579.

Organizational Change

8

Chapter objectives

The main objectives are to:

- identify and describe the various types of organizational change;
- understand the factors which either facilitate or inhibit organizational change;

(cont'd)

- explain the relation of organizational climate and culture to effective organizational change;
- describe the main characteristics of the change situation;
- consider change tactics that managers often use to bring about organizational change;
- describe the most common reactions to organizational change and explain why people tend to resist it.

Introduction

Changes in technology, markets and the world economy have meant that organizations have been forced to change dramatically not only what they do but how they do it (Furnham, 2002). Current issues range from managing mergers and acquisitions, downsizing and 'rightsizing', to business re-engineering or implementing new technologies (Fay & Luhrmann, 2004). Products and people skills are becoming obsolescent – a major task for all organizations is effectively managing change (Carnall, 1990). The psychology of organizational change is about various, very specific issues: the identity, ranking and weighting of the forces that act as stimulants to change and the sources of resistance to change, the main approaches to managing change, how organizations can become adaptive and learning systems, and how global forces effectively change.

The target of change can be both people and technology. It may focus on changing the structure of the organization or the way tasks are executed. It can be planned or unplanned.

Some changes occur gradually, others very dramatically. Small causes can have big effects.

Organizations and individual managers want changes in the way people think and act as well as in business processes. Change is both continuous and often ugly in organizations because of resistance. Clever business plans (about change) rarely survive the first attempts to put them into practice. Paradoxically, while it is often said that the aim is to improve well-being, the effect is often the opposite.

There are many drivers of change and vast sums are spent on change programmes but many fail. Although organizational change is pervasive, effective organizational change is rare (Armenakis & Harris, 2009). It has been estimated that in 2006 in the UK alone, $6 billion was spent on change programmes but around three-quarters of the programmes failed. Half or even two-thirds of all mergers and acquisitions are not successful (Cartwright & Schoenberg, 2006; Marks & Mirvis, 2001). The reasons are numerous and include being too complacent, failing to find real and powerful and important champions of change and not anchoring new processes in the corporate culture. They fail because of the change management process, be it design or delivery or simply a failure to understand the change psychology.

Some leaders attempt to bring about change to organizations, others change with organizations. Some focus on energy, others on tension. Some focus on 'mind-sets', others on potential. Change is about movement and involves complex and fundamental questions: Why is there a need for change? What is proposed? Who is involved in the process? Have all options been considered? What is the precise aim or goal?

Change is about innovation and adaptation. It often confronts all processes and procedures in an organization, asking fundamental questions about the basic goals and values of the organization.

Furnham (2005) has noted a number of predictions made less than 10 years ago (see Box 8.1). Of course we shall have to wait to assess their veracity.

Box 8.1   Work in 2020

- Shorter working hours
- Twenty-five per cent working from home
- Business 24 hours a day
- Privatized automated roads
- Rail renaissance – 350 mph trains
- Space shuttle to Sydney in two hours
- Precautionary saving for nonworking hours
- Virtual companies – 10 per cent of FTSE 100
- Contingent and core workers

- One month per annum – no work
- Easier commuting
- Online recruitment
- Entrepreneurial renaissance
- Growth of friction-free capitalism
- Personal digital assistants
- Massive increase in PC power
- Community work one day per week
- Global personal networks

Box 8.2 lists some further speculations about changes from the world of yesterday to that of tomorrow (or today). Many of these are simplistic catch-phrases which can, and should, be challenged. Things change in different sectors for different reasons. Globalization, mechanization and legislation have changed some jobs dramatically while others remain almost untouched by the twenty-first century.

Emphasis on what has changed in the business world leads to focus on what needs to change in the way that organizations operate. There have been changes in the workforce in terms of cultural diversity, skill experience and expectations, which differ significantly from one country to another.

Box 8.2   Speculations about the old and the new world

Old world	New world
• Wired	• Wireless
• Office hours	• 24/7 – open all hours
• Corporate headquarters	• Satellite companies
• Local/global markets	• Web-based
• e-excitement	• e-fatigue
• Surplus of youth	• Surplus of wrinkles
• Departments and divisions	• Flexible team
• Paid for attendance	• Paid for output
• Attentive to boss	• Attentive to customers
• Boss is supervisor	• Boss is coach
• Boss is scorekeeper	• Boss is leader
• Command, control and mistrust	• Networks, self-managed teams
• Labour, land and capital	• Knowledge, information and
• Fixed, hierarchical, stable	response time
• Loyalty, compliance	• Nomadic, equal, flexible
• Work/life separate	• Self-evaluation and responsibilities
• Norms, customs and laws	• Work/life blur
	• Relationships

Changes in customer expectations have clearly occurred, which normally means a rise in the quality and reliability of products, and the excellence of service demanded. It seems that there are consistent changes in the size, structure and international focus of organizations, and the managers needed to run them. Economic, legal, social and competitive forces mean that companies have to adapt, reinvent themselves and re-engineer simply to survive, let alone prosper.

Inevitably there are macro, sociopolitical changes in economic conditions governed by new inventions (the electronic revolution), raw material (the exhaustion of certain assets), and political cooperation and competition.

Such change has meant pressures and challenges facing both individuals and organizations. Individuals have to get used to no more jobs for life. They have to think of work as something you do, not somewhere you go to. They need to think of themselves as being employable, not being employed. They need to take more, if not total, responsibility for their own learning and development. Organizations face greater global competition, faster reactions and reduced product life cycles. They face a different workforce and therefore need to be flexible in the ways they manage their people.

Changes have taken place in working practices, processes, design and materials management. In the private sector Heller (2002) has identified seven major changes that have directly impacted the profitability of firms. These include changes in the desirability (fashion) for particular products and services, changes in product price, changes in market size, changes in promotion awareness and availability, changes in the distribution of goods and service, changes in field support from suppliers and changes in labour and operating costs.

Some change is proactive, other times it is reactive. Groups and organizations try to bring about change but change is also forced upon them. There is also episodic change, which is infrequent, discontinuous and occasional, versus continuous change, which is ongoing, evolving and continuous.

The targets and context of organizational change

The targets of change are frequently the trio of organizational structure, the technology and the people. There are often both internal and external pressures for change. Organizations must have the courage to change the things they can change, the tolerance and adaptability to leave unchanged the things they cannot change and the wisdom to know the difference. Many hope to be adaptive and flexible. A major determinant is readiness for change (Armenakis, Harris, & Mossholder, 1993; Armenakis & Harris, 2009). One objective is to eliminate the typical structure in favour of an ever-changing network of teams, projects, alliances and coalitions, which adapt appropriately to internal and external forces. Organizations cannot change everything. They can, with difficulty, persistence and determination, change their goals and strategies, technology, structure and people.

It is useful to distinguish between planned, intentional, goal-orientated change and that which inevitably occurs. Change may be at different levels and applied to culture, structure, technology and products, as well as individual behaviours. Perhaps the four most common pressures to change are:

1. *Globalization*: There is an increasing global market for products, but, in order to compete effectively in it, many organizations have to change their culture, structure and operations.

2. *Changing technology*: The rapid expansion of information systems technology, computer-integrated manufacturing, virtual reality technology and robots; the speed, power and cost of various operations have changed remarkably.

3. *Rapid product obsolescence*: The shortened life-cycle of products occurs because of innovations and thus leads to the necessity to shorten production lead times. Hence organizations have to adapt quickly and constantly to new information, and facilitate transitions to new forms of operations.

4. *Changing nature of the workforce*: Depending on the demographic nature of the country, there are many important and noticeable changes.

Others, like Robbins and Judge (2010) have mentioned factors like economic shocks (e.g., sudden massive increase in the oil price) as well as competition from abroad. The influence of environmental factors such as industry regulation and market concentration on organizational adoption of change has also been detailed by Wischnevsky, Damapoour, and Mendez (2011).

Hartley (2002) has provided a useful framework for understanding organizational change which has four mutually interacting parts:

1. *The context*: External including political, social and economic forces and internal including organizational size, structure, culture and history.

2. *Leadership*: Whether the key agents of change tend to be change strategists, implementers or recipients.

3. *Management of the change process*: The strategy and vision for change, the engagement of the different stakeholders, the timing and phasing of change and whether the change is essentially cultural or structural.

4. *Outcomes of change*: Intended and unintended and how easy they are to measure.

Change is both ubiquitous and constant. Since it can be planned or not planned, some organizations are proactive and others reactive. Change can also come from the inside or the outside, or both.

There are a variety of things that can (and often need to) be changed in an organization (Randolph & Blackburn 1989). At the environmental level these include an attempt to change laws, entry requirements to the market, one's niche in the market or indeed the competition. At the organizational level one can change (with difficulty) the organization's goals, strategies, culture, technology, processes and structure. At the group level it may be possible to change group composition and cohesiveness, as well as leadership and conflict management styles. Finally, at the individual level, most managers have attempted to change attitudes, commitment, performance, skills and motivation.

Change tactics can be described on various dimensions: quick versus slow, unilateral versus participative, planned versus evolving and aiming to eliminate resistance versus pacification. The choice of strategy inevitably depends on many things, including the importance of the required change, the distribution of power in the organization, the management culture and style, as well as the perceived strength and source of the resistance forces. Robbins and Judge (2010) note that it is fundamentally important to ask who in any and every organization is responsible for managing change activities. Who, in short, are the change agents: external consultants, top management, supervisors?

Besides the factors that seem to facilitate and encourage organizational change, we should note that resistance and reluctance to adopt – or even get involved in – change are common reactions of organizational members (King & Anderson, 2002). Individual employees tend to fear the uncertainty that surrounds change and often distrust the change agents (see Box 8.3). They are more accepting of change when it is understood; it does not threaten security; those affected have helped create it; it follows other successful changes; it genuinely reduces a work burden; the outcome is reasonably certain; the implementation has been mutually planned; top management support is strongly evident.

Box 8.3   Factors for and against change

Factors

For change (that facilitate, drive, encourage)

- Repealed or revised laws or regulations (often government-based) that lead to new opportunities, markets or ways of operating;
- rapidly changing environment (geographic, market, political situation) that makes old methods, processes or products redundant;
- improved technology or technology that can do things faster, cheaper and more reliably;
- new product development or selection by consumers;
- changed workforce (e.g., more educated, more women) with different demands and skills;
- more technically trained management who appreciate the possibilities of, and for, the new technology;
- organizational crisis (e.g., impending bankruptcy, purchase) that requires change of necessity;
- reduced productivity or product quality that leads to a change;
- reduced satisfaction or commitment by staff, which ultimately forces a crisis of morale and reduced productivity;
- increased turnover, absenteeism and other signs of organizational stress.

Against change

- individual distrust of change agents, be they consultants, new managers or technocrats;
- individual fear of change, especially fear of the unknown or fear that personal or occupational security will be challenged;
- individual desires for maintaining power in the present structure;
- individual complacency and believing all is well;
- lack of resources to support change so that early efforts collapse;
- conflict between individual and organizational goals;
- organizational inertia against changing the status quo.

Individuals and groups, like organizations as a whole, need to experience different things during the process of change. Old beliefs and behaviours need to be challenged, rejected, unfrozen and the new patterns established.

Change involves the unfreezing of old ways, the change then being established and the refreezing into a normative pattern. When does change occur and when not? Whether or not an organizational change will be made depends on members' beliefs regarding the relative benefits and costs of making the change.

In order to evaluate the efficiency of an intervention programme, researchers often give questionnaires to those involved before and after the change process. Golembiewski, Billingsley, and Yeager (1976) proposed that changes in numerical ratings on the questionnaires typically used in evaluating interventions confound three types of change: alpha, beta and gamma change. 'Alpha change' is a shift in the numerical rating that reflects real change in the target of the intervention. 'Beta change' is a recalibration of the scale. 'Gamma change' is the redefinition of the construct underlying the scale.

There are many types of organizational change. Burke (2002) has listed six: revolutionary versus evolutionary, discontinuous versus continuous, episodic versus continuing flow, transformational versus transactional, strategic versus operational, total system versus local option. Change operates at the level of the individual, the working group and the organization as a whole. Strategies for change work differently at the different levels. You change individuals by training, coaching, appraisal and change selection and recruitment strategies. You change work teams by team-building processes and encouraging self-management. You change organizations by focusing on culture, structures and processes.

Over the years, various different approaches to organizational change have been proposed. These include the well-known three-step model of Lewin (1951) that involves unfreezing the status quo, moving to a desired end state and refreezing or setting in place new processes, procedures and, sometimes, people. It also involves a close analysis of both the driving and restraining forces that bring about change.

Kotter (1995, 2007) essentially extended this model with eight steps: the first four are unfreezing, the next three change and the final freezing.

1. Establish a constant sense of urgency by creating compelling reasons for why change is needed.
2. Form a coalition with those with enough power to lead the change.
3. Create a new version to direct the change and strategies for achieving the version of the new organization.
4. Clearly communicate the vision throughout the organization to all those relevant to the process.
5. Empower others to act on the goal by removing barriers to change and encourage appropriate risk-taking and creative problem solving.
6. Plan for, create and reward short-term 'wins' that move the organization towards the new structure and process.
7. Consolidate improvements but reassess changes and make necessary adaptations in the new programmes.

8. Constantly reinforce the changes by demonstrating the relationship between new behaviours and organizational success. Change sticks when it is rooted in social norms, shared values and is reflected in the 'way we do things around here'.

Critical mistakes that change leaders often do in each of these eight phases of change are presented in Box 8.4.

Box 8.4   Critical errors related to each of the eight steps of change (Kotter, 2007)

Steps of change	Critical errors
1	• Not establishing a great enough sense of urgency
2	• Not creating a powerful enough guiding coalition
3	• Lacking a vision
4	• Undercommunicating the vision
5	• Not removing obstacles to the new vision
6	• Not systematically planning for and creating short-term wins
7	• Declaring victory too soon
8	• Not anchoring changes in the organization's culture

A third approach applies traditional organizational development methods such as survey feedback or process re-engineering. A more recent method is appreciative enquiry, which comes out of positive psychology. Positive psychology recommends a strength-based approach to change. The idea is to identify strengths, namely things that one is good at, and aim to exploit these more efficiently. The appreciative enquiry school aims to strengthen an organization's capacity to bring about change.

A central feature of this approach is to focus on positive emotions and experiences, which help people to embrace change.

Factors associated with organizational change

Some factors make organizations ripe for, and amenable to, change, but render others much more difficult to change in fundamental ways. Although these factors may include wider macroeconomic reasons (such as increased competition from the Third World), legal changes (protecting certain groups or markets or prohibiting products) or sociological changes (in attitudes to particular issues), it is simplest to divide these into various organizational and personal characteristics (Westwood, 1992).

Organizational factors

Centralization of decision-making: Where decisional prerogatives are concentrated at the highest levels of the organization, there is a natural tendency for those in authority to try to maintain and protect their position of power and to resist change. However, the likelihood of change in organizations, especially small ones run by owner-managers, depends in large measure on the personality characteristics of the person(s) at the top. In the hands of progressive and dynamic leaders, organizations tend to be quite flexible and adaptable. Radical individual leaders can also change large organizations, but centralization is usually a result of, and a contributor to, anti-change bureaucracy.

Organizational hierarchy: Tall organizations with high degrees of differentiation in terms of social status, administrative position and compensation levels tend to exhibit less change than do organizations with flat structures. In highly hierarchical organizations, people who are high up on the administrative ladder are typically insulated from operational problems that may require change. They have also spent a long time getting there and feel they deserve their current status. Such organizations tend to be unresponsive to changing forces within, and sometimes outside, the organization. This may account for the current enthusiasm for de-layering and downsizing middle-management jobs, although there is now much doubt about the wisdom of downsizing.

Degree of formalization: The greater the extent to which organizational activities are governed by formal rules and procedures, the less flexible the organization is and the less likely it is to respond readily to external changes. Local, national and international laws and customs may well inhibit change. Of course formalization is a factor that may be conducive to the implementation of change.

Degree of professionalization: The degree of professionalization of organizational members is understandably high in such organizations as law offices, medical clinics and engineering firms, and comparatively low in most mass-production manufacturing companies. Sometimes, because of their commitment to knowledge and quality of performance, professionals tend to favour continuous adaptation to changing technologies, and therefore exert a slow but positive influence on organizational change. But many are independently minded and can cause much internal disagreement. Thus, advertising and engineering firms tend to be more given to change than are law firms and financial institutions, which tend to be more tradition bound, partly because of the speed and nature of change in the profession. Because they have more to lose (years of poorly paid training), some professionals are strongly against change of any sort, because they want to recoup their losses.

Complexity: Organizations that undertake wide-ranging tasks or produce multiple products usually perceive a greater need for change than do organizations with simple structures and processes. Complex systems interact with many segments of the external environment, and the adaptive process therefore requires many and more frequent organizational changes. Furthermore, they assume the habit of change more easily. But complexity of operation and structure certainly mitigate against speed and ease of change.

Organizational size: Small organizations tend to be less formal and less differentiated and therefore more flexible. Moreover, smaller organizations typically have fewer resources committed to specific activities or processes, and therefore incur relatively few sunk costs of change compared to large organizations. On the other hand, large organizations have the ability to absorb a possible failure of a change attempt because they have many resources, which, in turn, encourages adaptability and change.

Age of the organization: The older the organization, typically the greater the degree of formalization and standardization of procedures, and therefore older organizations tend to be less flexible. They have more formal and established commitments to their external environments (in the form of contracts or working arrangements with trade unions, suppliers, competitors, regulatory agencies and other entities with which they regularly interact), thereby limiting their opportunities for change somewhat. But having seen the need for change previously, and having done so (simply in order to survive), they may have accumulated the experience necessary to cope with change more effectively. Indeed, it may be that being in an old organization (staying alive in the business world) one has to be change-oriented.

There is a growing argument that organizational culture is central to understanding the processes that lead to successful organizational change (Detert, Schroeder, & Mauriel, 2000). Culture is considered to impede or facilitate organizational change by shaping the way employees resist or adapt to change. Senior (2000) also makes a lot of the role of organizational culture in the change process. She sees culture as a web of various factors like power structures, organizational structure, control mechanisms, rituals and routines, stories and symbols. She distinguishes between segmentalist and integrative cultures. The former are specialistic, compartmentalized organizations with many different departments. They tend to avoid both confrontation and experimentation and have weak coordinating mechanisms. They differ from the more outward-looking, experimenting integrative cultures that are more holistic and future-oriented in their beliefs. The latter are more cooperative and happy to challenge the norm and hence are more change-oriented.

Previous research on the role of culture and climate on organizational change has shown that a climate for initiative – that is, a proactive working environment where employees are encouraged to take initiatives, as well as risks – facilitates changes in organizational processes (Baer & Frese, 2003). Similarly, computerized technology adoption was shown to be successful in the case of manufacturing plants holding a strong climate for implementation (Klein, Conn, & Sorra, 2001) and strong human relations values (Jones, Jimmieson, & Griffiths, 2005). Finally, cultures that are externally oriented, paying attention to innovations implemented by other organizations in their sector, to customer demands, to technology advancements and to changes in the economic and legal environment, are considered to be 'adaptive cultures' that promote successful organizational changes (Denison, Haaland, & Goelzer, 2004; Denison & Mishra, 1995; Kotter & Heskett, 1992).

With regard to the issue of how organizational cultures change, Brown (1998) has put forward four key factors:

- *Crisis*: An organization experiencing a crisis is what often initiates most mechanisms of culture change.
- *Leadership*: The role of leadership in culture change is essential to recognize the nature of the problem, formulate a coherent strategy and action plans, establish new roles and responsibilities and manage conflicts.
- *Success*: For a new culture to become established it must be identified as the factor that solves the initial crisis.
- *Learning*: Culture change is in essence a process of re-learning, that is, the search for new cultural possibilities.

Burke (2002) has noted that there are four types of change based on category (planned vs unplanned) and order (first vs second). Hence, change can be developmental, evolutionary, transformational or revolutionary. As most is unplanned, he concentrated on evolutionary and revolutionary change. Further, he notes that this occurs at each of three levels: individual, group and organizational.

Personal characteristics

Age: Normally, younger people are more inclined to initiate and accept change than are older ones. They tend to be less risk-averse and are more willing to try out new things. More importantly, being new and low-ranking in the organization, young people have little to lose from change. For their part, older members of organizations tend to be more set in their ways, have much stake in the status quo and therefore tend to be more wary about change. Along with chronological age is deference to age, which may inhibit change. To the extent that older more conservative people occupy leadership roles in organizations, and to the extent that organizational members acquiesce to or despise them, organizational change may be slow in coming. A company's age profile may give some indication as to its attitude to change, and more particularly the age profile of its decision-makers.

Training and education: Well-trained and better-educated people tend to be more progressive in outlook and have a better appreciation of the need for the most appropriate time to set in motion effective strategies of change. They can be aware of the potential impact of change on the organization and have a clear understanding of the cost of implementing change. They base their judgements more on facts and analysis than on personal values and sentiments, and usually have more confidence in their ability to learn new skills.

Rank: People of rank and status at the upper reaches of the administrative hierarchy, along with those who wield power and authority, tend to be quite cautious in adopting change, for fear of losing their power and resulting rewards. Yet, the successful implementation of change in organizations requires the active involvement and support of the people who make the major decisions in the organization. For good or bad, organizational managers play a key role in the change process.

Values and beliefs: Certain values, such as conservatism, belief in a just world and work locus of control, may be expected to relate quite specifically to attitudes to, and indeed phobia about, change.

Management courage: To be successful, organizational change requires courage. Furnham (2002) argued that successful change-oriented managers need three types of courage: the courage to accept failure when their change efforts fail for whatever reason; interpersonal courage to confront poor performers and where necessary deliver bad news; and the moral courage to uphold ethical and moral decisions and eliminate various forms of corruptions and counter-productive behaviour.

Quite simply, habit, fear, need for security, self-interest, a different assessment of the selection and natural conservatism often drive people to resist change. But it may be that attitudes to change are culture- and sector-dependent. Consider the following four questions and the extent to which they are culturally determined:

1. Do people believe that change is possible (let alone desirable)? Some fatalistic cultures may not believe it as strongly as those infused with instrumentalist beliefs. That is, for some, change is instituted externally and one must wait patiently for it to happen.
2. If change is possible, how long will it take and when will it seem necessary to change again? This relates to cultural difference in reactions to time.
3. Do some cultures resist more than others? This may be determined by how much a culture values tradition and is past-oriented as opposed to future-oriented.
4. Do cultures influence how changes can or should be implemented? This refers to top-down autocratic versus bottom-up democratic attitudes to change.

In some countries change is managed at the organizational level through restructuring, the introduction of new reward systems and attempts to change the corporate culture. Other interventions may be based on technology, job design and concern about socio-technical systems. Finally, some organizations prefer to focus on the individual through such things as sensitivity training, feedback and personal performance and team-building.

One very popular 'people' approach to change is organizational coaching and mentoring for specific, usually senior, people in the organizations. Passmore and Anagnos (2009) note various differences between coaching and mentoring, one of which is that the former is more performance-focused while the latter is more career-focused. They note the lack of robust empirical evidence concerning the efficacy of coaching to actually change performance over the long term. They also note its rather 'fuzzy' theoretical basis, drawing on such models as personal counselling, goal setting, adult learning, career counselling and techniques from sports psychology.

Characteristics of the change situation

Senior (2000) believes that an organization's capacity to change is a function of eight interrelated factors: general attitudes to criticism, conflict, sharing information and experimentation; the degree to which it is willing to give people autonomy and support them in their actions; the degree to which it encourages or disapproves of the discussion of sensitive issues openly; and finally management's openness to new ideas, especially from below. Thus the organizational culture affects attempts to change all sorts of functions, from appraisal and mentoring to innovation and decision-making. Thus one needs to match the change strategy to the culture which dictates the preferable or 'right' approach to change.

Certain aspects of the change itself affect the likelihood of its being proposed and the chances of its successful implementation. Some of these are objective and can be reasonably well managed, whereas others are based more on perceptions and attitude (Westwood, 1992).

Cost: Other things being equal, the higher the costs associated with a particular change proposal, the less likely that it will be put into effect. Cost is a major consideration in the installation of a computer-based management information system, or in the expansion of plant capacity. But once cost–benefit calculations are done, over a particular time-period even the highest-cost programme may look reasonable if not essential. Ultimately, the cost of not changing may be higher than the cost of change, although this calculation is difficult, speculative and often avoided.

Riskiness: The resource requirements and ultimate results of a change proposal are often difficult to ascertain in advance. As a rule, the less certainty surrounding a particular change, the less likely it is to be considered. This follows from the fact that people and organizations are all risk-averse in varying degrees. The 'no-pain-no-gain' philosophy of the 1980s has made more organizations less overtly risk-averse, but once they have introduced a costly and unsuccessful change, the experience of 'having their fingers burnt' makes them very cautious.

Adaptability of the change: Changes that are irreversible, or those which are difficult to modify once started, stand less chance of being adopted than changes that are easily adaptable. Note the way that some countries make changes in their currency or the use of the metric system. Some have a period when a 'dual system' operates, tending to favour adaptation, whereas sudden change favours more innovative behaviours. Many argue that adaptability is an enemy of change because it allows those who resist change never fully to come to grips with changed circumstances.

Magnitude of the change: Changes that require substantial time and resources to implement, and those that result in major transformation of organizational structure and processes, are more difficult to adopt than those that entail little effort and few resources, or have minimal impact on organizational life. Moreover, the larger the size of the change, the greater the degree of risk associated with it. In this sense, all these factors listed above are interrelated.

Type of change: Administrative changes are those that alter positions, responsibilities, reporting relationships and compensation, whereas technological changes are those that affect the process by which inputs are transformed into outputs (Damanpour, 1991). These two types of change are, typically, implemented through different procedures. Administrative changes are typically initiated and enforced by the organization's top decision-makers, and technical changes are conceived and implemented by its technical, professional and operational staff. Administrative changes elicit more objections and controversy than do technological changes and are therefore more difficult to implement.

Organizational change strategies

Over the years, there have been many methods or interventions proposed to bring about permanent, structural and successful organizational change. Landy and Conte (2004) have noted that these different methods have similar things in common. First, they are strategic, in the sense they try and refocus all groups into achieving very specific organizational goals. Second, they are nearly always group- or team-centred, rather than attempts to change individuals. Third, they are empirical in the sense they try to set up sophisticated data collection gathering and analysis to give precise feedback on all the changes. Fourth, they attempt to be participatory, encouraging the full engagement of all parties. Fifth, they are always very clearly quality-focused in the sense that they agree to make processes, products and services more efficient and effective. These methods include:

- *Management by objectives.* This moves the emphasis from managing by years of service to actual performance. This involves setting clear objectives and measuring various aspects of performance against these objectives.
- *Matrix organization.* This is where individuals and groups have dual reporting relationships where they are part of both particular project teams but also regular members of traditional specialist departments. Thus, people may be members of more than one group at the same time.
- *Total quality management.* This is a work-group-focused approach to encourage and support innovation to meet new customer demands. The idea is to get individuals to suggest and implement new strategies and processes that streamline business and help productivity.
- *Six sigma systems.* This was initially aimed specifically at manufacturing organizations that had quality control problems and many defects. The idea is that

everything should be aimed at doing it right the first time, thus making all processes efficient and integrated.

- *Lean production manufacturing.* This focuses on reducing costs and wasted time. It has also been called just-in-time management.

Burke (2002) believes there are three very basic strategies aimed at change. These are:

1. *Empirical-rational*: Based on the idea that in response to an appeal to people's rational self-interest, they will be prepared to change.
2. *Normative-re-educational*: Based on the idea that people are prepared to learn and are interested in conforming to subgroup norms.
3. *Power-coercive*: Based on the idea that people respond to political and economic incentives and sanctions.

Furnham (2003) has identified seven organizational change strategies that senior managers often use to change organizational culture. Various points need to be made: First, the choice of strategy is part function of the culture of the organization as well as the personality and values of the change agents. Second, it is both possible and likely that organizations try more than one strategy, either at the same time or sequentially. Third, there may be other preferred strategies not specified here. Next, it is difficult to assert confidently and with empirical support that one or more strategy is clearly more successful than others. Fifth, whatever strategy or strategies are employed it takes sustained effort, concentration and pressure to bring about the change.

The fellowship strategy

The fellowship strategy relies heavily on interpersonal relations, using seminars, dinners and events to announce and discuss what needs to be changed and how. People at all levels are listened to, ideally treated equally and conflicting opinions and anxieties are expressed. This 'warm and fuzzy' approach emphasizes personal commitment over ideas. However, the process may have serious problems getting under way, if at all. Because this strategy is averse to conflict, it can miss crucial issues and waste time. It rarely succeeds in changing culture alone.

The political strategy

The power structure is targeted by attempting to influence the official and unofficial leaders: the 'keepers of the culture'. The strategy seeks to identify and persuade those most respected and who have large constituencies and who therefore shape the culture. Political strategies flatter, bargain and compromise to achieve their ends, which is usually the introduction of new methods that reflect different values. But this de-stabilizes the organization because of continuing shifts in people's political stances. Maintaining credibility can be difficult because the strategy is often devious and paradoxically often is the very opposite of the values that the new company is proposing in the new culture.

The economic strategy

This strategy believes that money is the best persuader to change values and behaviour. Everyone has a price: a serious increase or decrease in money will change behaviour which reflects the values of the new culture if sufficiently incentivized. That approach assumes that people act more or less logically, but that their logic is based on entirely economic motives. However, 'buying people off' can be costly and the effects short term. The strategy also ignores emotional issues and all questions besides bottom-line profit. It too often is a strategy at odds with the new desirable cultural values of the organization.

The academic strategy

The academic strategy assumes that if you present people with enough information and the correct facts, they will accept the need to change and understand how to do it. The academic strategist commissions studies and reports from employees, experts and consultants. Although such strategists are happy to share their findings, it is difficult to mobilize energy and resources after the analysis phase. 'Analysis paralysis' often results because the study phase lasts too long and the results and recommendations are often out of date when they are published. Also, most managers do not really know what they should do, to whom, how or when. Many people often feel left out and ignored by the consultant academic.

The engineering strategy

This technocratic approach assumes that, if the physical nature of a job is changed, enough people will be forced to change. It is the process re-engineering approach. The strong emphasis is on the structural aspects of jobs: what people do, how and why they do it and what the realistic alternatives are. A major channel of communication, such as the usage of an intranet, can prompt structural change, but fails to commit most people. Technology changes how, when and why people communicate. It determines the speed and the cost of jobs. Such change can also break up happy and efficient teams. The strategy is limited because only high-level managers can really understand it, it is impersonal and it ignores the question: 'What is in it for me?' It can work well once those who can't change leave.

The military strategy

The military strategy is reliant on brute force. The emphasis is on learning to use the weapons for fighting the law, the union and the media. Physical strength and agility are required, and following the plan is rewarded. But the change-enforcer cannot relax, in case the imposed change disappears. Furthermore, force is met by force and the result is ever-escalating violence. It only ever works when organizations are in real crisis and seriously struggling to survive.

The confrontational strategy

This strategy believes that if you can arouse and then mobilize anger in people to confront the problem, they will change. Much depends on the strategists' ability to argue the points, as well as being able to stir up emotions without promoting violence – and control them. This approach encourages people to confront problems they would prefer not to address, but tends to focus too much on the problems and not on the solution. Anger and conflict tend to polarize and can cause a backlash.

Reactions to change

Inevitably, organizations are most concerned with resistance to change, which will be manifest in everything from strikes and sabotage, to a drop in motivation and morale, to no participation in, and commitment to, change initiatives. There is both individual resistance and organizational resistance for a variety of well-known and anticipatory reasons.

Change in organizations can be aimed at the individual, the team/group or the organization as a whole level. Change at the group level involves a number of ideas and processes. Groups, like individuals, often start by vigorously resisting change. Burke (2002) has suggested four very typical responses to attempts to change the structure, functioning or make-up of work groups. First, there is protectionism, where groups muster 'arguments' plus guilt-inducing evidence to resist all change. Next, there is the closing of ranks where groups become interpersonally stronger and dedicate themselves only to resist outside forces of change. Next, groups may try to change allegiance or ownership to remain the same. They may also demand leadership change in the hope that new, stronger leaders will successfully resist change.

Sometimes, groups avoiding or resisting change will simply believe 'this bad time will (soon) pass'. They may also craftily attempt diversionary tactics.

Organizational change causes powerful emotions, from a sense of liberation to depression and humiliation. People's support of, or resistance to, change depends heavily on how they answer the following five questions:

1. Will this change cause me to gain or lose something of value?
2. Do I understand the nature of this change?

3. Do I trust the initiators of this change?

4. Do I agree with the advisability of this change?

5. Given my personality, personal values and attitudes, how do I feel about this change?

How they answer these questions may lead to one of seven responses (Greenberg & Baron 1990):

1. *Quitting*: The most extreme reaction an employee shows to a change is to leave the organization. For example, following the introduction of a major organizational change, such as a merger or a transfer in job assignment, many workers leave because they believe the change is so obnoxious that staying would be intolerable. Sometimes organization members depart even if the change is a good one, because they find it personally difficult to cope with the change. Early retirement is a convenient and acceptable way to 'let people go' who are unhappy with organizational change. Although leaving an organization may be the most extreme reaction to change, it is not necessarily the most damaging one to the organization. Indeed, things probably proceed more smoothly if the most adamant opponents of a change leave rather than stay to fight it.

2. *Active resistance*: Workers who actively resist a change may try either to prevent it from occurring or to modify its nature. At its extreme, active resistance sends the message 'No, I will not do this'. Active resistance often goes beyond personal defiance and includes attempts to encourage others to resist the change. Many organizational changes have been scuttled by active employee resistance. A strike is a good example of group-oriented active resistance.

3. *Opposition*: Somewhat less extreme than active resistance is behaviour that can be labelled 'opposition'. Usually somewhat passive in nature, opposition behaviour might result in no more than simple 'foot dragging' to delay implementation or to bring about a scaled-down version of a proposed change. Opposition is a tactic commonly used by those who control resources that are necessary for the change to be made. By withholding essential resources, people can slow or modify a change quietly without having to make their dislike for the change known actively or aggressively.

4. *Acquiescence*: Opposition reactions tend to occur when those affected dislike a change and engage in passive resistance to delay or modify it. Sometimes, however, those opposed to a change feel powerless to prevent or alter it and they allow the change to occur without interference. This acquiescence to an unwanted change may arise from an impending sense of its inevitability – like death or taxes. People put up with the inevitable as best they can, shrugging their shoulders, gritting their teeth and steeling themselves

to face the inevitable. They hardly welcome the change but understand its inevitability.

5. *Acceptance/modification*: Employees who demonstrate an acceptance/ modification response accept a change to a certain extent but have some reservations about it. For example, suppose a manager has been told that her employer intends to move the company's headquarters to another European capital. She supports the idea of moving operations because local taxes and other restrictive ordinances are hurting the company's ability to compete in the marketplace. On the other hand, she is worried that the change may alienate many of its major customers and adversely affect its supply and delivery systems. At a personal level, she would rather not move her family too far from friends and relatives. One option available is to try to persuade her employer that there are sound reasons for finding a different site in the same country. Acceptance/modification responses to change usually can be characterized as bargaining over details (albeit, perhaps, important ones), rather than over principles.

6. *Acceptance*: This type of reaction is likely when people are either indifferent towards the change (i.e., they do not dislike it), or they agree with it. Acceptance reactions to change are characterized by passive support. If asked whether they like the change, for example, workers might agree that they do – but they are unlikely to volunteer such information. If asked to participate in the change, they will cooperate – but they probably will not initiate participation. They may see change as inevitable or that their jobs ultimately depend on it.

7. *Active support*: In this situation, organization members choose to engage actively in behaviours that increase the change's chances of success. Active supporters often initiate conversations, explaining why they support the change and think it is a good idea. They embrace, welcome and even rejoice in change.

Resistance to innovation and change occurs for different reasons. Managers may consciously or unconsciously resist the relearning and adaptation process that is part and parcel of change.

Insecurity may develop when changes occur. Sometimes this insecurity is caused by economic factors. Lower-level workers fear that automation will result in unemployment. Higher-level employees might view change as a threat to their status and eventually to their economic well-being. For example, doctors might resist the professional acceptance of paramedical personnel for fear that the increased volume of work paramedics would reduce the amount of work performed by physicians.

People often resist change because they believe that change is not in the best interest of the team and/or the organization. However, people occasionally do not change although it may be in their best interests to do so. The following is a checklist of factors that account for why this happens:

- *Because of ignorance*: Often, concerned individuals are simply not aware of the changes taking place. Manufacturers may continue to use a certain production process because they are unaware of a better method.
- *By default*: Sometimes people may reject a change, even though they are aware of another better technique, with little justification except a desire not to learn to use a new method.
- *On the basis of the status quo*: Change is rejected because it will alter the way in which things have traditionally been done.
- *Because of social reasons*: A manager may refuse to change because of a rationalization that the people within and society outside the organization will not accept it.
- *On the basis of interpersonal relations*: Because friends and even competitors have not accepted the change or are threatened by it.
- *Through substitution*: Another process or technique is selected in favour of the proposed change, because it seems easier, safer and less threatening.
- *Because of experience*: People reject a change when they try it but do not like it, or do it badly, wrongly or half-heartedly, thus self-fulfilling their prophecies.
- *Through incorrect logic*: People may reject a change on supposedly 'logical' grounds without having well-founded reasons. Collective rationalization is strong when passion is involved.

In short, people sometimes resist change through habit and the inconvenience of having to do things differently. Fearing the unknown, insecurity or indeed economic implications (having to work harder) are main causes of individuals resisting change. Resistance to change, on the other hand, may also be well-justified as, for example, in the case that the decision makers are removed from those at grass roots implementing the changes. In his force field analysis, Lewin (1951) believed all organizations were in a state of equilibrium as a consequence of various forces, some pushing for change and others resisting it. His technique was to attempt to identify all the salient forces for and against change, and next identify those that seemed controllable. Once the most important controllable forces were identified, they could at least be worked on. Lewin's process was then a three-step procedure: first to unfreeze the organization by reducing the forces holding the behaviour in the organization as stable; next to change structures and procedures; and then to refreeze by stabilizing the organization at a new state of equilibrium.

Essentially, most organizations are eager to create organizational culture that copes well with change and innovation. As Robbins and Judge (2010) note, there is data on innovative organizations. They tend to be structurally flexible; they give their managers long versus short tenure; they have a lean and mean nature with few resources and they have good internet communication. Culturally, they reward success and failure, the latter because it encourages risk taking.

They promote development, learning and training. They encourage individuals to become change agents.

Most of all, successful organizational change involves turning organizations into learning organizations that have the capacity and will to continuously change. It is proactive and not reactive, aiming to correct mistakes but modifying all processes and procedures which cause them. Learning organizations aim to prevent fragmentation into silos, competition which undermines cooperation and reactiveness rather than risk-taking proactiveness.

Organizational cultures that are adaptive and change-oriented know about the stress associated with change and the delicate balance between demands and resources. Inevitably, stress arises but it is not long-term or dysfunctional.

Summary

Burke (2002) points out that there is always a paradox in planned organization change because it almost never goes to plan. He notes that the ability to change is essential to organizational success and survival. He favours a biological metaphor of the organization as a system which is commonly adopted. Further, he points out, as have many others, that you do not change corporate culture by trying to change culture. Rather, you focus on specific behaviours. Trying to change values and beliefs is 'fraught with difficulty, resistance and strong emotion' (p. 13). Beliefs follow behaviour.

The targets of organizational change are most often the structure, the technology and the people. It is important to distinguish between the process of change (i.e., how it is achieved) and the content of change (what is being changed). Inevitably, change agents need to focus on specific factors and procedures that maximize change. It is also advisable to have some model that allows one to understand the relationship between various organizational factors and predict what will happen in the future. Most importantly, it is essential that the change agents put in place a number of metrics so they can get some clear feedback on the progress on the change strategies at various crucial points. It also takes a determined, courageous leadership to plan how to launch and sustain change to ensure the survival and success of the organization.

External factors to the organization often require internal changes in organizations. The culture, function and history of the organization and the type of people in it dictate how change is best done. The leadership in the organization as well as its structure, reward systems, attitudes to training and development, size and, perhaps most of all, its history of performance are all crucial factors in how, indeed whether, it successfully adapts to change. Management has at its disposal a number of change strategies that can be utilized to achieve sustainable change, such as the fellowship, the academic or the economic strategy. Indeed a combination of various strategies seems to be the best way to proceed with change management after taking into account the cultural, structural and technical aspects of a particular organization. Resistance to change is a common reaction of organizational members to change management programmes grounded primarily on the uncertainty associated with change especially when change agents have not earned members' trust.

Questions

1. Describe some types of organizational change.
2. Which are the factors that facilitate or inhibit organizational change?
3. How are organizational climate and culture related to effective organizational change?
4. List the main characteristics of the change situation.
5. Which are the change strategies that management can use in order to bring about organizational changes?
6. Which are (a) the reasons for resistance to change and (b) most common reactions reflecting resistance to change?

Case study

Resistance to change in a nursing home for the elderly

Hazel Hill is a private nursing home in Britain having an excellent reputation for providing a friendly and caring environment for highly dependent elderly residents of both sexes. Most of its residents are not able to care for their own personal hygiene requirements, dress or feed themselves, take themselves to the toilet, or even walk. Staff seems to cope well with both verbal and physical violence on a daily basis.

The managers, who are also owners of the home, have decided to introduce the National Vocational Qualification (NVQ) training and assessment established by the UK government. NVQ is a standardized proof of competence in a candidate's area of work assessed in their place of employment by trained assessors employed in the same workplace. It has five levels ranging from basic (level 1) to managerial (level 5) competencies. Management decision towards the implementation of this change was primarily a result of pressure from the outside. The local authority's Social Services Department that constitutes the major purchaser of care at Hazel Hill informed all private residential homes that they had to provide a policy document on staff training. NVQ is seen as key to establishing a formal training policy for the home, as well as a way to meet the assurance standards required for quality certification.

It is interesting to focus on the reactions to NVQ training and qualification of two key groups: the managers/owners who have introduced it, and

(cont'd)

those members of staff who are NVQ candidates. The three managers expect that members of staff will resist the introduction of the NVQ training and assessment, and consider this reaction a serious problem that they have to deal with. However, they also exhibit a rather contradictory stance towards the innovation. Although they were initially enthusiastic about the potential benefits of the training, and encouraged staff to take it up, they do not like the thought of the home changing significantly. The have also assumed that staff will strongly resist the introduction of this new policy, and have overestimated the amount of resistance, being disproportionally influenced in their perceptions by a vocal minority of organizational members. Their expectations of resistance to change may be seen to have acted as a self-fulfilling prophecy, in that they adopted an implementation strategy that was perceived to be overly coercive and not sufficiently informative.

Looking at personnel reactions to change, staff members who are NVQ candidates have a wide spectrum of responses towards the new training and assessment policy ranging from active resistance to adoption. Staff views of the pros and cons of NVQ depend heavily on what the individual employee most values in his/her working life at Hazel Hill. For example, placing a high value on patient care and doing one's job well are associated with a positive attitude towards the new training scheme, whereas being concerned with one's individual well-being, financial income and work status are indicative of a negative evaluation to the innovation. Moreover, evaluations of the innovation are not always translated into a matching response as organizational members think of the strategies and resources available to them before acting; in particular, their perceptions of how powerful and influential they are in their work environment seem to be a strong determinant of voicing negative attitudes.

Taking an organization as a whole perspective in making sense of responses to change in Hazel Hill, it is useful to think of the metaphor of 'family'. The managers/owners play the role of caring but firm parents of staff members; for example, management help employees out with personal loans on generous terms or pay for the organization of social events. As often happens in families, the staff can be highly critical of their managers without weakening their sense of identification with the family. Newcomers are seen as potentially distracting the attention of parents/managers and therefore old members of staff tend to be hostile towards them. Finally, the rigid role and responsibilities in the elderly home resemble that of a traditional family where most often roles are sharply defined and differentiated. If one accepts the family metaphor, a negative employee attitude to the new training and assessment can be interpreted as a reaction to the fact that they are being asked to prove something that they think should be taken on trust – that is, their commitment to doing their best for the home. Thus, for those employees who most value the family-like features of the home, strong and immediate resistance is a rational response.

(cont'd)

(1) Did managers/owners' belief expectations regarding the acceptance of change by Hazel Hill employees influence their change strategies?

(2) Individual employees seem to place most value on different aspects of the working life at Hazel Hill. Are these differences in value orientations among employees predictive of their reactions to change?

(3) How does the 'family' metaphor describe the culture at Hazel Hill? Is it useful in understanding employees' responses to change?

Source: Adapted from Meston and King (1996).

References

Armenakis, A. A., & Harris, S. G. (2009). Reflections: Our journey in organizational change research and practice. *Journal of Change Management*, **9**, 127–142.

Armenakis, A. A., Harris, S. G., & Mossholder, K. W. (1993). Creating readiness for organizational change. *Human Relations*, **46**, 681–703.

Baer, M., & Frese, M. (2003). Innovation is not enough: Climates for initiative and psychological safety, process innovations and firm performance. *Journal of Organizational Behavior*, **24**, 45–68.

Burke, W. (2002). *Organisational Change: Theory and Practice*. London: Sage.

Carnall, C. (1990). *Managing Change in Organisations*. Englewood Cliffs, NJ. Prentice-Hall.

Cartwright, S., & Schoenberg, R. (2006). Thirty years of mergers and acquisitions research: Recent advances and future opportunities. *British Journal of Management*, **17**, 1–5.

Damanpour, F. (1991). Organizational innovation: A meta-analysis of effects of determinants and moderators. *Academy of Management Journal*, **34**, 555–590.

Denison, D. R., & Mishra, A. K. (1995). Toward a theory of organizational culture and effectiveness. *Organization Science*, **6**, 204–222.

Denison, D. R., Haaland, S., & Goelzer, P. (2004). Corporate culture and organizational effectiveness: Is Asia different from the rest of the world? *Organizational Dynamics*, **33**, 98–109.

Detert, J., Schroeder, R. G., & Mauriel, J. J. (2000). A framework for linking culture and improvement initiatives in organizations. *Academy of Management Review*, **25**, 850–863.

Fay, D., & Luhrmann, H. (2004). Current themes in organizational change. *European Journal of Work and Organizational Psychology*, **13**, 113–119.

Furnham, A. (2002). Managers as change agents. *Journal of Change Management*, **3**, 21–29.

Furnham, A. (2003). *Mad, Sad and Bad Management*. Guildford: Management Books 2000.

Furnham, A. (2005). *The People Business*. Basingstoke: Palgrave Macmillan.

Golembiewski, R., Billingsley, K., & Yeager, S. (1976). Measuring change and persistent to human affairs. *Journal of Applied Behavioural Science*, **12**, 133–157.

Greenberg, J., & Baron, R. (1990). *Behaviour in Organisations*. Boston: Allyn and Bacon.

Hartley, J. (2002). Organisational change and development. In P. Warr (ed.), *Psychology at Work* (pp. 399–425). Harmondsworth, UK: Penguin.

Heller, R. (ed.) (2002). *Manager's Handbook*. London: Dorling Kindersley.

Jones, R. A., Jimmieson, N. L., & Griffiths, A. (2005). The impact of organizational culture and reshaping capabilities on change implementation success: The mediating role of readiness for change. *Journal of Management Studies*, **42**, 361–386.

King, N., & Anderson, N. (2002). *Managing Innovation and Change* (2nd edition). London: Thompson.

Klein, K. J., Conn, A. B., & Sorra, J. S. (2001). Implementing computerized technology: An organizational analysis. *Journal of Applied Psychology*, **86**, 811–824.

Kotter, J. P. (1995). Leading change: Why transformation efforts fail. *Harvard Business Review*, **73**, 59–67.

Kotter, J. P. (2007). Leading change. *Harvard Business Review*, **85**, 96–103.

Kotter, J. P., & Heskett, J. L. (1992). *Corporate Culture and Performance*. New York: Free Press.

Landy, F., & Conte, J. (2004). *Work in the 21st Century*. New York: McGraw-Hill.

Lewin, K. (1951). *Field Theory in Social Science*. New York: Harper and Row.

Marks, M. L., & Mirvis, P. H. (2001). Making mergers and acquisitions work: strategic and psychological penetration. *Academy of Management Executive*, **15**, 80–92.

Meston, C., & King, N. (1996). Making sense of 'resistance': Responses to organizational change in a private nursing home for the elderly. *European Journal of Work and Organizational Psychology*, **5**, 91–102.

Passmore, J., & Anagnos, J. (2009). Organizational coaching and mentoring. In S. Cartwright and C. Cooper (eds.), *The Oxford Handbook of Organizational Well-Being* (pp. 497–519). Oxford: Oxford University Press.

Randolph, W., & Blackburn, R. (1989). *Managing Organisational Behaviour*. Homewood, IL: Irwin.

Robbins, S., & Judge, T. (2010). *Essentials of Organizational Behaviour*. Boston: Pearson.

Senior, B. (2000). Organisational change and development. In N. Chmiel (ed.), *Introduction to Work and Organisational Psychology* (pp. 347–381). Oxford: Blackwood.

Westwood, R. (ed.) (1992). *Organisational Behaviour*. Hong Kong: Longman.

Wischnevsky, J. D., Damapoour, F., & Mendez, F. A. (2011). Influence of environmental factors and prior changes on the organizational adoption of changes in products and in technological and administrative processes. *British Journal of Management*, **22**, 132–149.

Author Index

Subject Index

accommodating, *see* conflict management, strategies
achievement culture orientation, 165–9
adaptability, 169–73
aggressive/defensive styles, 108
appreciative inquiry, 190
avoiding, *see* conflict management, strategies

bargaining situation
  structure of, 62–3
behavioral norms model, 108
brainstorming
  production blocking, 39, 83
  production loss, 39, 83
  rules for, 38, 39, 82–3
brainwriting, 84

charismatic leadership, 138
cognitive styles, 75
collaboration, *see* conflict management, strategies
competing values model, 109
competition, *see* conflict management, strategies
competitive advantage, 159–60
compromising, *see* conflict management, strategies
conflict
  efficacy, 56
  and group performance, 50–4
  process of, 46–50
  relationship, 51
  resolution of, 57
  task, 51
conflict management
  and dimensions of intent, 58
  and dual concern models, 57
  strategies, 57–61
  styles, 57–61
confronting, *see* conflict management, strategies
constructive controversy, 54–7
constructive styles, 110
contending, *see* conflict management, strategies
contextual performance, 173
convergent thinking, 75
cooperation, *see* conflict management, strategies

creativity enhancement techniques, 82–5
cultural dimensions, *see* organizational culture, dimensions of
cultural innovation, 132–3
cultural leadership, 132, 140
cultural maintenance, 133–4
cultural potency, 152
cultural traits, *see* organizational culture, traits of
culture-environment fit *versus* adaptability, 172–3
culture-performance link
  and culture content, 157–69
  and culture-environment fit, 169–73
  and culture strength, 151–7
  and performance reliability, 156–7
  and person-organization fit, 173–4
culture of productivity, 159
culture strength
  definition of, 152
  operationalization of, 152–3

defensive styles, 110
divergent thinking, 75

emic approach, 116
error management culture, 166
etic approach, 116
evaluation apprehension, 83
external-view paradigm, 116

fixed pie error, 63
forcing, *see* conflict management, strategies
free-rider effect, 28

goal orientation, 109
group decision-making, 30–3
group dynamics, 3, 4
group performance, 24–9
group polarization, 30–1
group productivity, 24–6
group task
  categorization of, 24–5
  taxology of, 24–5
groupthink, 6, 31–2